1,001 Timely Tips for Clutter Control

Knowing What to Keep, When to Toss,
and How to Store Your Stuff

Publisher's Note

The editors of FC&A have taken careful measures to ensure the accuracy and usefulness of the information in this book. While every attempt was made to assure accuracy, some Web sites, addresses, telephone numbers, and other information may have changed since printing. We advise readers to carefully review and understand the ideas and tips presented and to seek the advice of a qualified professional before attempting to use them.

The publisher and editors disclaim all liability (including any injuries, damages, or losses) resulting from the use of the information in this book.

"Happy is the man who doesn't give in and do wrong when he is tempted, for afterwards he will get as his reward the crown of life that God has promised those who love him."

James 1:12

Contents

Before you begin

CLUTTER-
BUSTING
STEPS:

STEP 1
Cut the
clutter

STEP 2
Increase
storage

STEP 3
Get
organized

STEP 4
Keep it
clean

C lutter control can be easy. You just need a plan. And like any good plan, this one comes in small, easy-to-swallow bites.

That's the key. When your house is cluttered, you feel overwhelmed with the enormity of putting everything in order. But if you take one area at a time, and learn how to follow four simple steps, you'll have a neat-as-a-pin home in no time.

Your space and your clutter are unique, but the beauty of this plan is how easy it is to customize your organizing decisions and actions.

First, you're going to get the low-down on this step-by-step decluttering system. Then you can flip to the area in your home that's giving you problems. There you'll find reminders about these steps, as well as specific ideas and lots of tips for getting and keeping that space clean and organized.

If you can think of decluttering as a journey, then setting goals is your destination. Without one, you could wander aimlessly and endlessly through your chaos. But with an objective, it's so much easier to plot your course. In fact, many professionals say the first step to a clutter-free, organized home is having a plan to reach your goals. So that's what you're going to do in every space — first visualize an end result, then go through four easy steps to get there.

> "Clutter is anything we don't need, want, or use that takes our time, energy, or space and destroys our serenity."
>
> – Clutterers Anonymous

Make a wish list. Sit down for a minute and think about the space that needs cleaning and organizing. Get a piece of paper and actually write down how you'd like it to function. Make this a list so you can consider each idea individually. Keep in mind what you want or need to store in this area and how you want to access it. Be specific.

Be realistic. You may have a whole string of desires when you're finished, so now you must decide which ones you can realistically achieve. Take into account square footage, time, and money. Cross off those that are simply not practical right now. Or move them to another list of long-term goals.

Set priorities. When you're down to just your truly realistic goals, rank them based on your priorities. The number one goal should be the most important function of a room or space.

While you're evaluating the space, consider cosmetic and safety issues. That means think about what you can do to the room to make it more appealing and safer, like upgrading the lighting, painting, adding rugs, or improving access.

Further down the list will be those functions you'd like to achieve, if possible. The plan is to do everything in your power to accomplish at least your top-ranked goals.

For example, in your attic, you may end up with these as your top three objectives:

- store out-of-season clothes
- catalog family memorabilia
- locate holiday decorations easily

Identify your clutter problems. Pogo said, "We have met the enemy, and it is us." In the war on clutter, you truly are your own worst enemy. It might be appealing to blame the pandemonium on gremlins that sneak in at night, but the fact is, your own habits and lifestyle have gotten you in this mess. Rest assured, a few changes to your habits and lifestyle can get you out. Now get ready to face the enemy.

How decluttering will improve your life:
- ❏ more space   ❏ easier cleaning
- ❏ less stress   ❏ more free time

If you're reading this book, something isn't working in your home.
So the next step is to review what's currently going on in each
space. For example, when evaluating your attic, you may realize:

- You've got every piece of kindergarten artwork your now-grown children ever produced.

- Moths ate through your box of winter sweaters.

- You never seem to find the same Christmas decorations two years in a row.

Obviously, this list of issues could be quite long. That's OK. It
will help you focus on what you need to fix. And remember,
things like these can be fixed. So list away.

In most cases, your difficulties fall into one of three problem
categories.

Problem	Decluttering solution	
The bottom line is I have too much stuff.	Step 1 Cut the clutter	You'll evaluate and make a decision on everything in your space.
I don't have enough or the right kind of storage.	Step 2 Increase storage	You may need to forage around the house or buy containers uniquely suited for your belongings and your space.
I don't know what I have, where to put it, or the best way to store it.	Step 3 Get organized	You must arrange things within this space so everything is tidy, accessible, and stored more efficiently

4

Label your zones. Your list of objectives may naturally produce zones — major categories of items you need to store in the space, or in some cases, physical areas of a room. For instance, the attic example suggests these zones:

- off-season clothes

- family memorabilia

- holiday items

But your kitchen will have physical zones, like:

- pantry
- refrigerator and freezer
- countertops
- cupboards
- drawers

Zones are important because they will help you sort, group, and store like items. Each chapter will propose zones that are most likely to occur in that area. But you can create more or different ones, depending on your home and your lifestyle.

Set a timeline. Now you know your clutter problems and your zones. It's time to put them together so you can see just how big an organizing task you face.

Stand in the middle of your space and take a good, long look at your stuff. In your mind, try to get a feel for exactly how much belongs in each zone.

You don't want to start a decluttering project on a Friday afternoon if company is coming for dinner — you'll just end up frustrated with an even bigger mess on your hands. Then again, after filling in the timetable, you may discover the job won't be as time-consuming as you first thought.

You'll find a chart in each chapter with blanks for you to estimate how long you think it will take to accomplish each task for each zone. This is an important step. By assigning thoughtful, reasonable numbers, you may be pleasantly surprised. Remember *Step 2 Increase storage* may need to include time for shopping for new storage containers.

Here's an example that shows you'd need at least a full weekend to declutter a typical attic.

Zones	Step 1: Cut the clutter	Step 2: Increase storage	Step 3: Get organized
Off-season clothes	2 hours	1 hour	1 hour
Family memorabilia	4 hours	1 hour	2 hours
Holiday items	1 hour	1 hour	2 hours

So let's recap the things you need to think about and do before you ever begin decluttering a space. You'll find a handy reminder list just like this one in each room chapter. Don't rush through or skip this part.

Remember...

✓ make a wish list

✓ be realistic

✓ set priorities

✓ identify your clutter problems

✓ label your zones

✓ set a timeline

Now you'll learn about each of the decluttering steps plus how the *Step 4 Keep it clean* sections work.

Step 1 Cut the clutter

Remember, the bottom line here is you simply have too many things. The goal is to get rid of some of them.

Make a decision. As you attack each space, you're going to go through every item and assign it to one of these piles:

- keep
- toss
- donate
- sell
- pass on

> There are about 50,000 self-storage facilities in the United States and people are using them more than ever.

You can use boxes, trash bags, or laundry baskets to keep your items separated.

Follow purging rules. But wait. The whole plan could break down if you don't exercise some self-discipline during this step.

- *Decide quickly.* Make up your mind and keep moving. Don't dawdle or get sidetracked. Don't start flipping through photo albums or reading anniversary cards.

7

- *Handle items just once.* If you pick it up, you must place it in one of your decision piles.

- *Set limits.* The whole idea here is to purge. That's not always easy, but if you lay some ground rules ahead of time, you'll be less likely to wind up with everything sitting fat and sassy in your "keep" pile. So identify problem categories and set a number limit. For instance, make the decision that you may keep only three winter scarves. Or perhaps decide that if you haven't put up a particular Christmas decoration in two years, it must go.

- *Pass the "keep" test.* Many experts say if you want to keep an item, you must answer yes to one of these:

    Do I use it?

    Do I absolutely love it?

    Do I really need it?

    Things that don't fit into one of these categories you can eliminate from your house — and you won't even miss them.

- *Recognize garbage.* If it's beyond repair, unidentifiable, or not worth donating or selling, get rid of it.

You'll find a quick reminder of these clutter-busting rules in each room chapter.

Under dire circumstances, if you are absolutely torn by indecision — you simply can't bear to part with some items but you know you don't use them either — try this. Place these things in a box with a date label on the outside. Store this away somewhere for six months or even a year. If you haven't needed, wanted, or missed anything in the box, get rid of it. This may help you get over the decluttering hump.

Keep in mind

Make a decision:	Follow purging rules:
✓ keep	✓ decide quickly
✓ toss	✓ handle items once
✓ donate	✓ set limits
✓ sell	✓ pass the "keep" test
✓ pass on	✓ recognize garbage

Step 2 Increase storage

Sometimes you don't really have too much stuff, you just have it all over the place. That, too, is clutter. "Containing" your belongings so they are safe, clean, and together is critical.

Map your space. No two closets or kitchens or bathrooms are alike. And while most people face the same kinds of storage problems, you have a unique allocation of square footage to work in. Just think of it all as potential storage. And that means you're going to want to use every last square inch. So after you empty your space, you'll get out your measuring tape and go to work.

The best method is to use graph paper and assign one square for every square foot. This way you'll have an exact diagram of your bedroom, closet, garage, or other area. But if the very idea of all that computing leaves you lightheaded, forget it and just sketch in the walls, windows, and doors, plus their measurements.

Now plan your new storage based on your zones and the amount of things you have left after purging. Don't forget to think vertically — consider tall storage or even storage suspended from the ceiling.

Houses, on average, are almost two-and-a-half times larger than they were 50 years ago. The National Association of Home Builders says the typical American home has more than 2,300 square feet.

Shop for containers. This doesn't mean you have to spend a lot of money at a fancy home decor store. You might be surprised where you can find things that can hold other things.

The best place to start is in your own home. What have you got lying around the house that seems, at first glance, to simply be more clutter? Like baskets. They make great containers for everything from cotton balls in the bathroom to magazines in the family room. For a start, try picturing an item out of its current setting. A cherished vase that's buried in the attic might hold utensils beautifully on your kitchen countertop.

And then there are garage sales and flea markets — endless sources of odd boxes, pots, bottles, urns, jugs, cartons, and other containers to curb your chaos.

Be sure you take all your measurements with you when you go shopping for containers.

Just make sure your purchase is truly useful and suitable. Buying something that's all wrong for your plan and your space simply means you've added to your clutter problem. If you're not sure whether to drag something home, these questions could help you decide.

- Do you want your items in open containers or sealed ones?

- Will you want to stack them?

- Do you need to see what's inside or would you rather hide your items in an opaque container?

- Do you feel you have to coordinate containers with a certain decorating theme?

Remember...

✓ map your space

✓ shop for containers

You'll see this reminder for *Step 2 Increase storage* in every chapter.

Step 3 Get organized

What's the definition of frustration? Knowing you have something, but not being able to find it. Or perhaps it's finally finding something but discovering it's broken, smashed, eaten, mildewed, or otherwise ruined.

Pack properly. This is important. Simply loading items into boxes is not clutter control. Everything must be stored with like items or zone-similar items, packed appropriately, and then labeled.

Let your camera act as a labeler. Take a picture of a container's contents and tape it to the outside. This works especially well for containers that are stacked or hard to get to.

Label. Decide on a labeling system right now. Label machines are a good choice. They are extremely handy, versatile, easy to use, and not very expensive.

There are hand-held versions or those that are computer compatible. They can print on paper, plastic, metallic, or fabric tape and offer a wide range of fonts, symbols, and sizes. Buy them online or visit any office supply store or major retailer, like Wal-Mart.

> Take a snapshot of your newly cleaned and organized space. This simple trick will act as a reminder of all your hard work. Look at it every now and then and you'll be less likely to allow clutter to creep back into your life. Try it — you'll be so proud.

However, a hand-written label on masking tape is better than no label at all. Buy sheets of self-adhesive stickers, a black, indelible marker, and you're good to go.

Look for a box like this to remind you of the two important tasks in *Step 3 Get Organized*.

Remember...

✓ pack properly

✓ label

Step 4 *Keep it clean*

Step back and admire your accomplishment. The space is cleared out and organized. Everything is sorted, stacked, ordered, and labeled. The floor is free of clutter. Surfaces are tidy. You feel great, and you love your space.

Now that you have it this way, you want to keep it this way. It's easier than you think, especially since you've already done the hard part.

The secret: Take care of things now. Don't step over the towels on the bathroom floor. Hang them up or throw them in the washer. Don't toss the mail onto the kitchen counter. Open, sort, trash, and file it as soon as it comes into the house. Procrastination breeds clutter. But if you act on things as they happen, you'll find your clutter gradually disappearing.

And a clutter-free home is not only easier to clean, it will look clean even if it really isn't. It's one cleaning tip you can't live without. Emilie Barnes, author of *Cleaning Up the Clutter* and founder of *More Hours in My Day* time-management seminars, has a favorite saying: "Don't put it down, put it away." It's a simple tip that can create order out of chaos and make your house look like a pro cleans it.

The 10-minute plan. When it's time to clean, you'll find you can zip through cleaning chores that once took all day. In fact, just 10 minutes of speed cleaning a day can make your home livable again.

At the end of most room chapters, you'll find a cleaning chart (see following page). One column gives you a list of chores you should be able to complete in just 10 minutes. Then add a few weekly and monthly chores, and you've got one smart cleaning plan.

In addition, this section will give you plenty of fast and easy cleaning tips for each room. You'll learn how to clean smart, not hard. You'll find ways to accomplish several cleaning tasks at once and often with products you have around the house.

For instance, if you find yourself short of commercial cleaning products, reach for these six simple items. With them, you can

10-minute daily speed cleaning	Weekly chores	Monthly chores	Occasional chores
Clear off and wipe down all countertops	Replace all towels and cloths with clean ones	Clean out refrigerator, wipe surfaces, and replace box of baking soda	Wash curtains and windows
Put all dirty dishes into dishwasher	Vacuum then mop floor		Vacuum refrigerator condenser and grille

clean most of your house, top to bottom. You'll find specific cleaning tips using these natural marvels throughout the book.

Baking soda, also known as bicarbonate of soda or sodium bicarbonate, is a staple in most kitchens. Because it's made up of fine particles, it's mildly abrasive. That means if you mix it with a bit of water to form a paste, you can scour pots, pans, sinks, bathtubs, and ovens. And because it's absorbent, it's famous for soaking up odors. Try it on countertops, ceramic tile, cut glass, walls, and piano keys. Clean your hairbrushes and combs, deodorize your garbage disposal, and get rid of baked-on food. This powerhouse gently cleans just about everything.

Vinegar is sometimes defined as sour wine. In truth, it can be made from anything with sugar, usually some kind of fruit.

White vinegar is often called a household wonder cleaner. It's inexpensive, nontoxic, and useful for dozens of chores. It's the acid in vinegar that cuts through grease and germs and inhibits bacteria and mold. It will remove clothing stains, beat bathtub film and grout stains, and make your stainless steel sink shine like the chrome on an old Cadillac.

Bleach is simply a chemical mixture of chlorine gas, sodium hydroxide, and water. It's the chlorine that makes bleach such a great disinfectant — it kills disease-causing bacteria and viruses in your bathroom and kitchen and gets rid of mildew. Why bleach is a great stain remover is a little more complicated, but it has a lot to do with a chemical reaction that removes color. So not only can bleach make your laundry whites whiter and brighter, it can wipe out countertop stains.

Ammonia can be a tricky product to use because of the important safety measures you must take. The vapors can irritate — even burn — your skin, eyes, or lungs, so you always want to work in a well-ventilated area. And never use ammonia with bleach. This mixture produces a dangerous gas. But as a household cleaner, ammonia does a bang-up job deodorizing, bleaching, and cutting through grease, oil, and wax. Mix it with water to work wonders on windows, mirrors, stainless steel, concrete, and even your golf balls. Use it undiluted on bathtub rings.

Liquid hand dishwashing detergent wasn't invented until the 1950s, and you're probably wondering how people got along without it. Chemists call the major components of hand dishwashing detergent surfactants. These are basically organic chemicals that actually change the properties of water, helping to quickly wet the surface of whatever you want to clean and making the dirt easier to loosen and remove. Surfactants also keep oils trapped so they can't settle back on the surface and are easily rinsed away. Most hand dishwashing detergents cut grease and are biodegradable. Among other things, you can use these liquid detergents on carpet spills, fiberglass, and greasy laundry stains.

Mustard is the second most-used spice in the United States, surpassed only by pepper. Even though most people think of mustard only in terms of the popular, yellow hot dog accessory — you can eat all parts of the mustard plant and buy several types of mustard products. But did you know you can also clean with it? Dry, powdered mustard is often used to deodorize household items, although there is no definite chemical explanation. And since mustard, the condiment, contains vinegar, it is sometimes used to clean the same household items vinegar can clean. Just be careful. Mustard is considered a dye and will stain fabrics and some hard surfaces.

You may want to hire a professional organizer (PO) to help you. POs cover a wide range of expertise so look for one that matches your specific needs. Since personal recommendations are the best way to find any service professional, ask friends and family members for a referral. You can also check the Yellow Pages, your local chamber of commerce, and ads in newspapers and regional magazines.

The National Association of Professional Organizers will also give you the names of its members in your area, either via the Internet at *www.napo.net* or by phone at 847-375-4746. Other organizing associations include the International Association of Professional Organizers, the Organizing and Management Institute, and the National Study Group on Chronic Disorganization.

Interview several POs either on the phone or personally before you choose one. Ask them about their education, training, and experience, how they work, and what they can do to solve your particular problems. Ask prospective POs what they charge and if it's by the hour or by the project. Fees are generally $50 to $125 per hour depending on experience, geographic location, and competition.

CHAPTER 1
The Kitchen

The kitchen is the heart and soul of a home. It's where delicious meals are lovingly prepared and family and friends gather to spend time together.

But it's precisely because the kitchen is a central hub that you'll often find it crammed with stuff totally unrelated to food or eating. It's where you pause on your way to somewhere else and drop off things — like keys, mail, newspapers, bags, books, notes, laundry. You know. You've seen it.

When you walk into your kitchen, you want to find cleanliness and order. Your mission is to reclaim your kitchen and make it the heart and soul of your home once more.

What exactly are your goals for this space? Make a list of your own, but

Remember...

✓ make a wish list

✓ be realistic

✓ set priorities

✓ identify your clutter problems

✓ label your zones

✓ set a timeline

consider if, perhaps, you'd like to:

- know what food you have on hand at all times.

- find the proper cooking utensils when you need them.

- eliminate at least one junk drawer.

- create a general feeling of tidiness.

The kitchen is a fairly complicated area, yet it's easy to section it off into zones. For that reason, you should plan to declutter one zone at a time. Tackle just the pantry, for instance, and go through all the decluttering and organizing steps. You'll get a

Zones	Step 1: Cut the clutter	Step 2: Increase storage	Step 3: Get organized
Pantry			
Refrigerator			
Countertops			
Cupboards			
Drawers			

real sense of accomplishment from completing this one task and can then move on to the other zones.

Take your best guess on how long it will take you to complete each task for each zone. You may need to factor in time to shop for new storage containers. Remember, this is just an estimate to help you plan your kitchen decluttering project.

The pantry

Step 1 Cut the clutter

The pantry is one of your main food storage areas, or at least it should be. Open the door wide and take a good look at what's going on inside.

Keep in mind

Make a decision:

✓ keep

✓ toss

✓ donate

✓ sell

✓ pass on

Follow purging rules:

✓ decide quickly

✓ handle items once

✓ set limits

✓ pass the "keep" test

✓ recognize garbage

If you're storing nonkitchen items here, you better be able to make a good argument for each thing. Otherwise, get the newspaper recycling out to the garage and the spray starch into the laundry area. Now take each item out and decide its fate.

If you don't have a pantry, and you can't fashion one out of a small closet, you'll apply the same sorting and organizing principles to whatever cupboards house your dry goods.

SUPER TIPS for sorting through your pantry

Purge your pantry for charity. Go ahead and pass on those canned peas or other canned goods as long as they haven't passed the expiration date and they're in good condition. Organizations like the Boy Scouts of America conduct food drives every year. You can also call Second Harvest at 1-800-771-2303 or visit *www.secondharvest.org* to see if they have a donation center near you. If they're too far away, ask someone at your church to recommend a local, reputable charity for food donations.

Help conserve billions in energy costs. Recycle in-the-way items cluttering up your home — like junk mail or ugly glassware — and you'll help save electricity and promote energy conservation. According to the U.S. Department of Energy, producing something from recycled materials often takes less energy than making it from raw materials. For example, manufacturing new aluminum cans from recycled aluminum uses 95 percent less energy than making cans from scratch. Every ton of paper recycled saves enough energy to heat and cool the average home for around six months. Even recycling just one glass container saves enough energy to light a 100-watt bulb for four hours. As more items are recycled, more energy can be saved. So combine decluttering your house with recycling and you'll be pitching in to help conserve billions of dollars in energy costs each year.

Find out if your pantry is overstocked or understocked. Get advice from professional organizer Sheri Lynch, owner of the Atlanta-based home-organizing company, Order in the House. She recommends this four-item checklist to help you find and keep the perfect balance.

❑ **Supply list.** "Keep a tear-off list, and every time a pantry item is depleted, write that item on the list," Lynch says. "When you go to the grocery store, you'll always remember what you need to replace." In addition to Lynch's advice, you could also write up a full pantry inventory and cross off pantry items that make the "depleted" list. After awhile, check how many items have never been crossed off. The more you have, the more overstocked you probably are.

❑ **Small, clear containers.** "Small containers keep loose items, like seasoning packets or snack items, together and easier to find," explains Lynch. If you keep foods like sugar in clear containers, a quick glance will tell you whether you have enough.

❑ **A collapsible step stool.** "If you have high pantry shelves and no way to reach those items easily, you'll soon forget what you have stored there," Lynch says. "A step stool that can be collapsed and folded against the wall or between cabinets helps you maintain order on the higher shelves."

❑ **Good lighting.** "It's impossible to have an organized pantry if you can't see what you have," Lynch explains. "Invest in good lighting."

Whip the "can't-find-time" dilemma. You started with big plans to get organized, but weeks have flown by and you can't free up a full day to organize your pantry. It's time to rework your organization plan. Break it down into small tasks and one or two-hour pieces. For example, instead of cleaning out the whole pantry, just try to get the top shelf done. Then plan when you'll do the next shelf.

Step 2 Increase storage

If your pantry setup is still exactly as the builder left it, it's time for you to get creative. Just as your clothes closet is not doomed to eternity with a single hanging rod, your food storage can go beyond basic wooden shelving.

Remember...

✓ map your space

✓ shop for containers

SUPER TIPS for storing in your pantry

Add bonus storage space inexpensively. For thrifty organization that's loaded with benefits, put an over-the-door shoe bag inside your pantry door. Clear vinyl shoe pockets can be a handy place to store dry goods, and you'll be able to find anything with just a glance. Don't worry about small pocket sizes, either. If that box of cornstarch won't fit, just repackage it in a resealable sandwich or quart-size baggy and label it. Best of all, these shoe organizers come in several sizes, so buy exactly what you need or leave room for expansion. Just remember to attach the bottom corners of the shoe organizer to your pantry door so it won't swing wildly when the door opens.

Reclaim hard-to-reach spots. If you can't reach the cans at the back of your pantry shelf, make them come to you with an inexpensive turntable or Lazy Susan. Add one to a shelf or corner to make items easier to find. It's almost like doubling your storage space. Measure the width of a can before you buy so you'll choose one wide enough for canned goods. If you find one big enough for two rings of cans, put taller items in the inner ring so you can see all your canned goods better.

Divide and conquer with shelf organizers. Get more storage from the empty space underneath your shelves. Use freestanding or stackable wire shelves or try those under-shelf wire baskets that hang by long, sturdy hair-pin-shaped handles. You can also get more from your shelves and cabinet bottoms. Enjoy the drawer-like convenience of roll-out trays and baskets. And don't forget those expandable "bleacher-style" three-tier shelves and double-decker turntables. These can help you put hard-to-reach or hard-to-see spaces back to work so you can store more items neatly.

Sidestep a spaghetti disaster. Watch out for that opened spaghetti box. The slightest bump or tilt could send pasta flying in all directions. You can switch to better spaghetti storage containers — those clever little canisters that stacked chips come in. Just clean out the canister and tape on either a text label or a pasta picture from a newspaper ad. If you still grab your spaghetti canister when you want stacked chips, try decorating the canister with a snazzy sheet of shelf liner.

Frustrate pantry pests. Try this bug-busting freebie. Save up a summer's worth of plastic ice cream buckets and give them a good cleaning. Store your baking goods and grains in them and label each one appropriately. Your sealed-in goods will stay fresh longer and those pesky bug bandits will soon discover the free lunches are over.

Straighten out packet pandemonium. You may be surprised at how many packets live in your pantry — packets for gravy, seasonings, gelatin desserts, sauces, and more. The list may seem endless. But organizing them can be a snap. For small packets, consider a checkbook box, a box for individual-size tea bags, or that long, square-bottomed plastic tray from a cookie box. You can even create a decorative look by trimming the box sides with scrapbooking scissors or pinking shears. For larger packets, cut off the top of a tissue box. Other options include shoe boxes, store-bought plastic or wicker baskets, and supermarket berry baskets. Just be sure to leak-proof all baskets or boxes by lining them with plastic wrap before you use them.

Square off to maximize a packed pantry. If you put lots of round storage containers in your pantry, the space between them will just go to waste. Stick with square and rectangular containers so you get less wasted space in between and more storage.

Expand your pantry without remodeling. Line the inside of your pantry door with over-the-door or door-mountable wire racks and you'll get storage that's perfect for frequently used items. Try a small, inexpensive spice rack, a four-level rack for canned goods, or a pricier six-tier door-spanner. But before you shop, measure your pantry door, as well as the largest and smallest items you plan to store. You'll want to check that the shelves are deep enough and wide enough to hold what you need — whether it's plastic wrap or a row of large cereal boxes. You also don't want smaller items to slip through the wire bars. If the rack's tiers aren't adjustable, also check for enough room between the shelves.

After hearing how bathroom heat and moisture can affect medicine, you moved your medication to the kitchen. Just don't forget kitchens have heat and moisture, too. Be sure to store your medicine away from the stove and sink. Instead, choose a cool, dry place where they can be kept out of the reach of children and pets. If your pantry is well lit, it may be a good place.

Build a space-saving bottle organizer. Improve the way you store soda bottles, wine bottles, or even alcohol-free sparkling cider. Buy 6-inch PVC piping and cut it into 14-inch mini-pipes. Place a box or crate on its side and stack your mini-pipes inside. Slide bottles into the mini-pipe slots and you've got great storage on the cheap.

Step 3 Get organized

Even if you must keep the blender and the aluminum foil in your pantry, you can still have a well-ordered space. By

Remember...

✓ pack properly

✓ label

grouping like items, you'll be surprised just how much stuff will fit and how easy it will be to find everything.

SUPER TIPS for organizing your pantry

Organize shelves like a pro. After you've emptied your pantry and purged what you don't need, pick out the items you use most often, as well as the ones you don't want to forget about. Put these on your "prime real estate" shelves. These shelves are the ones between knee and forehead height, and they're the easiest to reach. And remember, shelves nearest eye level are also the easiest to see. Keep your heaviest items between neck and hip height to make lifting less difficult. Put rarely or occasionally used items near the floor or on high shelves.

Block clutter from creeping back in. Your pantry could quickly turn into a mess if your family doesn't remember where everything belongs, but you can prevent that. Just label each section of every shelf to show what goes there. Your labels can be the same size as the shelf edges, or they can extend slightly below the shelf. Just make sure each label is easy to read and your family knows whether it refers to the shelf above it or the one below.

Brighten up a dark pantry. A dim, gloomy pantry is not only depressing, it's a tough place to find anything. Transform your pantry interior with a quart of light-colored, high-gloss paint. The shiny, bright color helps walls and shelves reflect light better so you can see what's on the shelves more easily. If you don't want to paint, use sewing pins to hang sheets of aluminum foil on the walls between your shelves. If your pantry has no lighting and no outside light gets in, attach a battery-powered stick-on light to the underside of a shelf.

The refrigerator and freezer

Step 1 Cut the clutter

It's probably true you won't have much in your DONATE, SELL, or PASS ON piles when you're through decluttering your refrigerator and freezer. Even die-hard garage salers will snub the rib roast with freezer burn and the limp celery. That's OK. It means your decision-making process just got simpler: KEEP or TOSS.

Keep in mind

Make a decision:

✓ keep

✓ toss

✓ donate

✓ sell

✓ pass on

Follow purging rules:

✓ decide quickly

✓ handle items once

✓ set limits

✓ pass the "keep" test

✓ recognize garbage

But the purging rules just became more important. After all, if you put back every type of pickle relish you hauled out, the "after" picture will look suspiciously like "before."

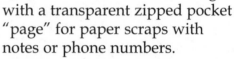

SUPER TIPS for sorting through your fridge

Shape up a paper-plastered fridge door. Start by trashing any out-of-date items or items you no longer use. Then move calendars, phone lists, schedules, and other often-used items to the side of your refrigerator. Or put them all in a three-ring "Quick Reference" binder, along with a transparent zipped pocket "page" for paper scraps with notes or phone numbers.

Toss without a thought

Pantry and refrigerator:

✓ food that's moldy, smelly, or slimy

✓ any normally firm food that has turned soft

✓ leftovers more than three-days old

Cabinets, counters, and drawers:

✓ chipped or damaged dishes, glasses, or mugs

✓ broken appliances

✓ burnt, rusty, or damaged pots, pans, and bake ware

✓ broken utensils and gadgets

Turn refrigerator art into a heartwarming keepsake. Take all the photos and children's artwork off your fridge, buy a scrapbook, and create special pages for each item. You can do it inexpensively or buy special scissors, stickers, and accessories from a scrapbooking store.

Round up outdated food. All expiration dates aren't created equal. Foods with a "use by" date must be used before that date to ensure peak flavor and quality. Foods with a "sell by" date or no date must be cooked or frozen within a certain number of days after purchase. The following list tells how many days each food should last in a refrigerator set below 40 degrees Fahrenheit.

Food	# days in fridge
bacon (opened)	7 days
butter	1-2 weeks
beef, veal, pork, and lamb	3-5 days
buttermilk	1-2 weeks
canned ham labeled "keep refrigerated" (opened)	3-4 days
cheese, unsliced (opened)	3-4 weeks
cheese, sliced	2 weeks
cooked sausage	3-4 days
sweetened condensed milk (opened)	4-5 days
cottage cheese	1-2 weeks
cured ham (cook-before-eating)	5-7 days
eggs	3-5 weeks
egg substitute (opened)	3 days
egg substitute (unopened)	10 days
evaporated milk (opened)	4-5 days
ground meat	1 or 2 days
hard boiled eggs	1 week
hot dogs (unopened)	2 weeks
hot dogs (opened)	1 week
lunch meat (opened)	3-5 days
margarine	4-6 months
sausage from pork, beef or turkey (uncooked)	1 or 2 days
Parmesan (grated) cheese	2 months
poultry	1 or 2 days
processed cooked sausage	3-4 days

Step 2 Increase storage

Short of buying a second refrigerator or freezer, you're stuck with a finite amount of space — and no possibility of a build-out. That means you have to get storage savvy in a hurry.

Remember...
✓ map your space
✓ shop for containers

SUPER TIPS for storing in your fridge

Tap into unused freezer space. Lack of shelves steals away lots of space in the top half of your freezer. Learn a lesson from side-by-side refrigerators. They have handy, space-saving freezer shelves and yours can, too. The same inexpensive wire racks and baskets that organize cabinets can help you use all the storage space in your freezer — instead of just the bottom half.

Uncover hidden fridge items faster. An affordable turntable or Lazy Susan can help keep bottles and condiments arranged neatly in your refrigerator or prevent perishables from going bad before you find them again.

Get tight-sealing plastic tubs for free. Instead of spending money on plastic storage containers, like Tupperware, hang on to plastic margarine and whipped topping tubs. They seal up nicely and offer terrific refrigerator and freezer storage for leftovers.

Free up space with clever liquid storage. Freezing liquids doesn't have to lead to bulky, hard-to-find storage containers. Replace Titanic-size freezer containers with tight-sealing freezer bags. Let them freeze flat so you can store them like file folders — or freeze them in a coffee can. For smaller amounts, pour the liquid into an ice cube tray and freeze.

Step 3 *Get organized*

Know what's in your refrigerator, be able to put your hands on it, discover it's still edible, and you'll save money. That's right, you'll buy fewer duplicate items and throw away less from spoilage.

Remember...

✓ pack properly

✓ label

Get ready to learn how to organize your cold foods and label them logically.

SUPER TIPS for organizing your fridge

Keep track of leftovers easily. Here's a great idea for keeping track of what's in your refrigerator and freezer and when you put it there. Anytime you store leftovers or perishables, list it on a magnetic, erasable, dry marker board, along with a "best before" date or the date it went in your refrigerator or freezer. You can even have separate boards for your refrigerator and freezer. You'll save money because you'll use foods before they spoil, and your family will stop holding the refrigerator and freezer doors open to see what's in there. Just don't forget to erase items from the board after you've used them.

Save time and money when you organize your refrigerator. It's easy — just group like items together. Say sayonara to endless scrounging through your fridge for a buried item. After you assign each group a home, you'll

Be prepared for disasters and health emergencies. Put a copy of health and contact information in an envelope labeled "Medicines and Emergency Contact Information." Keep one posted on your refrigerator and put duplicates near phones. Here's a list of vital health information you must have at your fingertips at all times. Include the following for each member of your household.

❑ name and birth date

❑ home contact information, including address, phone number, and e-mail address

❑ work or school contact information, including address, phone number, and e-mail address

❑ cell phone numbers

❑ insurance information

❑ doctor's name and phone number

❑ names of specialists regularly visited, including phone numbers

❑ drug and food allergies

❑ medications and dosage schedules

❑ pharmacist's name and phone number

❑ whether the person wears glasses, contact lenses, hearing aids, or dentures

❑ emergency contact information

instantly know right where to go for anything. And never again will you uncover luncheon meat gone bad or duplicate jars of mayo. Grouping items stops food disappearances cold, which helps you save money.

Rescue food from going to waste. Before you make your grocery list, find the oldest items in your freezer and move them to the front. Throw out anything that has been in there longer than recommended by food experts. Then plan how to use the older items before making this week's grocery list. That means less food wasted and more money saved.

Extend the shelf life of eggs and milk. Tucking eggs in those little egg slots in your refrigerator door makes them go bad faster. And milk stored in your fridge door deteriorates more rapidly, too. Keep milk and eggs — as well as refrigerated cookie dough, biscuits, rolls, and pastries — on your refrigerator shelves.

Kitchen countertops

Step 1 Cut the clutter

Countertops, and the chaos that's on them, are the first things you see when you enter a kitchen. Your pantry may be perfect, your cupboards immaculate, but if your counters are a jumble of papers, appliances, dishes, and knickknacks, no one will notice. And since no kitchen has enough counter space, how can you waste even one square inch of yours under clutter?

Keep in mind

Make a decision:	Follow purging rules:
✓ keep	✓ decide quickly
✓ toss	✓ handle items once
✓ donate	✓ set limits
✓ sell	✓ pass the "keep" test
✓ pass on	✓ recognize garbage

Clear off your counter and keep it clear, and you will feel better and more productive every time you walk into your kitchen. Who knows, you just might feel like cooking dinner.

The issue of mail and daily paper clutter is addressed in *Chapter 4 The Home Office*. Many people take care of finances and correspondence from the kitchen counter, but a casual setup like this naturally creates untidiness. If you can't carve out a separate office but must dedicate a portion of your kitchen to bill-paying and other office duties, make sure you allow for appropriate storage.

SUPER TIPS *for sorting out your countertops*

Do away with cookbook clutter. Don't let cookbooks take over your valuable storage space. Instead, copy or cut the best recipes from each book. Then make a "best recipes" collection in a three-ring binder, scrapbook, photo album with liftable sheets, or blank journal. Now you can donate or pass on undamaged cookbooks and toss the damaged ones. If you're tempted to hang on to a cookbook because you might need a recipe next Thanksgiving, consider this.

Chances are you — or your kids or grandkids — have access to the thousands of recipes on the Internet. You might never need a cookbook again.

Clear off countertops with ease. Clearing off countertops might be easier than you think. Ask yourself whether any items on your countertop could go in your cabinets, pantry, or on a shelf or wall.

Tailor countertops for how you live. Pull every item off your countertop and put it in a temporary holding area. Anything you or your family uses within three days can return to the countertop. On day four, sort through the items left in your temporary holding area. Assign each one to be donated, sold, given away, tossed, or stored in a new place.

Step 2 Increase storage

You've purged everything unnecessary from your countertops and now you're left with the bare essentials. If it's got to stay on your counter, work hard to make it look good. If you can, put it inside or under something attractive and clean.

Remember...
✓ map your space
✓ shop for containers

SUPER TIPS for storing on your countertops

Find a handy home for small appliances. Some fancy kitchens have an attractive "appliance garage" on or near the counter. Not only can you create similar storage, but you may also recover counter space. Just fashion your own "appliance hangar" by assigning one part of your cupboard for small appliances. They'll be within easy reach, and you'll love how your counter looks without the clutter.

Corner some extra space. Keep your counters as free of objects as you can. But when you must store items on the counter, put them in the corners enclosed by two walls. You're less likely to use this area as a workspace, and you can even double the usefulness of such areas with two- or three-story wire shelf units tailor-made for corners.

Create temporary counter space anytime. Find a good deal on a cutting board wide enough to cover your sink. Whenever you need extra counter space, lay it over your sink until you're done. Then just clean the cutting board and put it away until the next time.

Look high and low for unused space. If your cabinets are packed and your often-used countertop items still take up too much space, maybe you need more storage. Scour your kitchen for empty corners or unused wall space and measure any free space you find. Then check flea markets and garage sales for bookshelves, a microwave stand, a TV stand, or the largest and sturdiest corner shelves that will fit. These can give some of your countertop clutter new homes.

Hang baskets to save space. Just as hanging baskets get plants off the ground, you can hang items to get them off your counter. Hang a wire or wicker basket on a wall. Hang a three-tier basket set from the ceiling for produce. If you can't hang anything, fill up a three-story rack or shelf that leans against your fridge or countertop walls. That's better than cluttering your counter.

Step 3 Get organized

This should be the easy part because, hopefully, now you don't have much on your countertops to organize. But for those things you simply must store there, arrange them efficiently and logically.

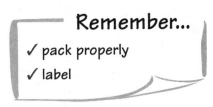

Remember...

✓ pack properly

✓ label

SUPER TIPS for organizing your countertops

End coupon clutter and menu mayhem. You can buy expensive custom organizers for menus and coupons — or you can rig up super substitutes for much less. Start with an inexpensive accordion file to organize your coupons. Then grab a hole punch to put menus in a three-ring binder. Stick sheets of scrap paper in the side pockets for writing down family orders.

Minimize countertop space hogs. Buy under-the-cabinet and wall-mounted versions of appliances and other counter-sitters whenever possible. Paper towel racks, coffee makers, can openers, and microwaves are just a few good examples of items that can be attached to walls or cabinet bottoms instead of hogging space on your countertop.

Kitchen cupboards

Step 1 Cut the clutter

What's lurking in the depths of your kitchen cupboards? Two fish poachers — how many does one family need? A mandoline — what is it anyway? And when was the last time you actually made your own yogurt?

There's no way around it. To cut the clutter in your kitchen cupboards, you must drag every single item out and decide its fate. Set some limits and follow the purging rules. If you do this properly, you may discover your kitchen really has all the storage space you need.

Keep in mind

Make a decision:
- ✓ keep
- ✓ toss
- ✓ donate
- ✓ sell
- ✓ pass on

Follow purging rules:
- ✓ decide quickly
- ✓ handle items once
- ✓ set limits
- ✓ pass the "keep" test
- ✓ recognize garbage

SUPER TIPS for sorting through your cupboards

Reclaim lost shelf space in four steps. First, match every lid with its container. Then sort out all the lid-deprived

containers. Determine which containers can quickly start a
new life as holders for things like drawer clutter, pencils,
mail, loose kitchen items, or loose items in another room.
Throw out or recycle all the others and toss any "orphan"
lids that don't have a matching container. Otherwise,
they're just stealing that extra storage space you've been
wishing for.

Show off holiday items then hide them away. That
Yuletide platter may live in your kitchen year round, but
you only use it in December. That's reason enough to store
holiday dinnerware and other seasonal items in your attic
or basement until they're needed. Think how much space
that will free up. Moreover, many holiday items make
good display pieces during their celebration time, so you
probably won't ever want them in your cupboards again.

Imagine cooking in a well-organized kitchen. You've
tried to purge items from your cabinets, counters, and
drawers, but you just can't let much go. Switch gears.
Think about what your kitchen will be like after you've
purged and organized. Look through magazines, newspapers, and Web sites for clever ideas. Start a folder for

How many pots and pans do you really need? A cooking professional recommends a 12-inch skillet with a lid, a 10-inch
sauté pot with tapered sides, an eight-quart stock pot, and a
four-quart sauce pan. But it pays to notice what you use most
often. "A single person who lives in a condo probably only
needs one skillet, one large pot, and one or two smaller pots,"
says professional organizer Sheri Lynch, owner of Atlanta-
based Order in the House. "A family of five that enjoys
gourmet cooking and has a large kitchen could still be organized even with many more pieces."

your ideas, clippings, and pictures. Use them to make a tentative overall storage plan for your pantry and kitchen items. Then you'll know what tradeoffs you're willing to make and purging will be easier.

Make deciding easy on yourself. You've cleared out your cabinets, and you're deciding what to keep versus what to donate or toss. If you catch yourself developing a huge "keep" pile or you repeatedly choose to "keep" items you're not sure about, add a "maybe" box. Use it for items you can't quickly or easily let go. After you sort all the other items from your cabinets, sort through this box. Decisions often come more easily then.

Step 2 Increase storage

Deep down inside, you want to rip out all your cupboards and start over. After all, those shiny new cabinets in the home stores have racks and bins, doors that tilt and slide, and trays that roll out and spin. It's an organizational dream come true. It's also a lot of money.

But what if you could store like the experts with only a little ingenuity and a few dollars?

Remember...

✓ map your space
✓ shop for containers

SUPER TIPS *for storing in your cupboards*

Regain storage space by hook or by crook. You may be surprised by how many kinds of hooks can help you reclaim space in your cabinets, counter, and pantry. You can use suction cup hooks, magnetic hooks, and adhesive hooks without touching a hammer and nails. Use these hooks, as well as the hammer-and-nails kind, to create storage on walls, refrigerators, vent hoods, and inside cabinets.

Create a spice rack from cardboard boxes. Buy three of those oversized boxes of aluminum foil, plastic wrap, or wax paper from a warehouse store. When they're empty, put one on top of another and place the third in front of them on your pantry shelf. Now you have a set of spice "bleachers" that resemble the expensive three-tier organizers you see in shops and catalogs. Just be sure to leave your heaviest spice bottles on the pantry shelf in case the boxes aren't strong enough to hold them.

Step up to the plate. Why dream of more storage when it may already be at your fingertips? If your high cupboards are empty because they're hard to reach, put them back into service with a step stool. They're the ideal spot for things you only use occasionally. Try turntables or pullout baskets and trays to help you reclaim corner cupboards and other hard-to-reach storage.

Catch sight of small bottles instantly. Good news for anyone who hates unloading an entire shelf to find one particular spice bottle. Put your spices on a rotating turntable, and you'll find whatever you need with a single spin. Buy a double-decker version if you have a tall storage space.

"File" your baking sheets. Don't buy an expensive maple rack for storing your baking sheets. Instead, look for a stair-stepped or "rising" office file organizer. If the space between the slats is wide enough, you can use it to store trays, cutting boards, pot lids, or any other long, almost-flat item.

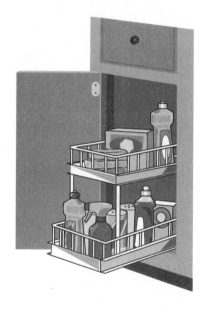

Try slide-out shelves for drawer-style convenience. Install sliding trays, shelves, bins, or baskets and you'll bring the back of your shelves and cabinets to you. No more fumbling around trying to reach something.

Patch up the holes in wire shelves. Wire shelves often have large, open spaces that smaller objects can slip right through. Here's an easy fix. Pull off a long sheet of plastic wrap. Cut it to match the width of your shelf and then wrap it around the shelf several times. Now you have a more solid surface to hold small items, and it's still transparent.

Stake your claim on under-the-sink territory. Unless the cabinet below your kitchen sink is full from top to bottom, you can probably add storage space. Install a triple swing-out towel rack to gain a convenient place for dish towels and cleanup rags.

Be on the lookout for clever storage racks. You'll find plenty of racks designed to attach to the inside of your cabinet doors. Many are ideal for storing cleaners, sponges, scouring pads, rubber gloves, lids, spices, or plastic wrap. Some can even hold a paper towel roll. Try one on the cabinet door under your sink. Before long, you may wonder how you ever lived without it.

Step 3 Get organized

Experts will tell you the most important storage rule in any kitchen is proximity. That means items should be close to where you use them — like dishware near the dishwasher and mugs near the coffeepot.

Remember...

✓ pack properly

✓ label

Rule number two — keep like items together. You'll save steps and frustration if you know all the glasses are in one cabinet, all the baking pans are on a single shelf, and if your measuring cup isn't with the mixing bowls, it must be in the dishwasher.

Make sure all family members are clued into these nifty little organization secrets. You'll get there faster if everyone is rowing in the same direction.

SUPER TIPS for organizing your cupboards

Put a lid on storage container clutter. Match up your lids and containers before you store them. Mark each lid with the same number as its matching container or use color codes. Then see which one of these storage ideas works for you.

- Use an old dish rack to file the lids.

- Divide a shoe box into compartments by cutting cardboard dividers to fit. Sort your lids by size and shape and then file appropriately.

- Designate a drawer for lids.

- Cut a cereal box in half lengthwise and drop lids in each half.

- Put all your lids in one basket.

Free up cabinet space and add a designer touch to your kitchen. Do this with your pots and pans — hang them from a pretty pot rack. Buy one at your favorite home improvement store. Add chains to help position the rack so your pots are within reach but above your head. Although hanging your pot rack above a cook top might seem ideal, it leads to grease-encrusted pots and a high risk of burns from reaching for the pans. Pick another spot — you'll like it better. Finally, make sure you can hang your rack securely from your ceiling joists or get your pot rack professionally installed.

Rig up a bargain pot rack. Suspend a short, wooden ladder or a sturdy wall grid from your ceiling joists using chains. Add S-hooks or other hooks, as appropriate, to complete your economical pot rack.

Store mugs in half the space. Hang half your mugs — or all of them — from hooks on the ceiling of your cabinet if space permits. Otherwise, hang them from the hooks of a decorative mug tree on your counter.

Kitchen drawers

Step 1 Cut the clutter

Count how many junk drawers you have in your kitchen. That's too many. Webster defines junk as "useless or worthless stuff; trash." If it's useless or worthless, what is it doing taking up valuable space in a kitchen drawer?

It's OK to have a drawer of useful and used kitchen gadgets, a drawer of silverware, or a drawer of kitchen towels. Get the term "junk drawer" right out of your head and vow that every item you keep will be worthy. Then treat it as such, with a clean, well-defined home.

Keep in mind

Make a decision:

✓ keep

✓ toss

✓ donate

✓ sell

✓ pass on

Follow purging rules:

✓ decide quickly

✓ handle items once

✓ set limits

✓ pass the "keep" test

✓ recognize garbage

SUPER TIPS for sorting through your drawers

Make junk drawer purging easier. Spread clean, white trash bags on an empty section of your kitchen floor.

Completely empty your junk drawer right down to the last thumb tack. Once you finally see what's in there, you'll probably spot plenty of items you've been meaning to throw out or move to another location.

Store items where they're used. Just because you keep it in your kitchen doesn't mean that's where you use it. As you sort through your things, ask yourself which items could just as easily be stored in another room — especially if that's where the item is usually used.

Step 2 Increase storage

If you can't even open a drawer because the spatula is caught in the whisk, which is tangled up with the can opener, which is jammed against the drawer frame, then "divide and conquer" is your new philosophy. Turn your turmoil into order with clever ways of containing your kitchen clutter.

Remember...

✓ map your space
✓ shop for containers

SUPER TIPS for storing in your drawers

Keep drawers ship-shape with free accessories.
You've won half the battle if most small items in your drawers are in containers. Don't miss out on these free "reusables" — baby food jars, checkbook boxes, resealable plastic storage bags, pill organizers, pill bottles, yogurt cups, and pudding cups. Clean and label them, if needed. Then use them to store twist ties, matches, birthday candles, batteries, and more.

Make an adjustable drawer organizer for free. Before you throw that box away, look it over. If cut short enough, would it be an ideal container for batteries or other loose items in your junk drawer? Then start cutting. That's a free drawer organizer. If you find enough good boxes, you could partition the whole drawer into useful compartments. Just remember to paper clip the boxes together so they won't slide around. As you add new boxes, rearrange the pattern so it continues to fit both the drawer and your storage needs.

Revamp a drawer with an egg carton. Don't waste your money on a small-items organizer for your junk drawer. Use an egg carton for free. Just lop off the top and you're ready to store twist-ties, tacks, corn-on-the-cob holders, rubber bands, small batteries, loose change, and more. Not only does this make grouped items easier to find, you can cut this organizer to fit, too. Clip the carton down to 4, 6, 8, or 10 cups if drawer space is tight.

Whip a messy drawer into shape. Organize a junky drawer in seconds with a plastic silverware tray. These trays come in different sizes, and they are easy on your budget, too.

Step 3 Get organized

Now for the fun part. You get to put things back into your clean drawers. Just remember to take a minute to think about how you use your kitchen and place items where they make the most sense. Potholders and

Remember...

✓ pack properly
✓ label

mitts should be next to the oven, silverware not too far from the dishwasher, and baking utensils near a work surface. Make a plan and stick with it, and you'll never face the muddle of a junk drawer again.

SUPER TIPS *for organizing your drawers*

Corral recipe clippings, cards, scraps, and scribbles. No more cut-out recipes strewn about. Use this trick to get organized fast. Sort cut-out or written-down recipes into categories and insert them in a photo album with liftable sheets. Use dividers to separate the categories, if possible. Otherwise, photocopy the recipes, three-hole-punch the pages, and put them in a three-ring binder with dividers. For best results, use two binders or albums — one for holiday/seasonal recipes and one for everyday recipes. Store the holiday/seasonal binder with other holiday items and keep the everyday book in your kitchen.

Tackle battery disorder. Expensive custom battery organizers are available, but you can get perfectly good battery storage at a better price. Store small batteries in the compartments of an empty tackle box. Large C and D batteries can fit in the bottom. You can also buy a three- to five-drawer plastic organizer that's about a foot tall. You can usually put one type of battery in each drawer.

Unearth decorative storage containers. If your decluttering has uncovered a flowerpot, planter, or vase that's not in use, line it with an attractive cloth napkin or tea towel and plunk in your manual can opener, tall utensils, or other kitchen gadgets. Not only can this clear drawer or counter space, it also makes a manual can opener readily available during power outages.

End plastic grocery bag overflow. Empty tissue boxes can do the job. Insert one plastic grocery bag as a starter. As you insert each additional bag, thread it through the previous bag's handles before pushing it into the box. This makes every bag easier to pull out later. When you tuck the last bag in, leave its handles sticking out of the box for easy access. When you've stuffed two tissue boxes full, keep one in your kitchen and another in your car.

Step 4 Keep it clean

Now that your kitchen is free of clutter, you'll find it's easy to keep it clean. The chart on the following page gives you a list of chores you can complete in 10 minutes. Add a few weekly, monthly, and occasional chores, and you've got one smart cleaning plan. Then keep reading to find plenty of quick and easy cleaning tips for your clutter-free kitchen.

SUPER TIPS for cleaning your kitchen

Throw in the towel to clean your microwave. Why use elbow grease to clean the inside of your microwave oven? A clever trick with a paper towel makes it clean itself while you tackle another chore. Soak a paper towel with water, drop it in your microwave, and "cook" it for four minutes. Wait two more minutes before opening your microwave. Once the paper towel has cooled slightly, use it to quickly wipe down the inside of your microwave, and you're done.

10-minute daily speed cleaning	Weekly chores	Monthly chores	Occasional chores
Return food, utensils, and pans to their homes	Replace towels and cloths with clean ones	Clean inside of fridge, including door seals	Wash curtains
Rinse sink	Vacuum then mop floor	Replace baking soda box in fridge	Wash windows
Empty trash	Wash throw rugs	Check ceiling corners for cobwebs	Vacuum refrigerator condenser and grille
Sweep floor	Clean stove drip pans	Wipe down kitchen cabinets	Clean exhaust fan
Wipe stove top	Dust top of fridge	Deodorize garbage disposal	Clean oven
Wipe microwave door	Clean inside of microwave	Dust ceiling fans and light fixtures	Check refrigerator pan
Close all doors and drawers	Wipe down stove backsplash		Wash out cutlery tray
Fold or hang dish towels			

Make fishy odors vanish. Dry mustard works great to neutralize odors. Just mix some dry mustard with a little dishwashing liquid to remove that nasty fish smell.

Bid purple price tag stains good-bye. Your laminate counter isn't doomed to wear a permanent purple patch. Spray on a generous amount of regular household or kitchen cleaner and let it set long enough to liquefy the stain. Then blot with a paper towel and rinse with water. Repeat this stain-busting trick until the stain vanishes.

Turn smelly glassware sunshine fresh. Make stinky bottles and glass containers smell clean and fresh. Just fill them halfway with water and one tablespoon of dry mustard and shake. Let the containers soak a few hours before rinsing.

Freshen your fridge with coffee grounds. Don't put up with unpleasant smells every time you open your refrigerator door. Tuck a bowl of coffee grounds in your fridge to chase away odors.

Try a trio of lemon-fresh tricks. You can clean cutting boards, copper cookware, and even tough faucet buildup with a lemon. Here's how:

❑ Grab a lemon wedge to help clean, deodorize, and bleach stains off your cutting board.

❑ Put salt on another wedge and use it to rub down copper pots and pans.

❑ Apply lemon juice to mineral deposits on your faucet. Let it soak for a while and then rinse. Repeat, if needed.

Happen upon a great fridge cleaner. The next time you change the baking soda in your refrigerator, save the old box. Baking soda scrubs almost as well as scouring powder, and it's great for removing refrigerator stains. Use baking soda and water to clean out your fridge, then check the door seals for mold. Use a bleach and water mixture to kill any mold you find.

Take a shine to club soda. You can make your stainless steel sink shine like new. Pour some club soda on a cloth and give your sink a good rubdown, then dry it with a clean cloth to prevent streaks. It also works great on vinyl floors.

Enlist dishwasher's help to battle greasy fan filter. Yuck! Greasy buildup in the fan filter above your stove can be disgusting! Get rid of it. Just remove the filter and stick it into the top rack of your dishwasher the next time you run a full wash cycle. When it's clean, simply return it to its home above your stove.

Show annoying allergens who's boss. This simple trick can keep allergens to a minimum and help keep the air in your home fresh for free. The secret? Keep humidity down so it can't fuel the growth of mold and dust mites. Close your windows except when you need to flush humidity out of rooms, like your kitchen. And make it a habit to clean out the drip pans for your air conditioner and refrigerator regularly.

Eliminate tarnish with mustard. When Angela C. of Peachtree City, Ga., found tarnish on her favorite copper pot, she raided the fridge. She snatched the yellow mustard jar and spread some over the stain. "You have to put it on and leave it," Angela says. After giving the mustard time to work, she rinsed the mustard — and tarnish — away. If you're out of mustard, don't worry. "Ketchup will work, too," she says.

Blot red drink stains to make them disappear. The moment you spot that red drink on your laminate counter, start blotting. Next, pour rubbing alcohol on any leftover spots and spread it around. Wait one minute and pour a little full-strength household chlorine bleach on the stain. Let that stand for a minute before rinsing thoroughly with clean water.

Prevent food poisoning from a surprising source. Don't forget to clean this important but overlooked part of every kitchen — your can opener. It can harbor dangerous bacteria that can cause food poisoning. Wash the can opener blade every time you use it. Scrub it with a clean toothbrush and some cleanser, then "open" a few layers of paper towels with it to make absolutely sure you've cleaned the blades thoroughly.

CHAPTER 2
The Family Room

You can call it a den or a great room, but whatever name it goes by, this room is where you truly do your living. It's where you fling yourself down on the couch and read a book or watch a movie. This is where the dog curls up and the cat naps.

Although this space should be comfortable and welcoming, it won't be restful if you have to shove aside newspapers just to sit down or if you miss your favorite program because you can't find the remote.

And even if you have a formal living room, don't guests always end up in this more lived-in space?

Now look at the space with a critical eye and decide what type of clutter problems you have. Then write down

Remember...

✓ make a wish list

✓ be realistic

✓ set priorities

✓ identify your clutter problems

✓ label your zones

✓ set a timeline

your goals for this space. Consider if you'd like to:

- gain control over magazines and newspapers

- organize your CDs and DVDs

- hide that hand-me-down afghan from company

- feel more calm and relaxed when you're in this room

When you're in the family room, you are most likely sitting down and enjoying the company of other people or engaging in a quiet activity. Look at the following table. Although you may have more or different zones, these are the two most common in a family living area.

Zones	Step 1: Cut the clutter	Step 2: Increase storage	Step 3: Get organized
Relaxing and entertaining			
Audio-visual equipment			
Additional zone			

Take your best guess on how long it will take you to complete each task for each zone. Don't forget to factor in time to shop for new storage containers. Remember, this is just an estimate to help you plan your living area decluttering project.

Step 1 Cut the clutter

Because your main living area is so visible and public, you must determine your clutter tolerance. If you don't mind a certain level — for instance, a stack of newspapers doesn't bother you — accept it and don't spend a lot of time and energy trying to fix that particular problem.

Keep in mind

Make a decision:
- ✓ keep
- ✓ toss
- ✓ donate
- ✓ sell
- ✓ pass on

Follow purging rules:
- ✓ decide quickly
- ✓ handle items once
- ✓ set limits
- ✓ pass the "keep" test
- ✓ recognize garbage

SUPER TIPS *for sorting the relaxing/entertaining area*

Reclaim your house from the Book Monster. Is your house being swallowed by books? For some people, parting with books is like letting go of loved ones. If you have plenty of shelf space, by all means keep them. But if more books live in boxes on the floor than reside on shelves, it's time to clean house. Decide whether you want to donate or sell your unwanted books. Set two empty boxes on the floor. Label one "keep" and the other either "donate" or "sell." You can even add a third box called "maybe" if you have trouble deciding which ones to keep. Quickly go through each shelf and toss books in the appropriate box.

Share your books with people in need. Donating or selling used books can make the decluttering process painless. These are just a few groups that might welcome donations. Don't forget — your donations are tax deductible, so get a receipt from the group you give them to.

- libraries
- schools
- assisted living facilities
- reading programs
- churches
- hospitals
- senior citizen centers

Make money off old books. While unwanted books sit on your shelves collecting dust, they could be earning you money. Consider these suggestions:

- Take them to a local used bookseller.
- Sell them in a garage sale.
- Sell them on the Internet through a used bookseller, like Amazon.com at *www.amazon.com.*
- Auction them through an online auction house, such as eBay at *www.ebay.com.*

All that junk in your family room could be a tax deduction in disguise. The Internal Revenue Service (IRS) allows you to deduct charitable donations to qualified organizations like these:

❑ federal, state, and local governments

❑ some charitable, religious, scientific, educational, or literary organizations

❑ groups working to prevent cruelty to children or animals

Call the group you would like to donate your items to. They can tell you if they qualify under the IRS tax code. Donations to individuals don't count.

You'll have to itemize your deductions using Schedule A of the 1040 tax form. And keep those receipts! For donations worth more than $250, you must have a receipt from the organization to claim a tax deduction. How much would you get for your items at a garage sale or flea market? That's the amount you can deduct, and the amount you should get the receipt for. If you donate more than $500 worth of items, you also need to fill out Form 8283 when you file your taxes. For more information, check out IRS Publication 526 or Tax Topic 506.

Clip and save favorite articles. Why save a whole magazine or newspaper when you only want a single picture or article? Clip it instead, then throw the rest away. Get an accordion folder or stack of loose file folders, and label them by interest, like gardening," "travel," "recipes," and so on. The more specific, the better. Clip and file as soon as you see a piece you want, and toss the rest. It's fast and easy, and you won't have to face an eyesore of old newspapers or feel guilty about having to go through them.

Cancel unread subscriptions. Everybody gets behind in their reading, but draw the line. Cancel a magazine subscription if you haven't read an issue in more than three months. You can often get a refund for the unused portion of your subscription. And never sign up for a magazine just to enter a sweepstakes. It will not increase your odds of winning. By law, you can enter a contest without buying anything.

Maximize space for current magazines. Overflowing stacks of old magazines are a common clutter problem in family rooms. Thin the dead wood. Pick an attractive container for your magazines and see how many fit in it. Limit yourself to only as many magazines as the container holds. Each time a new issue arrives, throw away an old one. Arrange issues chronologically with older ones in the back, so you can quickly toss. Or set a number and limit yourself to that many magazines. The same rules apply — when a new issue arrives, an old one has to go.

Toss without a thought

- ✓ old board games or card games no one plays anymore
- ✓ broken trinkets and knick-knacks
- ✓ books you have read and don't plan to read again
- ✓ anything you can't identify

Rethink family room furniture. Broken furniture or furniture you don't like should not live in your family room. Maybe your tastes have changed. Maybe you never liked that couch to begin with. Maybe your spouse keeps promising to fix the table and never gets around to it. Take an honest look and decide which pieces, if any, you would like to part with. Perhaps the piece is in good shape, but it doesn't fit with the room's decor. In that case, try it in a different room. And remember, comfortable couches and chairs can be recovered. Donate unwanted furniture to a local charitable organization, give it away, or sell it at a garage sale.

Create the illusion of more space. Forget about remodeling. You can create the illusion of space without spending a fortune. Here's how:

- Choose light colors for your walls and furniture.
- Keep colors within the same color family.
- Go with light-colored, hard-surface flooring that blends into your wall color.
- Use contemporary furniture and decor with simple, clean lines.

Stop storing other people's stuff. Are you still housing stuff for your grown children? Items for family or friends? Give it back and be firm. Tell them if they don't want it you will be happy to get rid of it for them. If they want to look it over first, ask them to take it home and go through it, so you can get it out of the way and continue clearing clutter.

SUPER TIPS *for sorting your audio-visual equipment*

Choose soft storage for CDs. Jewel cases — the hard, plastic cases that house CDs — take up lots of space. Consolidate your music collection by switching to a soft CD binder. CD binders are like soft books with plastic sleeves inside for holding the delicate discs and the booklet that comes with each CD. Some binders hold hundreds of discs. Switch to this storage method, and you can pitch those jewel cases for good.

Rent — don't buy — DVDs and videos. Why buy a movie you will watch only once or twice? Renting costs a fraction of the amount, and more and more rental services have eliminated late fees. Brick-and-mortar stores, like Blockbuster, carry most new movies, but they may charge more for their rentals. Newer mail-order rental programs, like Netflix, are generally cheaper and offer more movies. Netflix allows you to rent as many movies as you want for a low, flat, monthly fee. You can sign up for a free trial at *www.netflix.com*. Choose several movies you'd like to see, and Netflix will mail them to you. Watch them, and when you're done, simply mail them back. Postage both ways is free, and you can keep the movies as long as you like. Netflix does not charge late fees. You must have Internet access and a DVD player to use Netflix.

Fix appliances or get rid of them. Stop promising you will get the VCR fixed, or replace the needle on that old turntable. Give yourself or your spouse one more week to fix it, then let it go. Some items cost more to repair than replace, so factor that into your decision.

Step 2 Increase storage

Do you like everything out of sight? If so, don't install open shelving. Go for closed containers and hidden storage.

Remember...

✓ map your space

✓ shop for containers

And decide if your storage must match a decorating theme. You may not be happy with wicker or wooden baskets if you're a chrome-and-glass kind of person. Remember, there are storage options to suit every taste and every budget.

SUPER TIPS for storing in the relaxing/entertaining area

Put an end to visual clutter. Going vertical can create lots of space for storage, but before you start building or buying, decide which kind is best. Open storage, like bookcases, curio cabinets, coat racks, shelves, and any other visible storage, works best for neat, well-ordered objects, such as framed photographs, rows of books, CDs, or tasteful vases. Storage cabinets, trunks, drawers, and anything else you can close are good at hiding messier items, like papers, clothes, or blankets. Consider what you need to store, then decide if it makes for a good display item. If not, choose a unit with doors or a lid so you can easily "shut out" the visual clutter.

Stow throws in tasteful hampers. Lightweight and attractive, wicker hampers are perfect for storing blankets, throws, floor pillows, and other soft lounge-about items you keep in your family room. Choose a hamper made in materials and shades that complement your decor. Be sure it's large enough to hold everything you plan to store in it. A small hamper could double as an end table, while a large wicker blanket chest could also serve as a coffee table or ottoman.

Store blankets and pillows in style. Need more space? Try this. Place a cedar chest in your family room for blankets, throws, and pillows, and let it do double duty as a coffee table or end table. You can lay a table runner or place mat on top to protect the wood from the scratches and water marks tables tend to collect.

Give a second life to old plant pots. Recycle an old planter as a magazine holder. Paint it in colors that work with your decor and show off your personal style.

Keep old magazines in line. If you absolutely must keep back issues of magazines, keep them organized and attractive in magazine holders. These tall, slim holders come in plastic, cardboard, or metal and a variety of colors, plus they fit perfectly on most bookshelves. You can even label them by magazine title or interest.

DON'T STORE...

✓ dishes, unless decorative

✓ food

✓ incoming mail

✓ office papers

✓ shoes

✓ coats

✓ laundry

Hide stuff in plain sight. Tight on storage space? Store items in a box under a coffee table or end table and drape a floor-length tablecloth, fancy sheet, or throw over it. You can whisk the cloth aside to reach items you need, and hastily hide the box when company comes. For a more fashionable look, sew tassels or beads along the cloth's edges. Or drape several cloths of different lengths, textures, and colors artfully across one another for a chic, layered look.

Make the most of sofa space. Right now, only dust bunnies live under your couch. Change that. Store long, low items, like board games, card games, or the extra leaf to your dining room table beneath the sofa. Briefcases and sweater boxes are perfect for holding loose items and slide easily under the couch. Plus, a briefcase has handles so you can pull it out and carry it with you. If you have trouble bending or kneeling, don't use this spot to store stuff you use often.

Wage war on overflowing bookcases. Why relegate all books to your family room? Consider spreading them around the house by placing shelves or small bookcases in other rooms. Keep cookbooks in your kitchen, children's books in the kids' room, and finance and work-related books with your home office. Put a night stand with a small shelf in your bedroom to store your current nighttime reading. You can still use the living room bookcases as the workhorses.

Double your space by hanging shelves. Most furniture is less than 5 feet tall, but most ceilings are at least 8 feet. Hang shelves 12 to 18 inches below the ceiling and use them to display photos, books, knickknacks, and plants. Some shelving units allow you to adjust the height of shelves, while others are stationary. Decide which look appeals to you.

Keep hobby supplies organized and handy. Create a hobby basket to hold all the items you need to work on your hobby in the family room. If you're an avid puzzler, you may want to store a pencil, puzzle book, and glasses in it. Knitters might keep knitting needles, yarn, and their latest project there. Set it beside the sofa or chair you like to sit in, and you'll have a convenient, pretty container for items you use often. To keep pets out of it, or to keep it looking tidy, choose a basket with a lid.

Increase storage without spending a fortune. You don't have to buy new furniture to create more storage. Go on a scavenger hunt through your house for old or unused furniture in other rooms, pieces that can double as storage, like bookcases, night stands, trunks, baskets, and even wicker laundry hampers. Paint can mask scrapes and imperfections inexpensively and help old pieces blend with your new decor.

SUPER TIPS *for storing your audio-visual equipment*

Sew a pocket for remotes. Stitch together a pocket to hold remote controls, magazines, and newspapers at your favorite chair. Make a pouch out of slipcover fabric, and leave a long flap from the top. Tuck the flap underneath the seat cushion of a chair or couch, and drape the pocket over the arm and down the side.

Double-shelve movies for more space. Too many movies and not enough shelf space? Double up by shelving them two-deep. Choose a deep-set bookshelf or media cabinet. Place videotapes and DVDs you seldom watch in the back row, and in front, shelve blank tapes and movies you haven't seen yet or plan to watch again.

Store CDs in shoe boxes. Recycle old shoe boxes as media storage. Remove the lid and file CDs in them with the title facing up. Use tabbed index cards to separate music by category, and slide the box onto a bookshelf for easy access. You can dress up the boxes by wrapping them in your favorite gift wrap or spray-painting them to match your decor.

Groove with new technology. All of your music can fit in the palm of your hand or the pocket of your pants, thanks to technology. Popular devices like the iPod and other MP3-players can hold entire music collections, but they are smaller than most remote controls. Generally, you use a computer to transfer music from a compact disc (CD) to the MP3-player. Once you save your music to the tiny device, you can even throw away or at least pack up all those CDs. The players are portable and come with tiny earbuds, so you can carry them with you and listen to music almost anywhere without bothering others.

Step 3 Get organized

Now that you have things to put all your things in, learn some tricks for arranging them. First, think about how your furniture is placed in this room. Traffic should flow easily in and out, as well as around couches

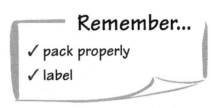

Remember...

✓ pack properly

✓ label

and chairs. Leave about 18 inches between your coffee table and seating. Make sure reclining pieces don't knock into walls or against other furniture.

Position the TV so you don't have to turn your head at an uncomfortable angle. Your eyes should hit just below center on the screen. Leave room for air to circulate around stereo and video equipment and for access to wires behind them.

Consider items you want handy while you're relaxing here. And think about having flat, clear surfaces near seating for drinks and snacks. Then pick soothing colors for this space and minimize fabric patterns. You'll rest your eyes and reduce that cluttered feeling.

SUPER TIPS *for organizing the relaxing/entertaining area*

Go pro with a label maker. Consider investing in a label maker if you need to label lots of containers and shelves for photographs, magazines, music, or files. These little machines are easy to operate, inexpensive, and available at Target and office supply stores. The labels look tidy, and you can enlarge the type to make it easier to read.

Spot unread books easily on your shelf. As you organize your bookshelves, slap a small, round, colorful sticker on the spine of books you haven't read. Do the same when you bring home new books. You will have no trouble spotting unread books on your shelf. Once you read them, peel off the sticker.

Lay tall books flat to maximize space. You want to make the most of bookcase space, but tall, oversized books can waste it. Give them their own shelf and lay them flat atop one another. Then lower the shelf above as much as you can. If you consolidate all your tall books this way, you may be able to add another shelf in your bookcase.

Display books and collectibles with style. Instead of cramming each shelf full of books, leave a little space on the ends, or even in the middle. Prop the books up with bookends, then stand a knickknack, framed photograph, or other attractive item in the extra space. Try alternating books with other objects to break up the monotony and show off both beloved books and collectibles to their best advantage.

Protect framed photos and art. Hang pictures or artwork in a low-humidity area away from sunlight. Showcase them with soft, ambient lighting, instead. Keep in mind most photographs look best hung at or slightly below eye level.

Cluster small pictures together. Small, framed photos look best together. Whether you hang them on a wall or stand them on a shelf, cluster small pictures together to make more of an impact. You can group them by theme, with framed vacation photos on a side table, and family pictures hung behind your sofa.

Hang large photos alone. Heighten the impact of large, framed photographs by hanging them alone rather than surrounding them with smaller pictures. The Eastman Kodak Company recommends hanging a large photo off-center over the sofa or other long piece of furniture. Balance it by placing another striking decorative object, like a vase or planter, at the other end.

Discover the secret to displaying collectibles. Don't settle for ho-hum exhibits of your collectibles. Create elegant displays in a snap with this decorator's secret. Place the tallest object in the center, then form a rough, triangle-shaped display around it. Surround the tall piece with medium-height items, and arrange the shortest objects around the edges.

Swap out collectibles if short on space. Don't have enough shelf space to show off all your collectibles? Rotate them out. Displaying a few well-chosen pieces is more striking. It leaves the room looking elegant and interesting rather than cluttered. Choose a few pieces to display now, gently pack and store the rest, and set a timeline. Every few months, pull out the stored knick-knacks, unpack a few, and put away the ones you've had on display. You can put the collectibles into several boxes labeled by theme if you have too many for one box.

SUPER TIPS *for organizing your audio-visual equipment*

Grab hold of elusive remote controls. Buy a few wide Velcro strips and start sticking. Place the soft, fuzzy side of a Velcro strip on the backs of TV, VCR, DVD, and stereo remotes. Then adhere the stiff, bristled side of the Velcro strip to a nearby surface — the side of your sofa or a place mat on an end table. Choose a spot within arm's reach of where you usually watch TV or listen to music. Stick the remotes on their corresponding Velcro strips when you finish using them, and you'll never have to hunt for them again.

Organize music for easy access. Whether you prefer CDs, records, or tapes, keep them organized. Group them by artist or musical category, like jazz, classical, and country. Store them in an attractive media cabinet or shelf near your stereo so you can easily change what's playing and put your music away.

Group videos for viewing pleasure. The same advice goes for DVDs and video tapes (VHS). Store them near your television on a shelf or inside a media cabinet. Organize them by title or category, like home movies, comedies, and exercise, whichever feels most natural to you. Be sure to return each to its proper place when you finish watching it.

Step 4 Keep it clean

Now that your family room is free of clutter, you'll find it's easy to keep it clean. A sample cleaning chart on the following page gives you a list of chores you can complete in 10 minutes. Add a few weekly, monthly, and occasional chores, and you've got one smart cleaning plan. Keep reading to find plenty of quick and easy cleaning tips for your clutter-free family room.

SUPER TIPS for cleaning your family room

Set a daily "clean routine." Schedule daily cleanup time just before bed and have family members pick up their own mess. Shelve books, take dishes back to the kitchen,

10-minute daily speed cleaning	Weekly chores	Monthly chores	Occasional chores
Remove items that belong somewhere else	Dust knick-knacks, lampshades, and artwork	Clean light fixtures	Wash windows
Straighten and fluff cushions and pillows	Sweep or vacuum floors	Turn or rotate upholstered cushions	Clean smudges off walls and light switches
Fold throws	Clean mirrors	Clean heating and air conditioning vents	Wash curtains
Place current magazines in their home	Dust TV screen	Wipe baseboards	Shampoo carpet
Put daily newspaper into recycling bin	Wipe windowsills	Check ceiling corners for cobwebs	
Dust table surfaces			
Straighten bookshelves			
Throw trash into trash basket			

return remote controls to their homes, and put away games and crafts. Need help motivating your family? Set a new house rule — no TV until the family room is clean.

Experience a better way to clean blinds. The most hated job in the house just got easier. Try one of these five simple ways to keep your blinds clean.

- *Lamb's wool dusters.* They contain lanolin, which attracts then traps dust.

- *Brush attachment* on your vacuum. It quickly sucks dirt off blinds.

- *Electrostatic disposable wipes.* These wipes are specially treated to attract and hold dust.

- *Lint-free cloth.* Wrap it around a spatula or ruler to sweep slats clean. Spray the cloth with dust-attracting spray or dip it in rubbing alcohol, and wipe across each slat. Don't use rubbing alcohol on wood blinds.

- *Fabric softener sheets.* They literally repel dirt and dust. Use one to wipe dirt off slats, or rub it over clean slats to keep them clean longer.

Remove glass stains with mustard. Make a mustard paste to clean away discolorations on glass or windows. Mix three parts dry mustard and one part white vinegar until it forms a paste. Apply it and rub until the stain disappears, then rinse the glass thoroughly with water. Wear eye protection when working with dry mustard as it can damage your cornea if it gets in your eye.

Freshen carpets with natural scents. Here's a recipe for a homemade carpet freshener you can make in a jiffy. Pour two cups of baking soda in a glass bowl and mash out the lumps with a fork. In a separate bowl, combine one cup of lavender flower buds and one cup of rosemary. Crush them to release their fragrance. Add them to the baking soda, mix well, and store in a glass jar or other airtight container. When you're ready to use it, sprinkle some on your carpet and let it sit for at least 10 minutes before vacuuming. You can substitute other herbs and even add essential oils to make it smell just like you want it to. For essential oils, add about 20 drops while stirring the baking soda, and let it sit for two to three days before using. This gives the oils time to dry. Otherwise, they may stain your carpet.

Before you clean your carpets, find out which methods work best and which to avoid. You have several options.

❑ **Steam cleaning.** Also known as hot water extraction, a machine sprays cleaning solution and hot water into the carpet, then immediately sucks it up along with dirt. Be careful not to overwet the carpet.

❑ **Dry extraction brushes.** A dry mix of detergents and solvents is applied to the carpet. The chemicals attach to dirt, and you vacuum all of it up.

❑ **Dry foam cleaning.** This technique uses a machine to whip detergent into a thick foam and work it into the carpet. Wet vacuuming then removes both soap and dirt.

❑ **Rotary bonnet method.** Also known as the absorbent pad method, a spinning pad absorbs dirt from the carpet. However, you must keep the pad lubricated with cleaning solution. Otherwise, it can distort the pile. Leave this method to the professionals.

❑ **Rotary shampooing.** This technique is similar to the rotary bonnet method, except carpet cleaner is sprayed onto the carpet before cleaning. Never use a rotary shampoo machine designed for hard floors on carpet. It can untwist the fibers and distort the pile.

Clean carpets like the pros. Carpet cleaning can be a real chore, but do it right and you can do it less often. For best results:

- Vacuum the area before cleaning.

- Put a preconditioning carpet cleaner on the carpet 10 minutes before cleaning to help loosen soil.

- Never use regular soap, laundry detergent, dishwashing detergent, or cleaners made for hard floors, like vinyl or wood, on carpet. They can damage the fibers.

- Avoid getting the carpet too wet. This can shrink the fibers, separate the backing, and pull apart seams.

- Turn on your air conditioning and ceiling fans and set up portable fans to dry carpets faster.

- Avoid walking on cleaned carpet or rugs until they are completely dry, often about 12 hours.

- Let carpet cleaning pros handle silk rugs and those made from natural plant fibers, such as jute, sisal, and ramie.

Say goodbye to fur-covered furniture. Rub a dryer sheet over furniture, carpet, and other surfaces to remove unwanted pet hair. It's quick, easy, and your furniture will smell great.

Dust lampshades more effectively. Vacuums don't always do a good job of sucking dust off cloth lampshades. Try a lint roller instead. Simply roll the sticky surface around the shade.

Go green for cleaner air. Plants add more than charm and greenery to a home — they also clean the air. New medical research finds English ivy is particularly effective at cleaning allergens, like mold and pet feces, out of the air. After spending 12 hours in a container of dirty air, English ivy had removed 78 percent of airborne mold and 94 percent of airborne feces. Keep in mind, English ivy is toxic if eaten, so place it out of reach of kids and pets. Other houseplants may also improve air quality. Consider adding these beauties to your decor.

- rubber plant

- peace lily

- gerbera daisy

- Boston fern

Cut down on dusting. Arrange books so their spines are even with the edge of the bookshelf. This prevents dust from gathering on the shelf.

Keep delicate items in curio cabinets. Cut down on dusting small items by displaying them in a cabinet with a glass door. Lighted curio cabinets are perfect for highlighting your favorite and most delicate pieces. You'll limit your weekly dusting and the risk of breaking something.

Save time and effort with this trick. Stash a "put away" basket behind your sofa or under an end table. Each time you find an item in the family room that doesn't belong there, drop it in the box. At the end of the day, carry the basket around the house, returning everything to its rightful room.

Wipe out clutter for good. Now that your family room is clean, you want to keep it that way. Put a to-go box in your hall closet and toss books, music, and other items in it as you decide to get rid of them. This way, things you no longer want won't clutter your now-clean space. Once the box is full, donate or sell everything in it and start a new one.

CHAPTER 3
The Dining Room

What's working in your dining room right now, and what isn't? You may be using this space for something other than dining — and wish you weren't. Because the dining table is a large, flat surface, it's natural to pile things on it or use it as a desk. Problems begin when you want to turn the space back into a dining room.

It's not ideal to have your dining room function as a home office — or anything else for that matter. But if this is your situation and you're stuck with it, make it work by coming up with dedicated storage.

There are tips in this chapter that may help you find a home for your non-dining items, but check out *Chapter 4 The Home Office* for more.

Make your wish list, imagining what you'd like to see happening in this space. Perhaps you'd like to:

- seat six for dinner on a moment's notice.

- display your grandmother's china.

- be able to put your hands on a complete set of napkin rings.

- feel a moment of pleasure instead of stress when you walk by your dining room.

Remember...

✓ make a wish list

✓ be realistic

✓ set priorities

✓ identify your clutter problems

✓ label your zones

✓ set a timeline

This room may be one of the easiest spaces to declutter and organize, especially if it is a dedicated space with no other purpose. That means anything that doesn't belong in one of your specific zones goes somewhere else.

Zones	Step 1: Cut the clutter	Step 2: Increase storage	Step 3: Get organized
Dining			
China and glassware			
Table linens			
Additional zone			

You may have other zones for this space. If so, add them to the table on the preceding page. Then take your best guess on how long it will take you to complete each task for each zone. Keep in mind you may need time to shop for new storage containers. Remember, this is just an estimate to help you plan your dining room decluttering project.

Step 1 Cut the clutter

A formal dining room can be a thing of beauty — gleaming wood, polished candlesticks, antique linens. But perhaps you need a comfortable, casual place for family and friends to gather every day. It can still be lovely. Just make sure the things you decide to keep in here, as well as your decorating theme, are a bit more durable.

Whatever your style, you need to get this room down to the basics. Remember, you're going to create several piles as you declutter. Besides these five — KEEP, TOSS, DONATE, SELL, PASS ON — you may need another one for items that will be moving permanently out of your dining room. Things like furniture

Keep in mind

Make a decision:

✓ keep
✓ toss
✓ donate
✓ sell
✓ pass on

Follow purging rules:

✓ decide quickly
✓ handle items once
✓ set limits
✓ pass the "keep" test
✓ recognize garbage

you've plopped in here over the years and the stacks of laundry, magazines, or newspapers.

SUPER TIPS for sorting the dining zone

Shrink table to expand dining room. Make your dining room look larger and less cluttered by removing a leaf from your dining room table. Real estate agents often recommend this tip for people trying to sell their homes. It gives buyers the illusion of more space — and it can do the same for you. Just make sure to store the leaf carefully. To save closet space, you can lay the leaf flat under your bed.

Extract extra chairs. Chances are you don't always need all the chairs grouped around your dining room table. Give yourself more space by removing the extras. Stash them in the basement, if the area is climate controlled. You can even hang them from pegs on the basement wall to save floor space.

DON'T STORE...

✓ toys

✓ paperwork

✓ mail

✓ videos or DVDs

✓ records or compact discs

✓ books

✓ magazines

✓ clothing

Rent to put a dent in clutter. You only entertain large groups of people a few times a year — maybe for Thanksgiving or Christmas. But you have to find spots to store all those extra chairs every other day of the year. Or do you? Consider renting or borrowing certain items, such as chairs, folding tables, and even punch bowls or other large serving pieces that you use only for big gatherings. It's cheaper than buying them, and you don't have to find a place to store them when the party is over. Look for party rental stores in your area.

SUPER TIPS for sorting china and glassware

Set limits on china sets. The phrase "the more the merrier" does not apply to your dining room clutter. How many sets of china do you really need? What about place mats, wine glasses, creamers, and sugar bowls? Set limits. Keep only those you use often. Get rid of the rest. Pass them on to your children or other family members, neighbors, or friends. You can even donate them to a worthy charity.

Rotate extra china for variety. Cramped china cabinet? Don't feel as if you have to display everything. Keep enough settings for daily family meals in your dining room and store the rest somewhere else. Put extra china in a closet, the attic, or basement, and retrieve it only when you have company. If you have — and want to keep — multiple sets of china, rotate them from the cabinet to storage. It can bring a welcome variety to your dining room.

Share heirlooms with family. It's hard to part with sentimental artifacts, like china that's been in your family for generations. Display, carefully store, and even use what you can — but don't clog up your dining room with heirlooms. Pass them on to

Toss without a thought

✓ table linens that don't fit any table in your house

✓ any items — plates, bowls, glasses, mugs — that are chipped or cracked

✓ linens that are permanently stained

your children, grandchildren, or other family members who will treasure them. You'll free up space for more useful items while keeping the tradition alive.

SUPER TIPS for sorting table linens

Save the day with pretty dish towels. Here's an easy way to solve your storage squeeze. Instead of cluttering up your sideboard with lots of place mats and fancy table linens, simplify things. For casual family dining, use pretty dish towels as place mats. They work great because they absorb spills and last a long time. Chances are your family won't object to the lack of formality.

Tailor tablecloths to fit needs. You have more tablecloths than you could possibly use but find yourself a little short on other dining room essentials. No problem. Just transform an old tablecloth into napkins, place mats, or table runners. You'll turn what was once clutter into something useful.

Break out the good stuff. Why keep fancy table linens stashed away for special occasions? They only take up space and add to your clutter problem. Make every day special and start using them. If you have too many linens, pass the extras on to your family or friends.

Step 2 Increase storage

Be as accurate as you can when filling in measurements on your dining room floor plan. You're going to need these if you want to add any pieces for extra storage. They'll also come in handy later when you're placing your furniture.

If your dining room must accommodate a second function, look for furniture that will not only look good in the space, but also store any necessary supplies — and, if you're lucky, act as a buffet or

Remember...

✓ map your space
✓ shop for containers

sideboard. You want items that are multifunctional. Don't think you're stuck using only traditional dining room furniture in this space. Creative use of bookshelves, cabinets, armoires, and fabric will help you organize and declutter.

In addition, whatever comes into this room with your blessing should have a designated home. For instance, if you've decided it's all right to keep magazines in your dining room, then make a place for them — besides the dining room table.

SUPER TIPS for storing in the dining zone

Assign your table double duty. Turn your dining room table into storage space no one can see. Just add drawers to the underside of the table. You'll have a super spot for linens and silverware. You can even keep paperwork and office supplies in the drawers if your dining room doubles as your office. You can find the equipment you'll need for this project at hardware or home improvement stores. Not the handy type? Consider buying a dining room table with drawers.

Hire a secretary to store supplies. Your home office — also known as your dining room — probably doesn't have the space (or the budget) for a secretary to answer the phone and type memos. But it's a perfect place for a secretary desk. This handy yet elegant piece of furniture provides not only a place to work but also plenty of storage space. When open, you have a solid writing surface and access to several shelves to hold your office supplies. When you're done working, simply close the desk. All your paperwork and supplies will be out of sight, and you'll be left with a beautiful piece of furniture in your dining room.

SUPER TIPS for storing china and glassware

Keep dining room extraordinary. Ordinary plastic storage containers can be very useful — but not in the dining room. Unless they can be kept completely out of sight, they will ruin the elegant atmosphere of the room. Instead, opt for items that provide storage and also look good, such as a cabinet, hutch, plate rack, or sideboard.

Build your own buffet. It doesn't take a big budget to spruce up your dining room and create more storage space. All you need is a couple of recycled base cabinets. Refinish or paint them to match your dining room's decor, and screw them together. Then top with laminate, tile, or painted or stained wood, or simply drape with fabric. Add some interesting hardware, perhaps legs, and you have a great buffet or dining room server.

Form hidden storage with fabric. Fabric can turn any storage unit into an elegant piece of furniture. If you're handy, you can build your own wooden buffet, with plenty of shelves. If not, buy inexpensive cube storage pieces, and piece them together to form a sideboard. Then cover your homemade sideboard with a great cloth or fabric drape. Under the fabric, you'll have wonderful hidden storage for serving pieces, glassware, linens, and other dining room items.

Bulk up storage space with built-ins. If you build it, order will come. Built-in shelves or cabinets can turn a plain dining room wall into a handy storage and display area. Shelves and drawers can hold your china, linens, and other serving items. You can even customize the shelves so they can hold oddly shaped items like punch bowls, or add doors to hide the items you don't want to display. It could be a costly project, but it's a great way to make the most of your space.

Pamper china with padded cases. If you don't mind spending money on commercial storage containers for your good china, look into the padded ones made especially for this purpose. These zippered cases come in a variety of shapes and sizes designed for specific pieces, including cups, saucers, and dessert or dinner plates. You'll keep your china intact while keeping it out of the way.

Think outside the hutch. Don't feel obligated to stick to traditional dining room furniture. Unusual items can work, too. For example, use an old dresser to store your linens and silverware. Be creative — and be on the lookout for older items you can "repurpose" to fit your dining room.

SUPER TIPS *for storing table linens*

Store linens under your seat. Fit more people — and more storage space — into your dining room. Swap some of your chairs for a wooden or upholstered storage bench. With the bench seating, you'll be able to fit a few more people around your dining room table. You'll also have a great place to keep your table linens.

Add an armoire. Who says an armoire is just for living rooms and bedrooms? Move an armoire into your dining room to hold your china, crystal, glasses, linens, platters, and other decorative pieces. You can even add extra shelves for more storage.

Turn napkins into decorations. No place to put your linen napkins? Display them in a decorative pot or bowl on top of your sideboard. The carefully arranged rolled-up napkins can even substitute for a floral arrangement.

Step 3 Get organized

You have the dimensions of your dining room — now measure all your furniture. Putting everything back is the fun part, but it can also make or break this decluttering project. Arrange the furniture and display your pieces wisely, and you're halfway home.

Remember...

✓ pack properly
✓ label

Group items by use and function. Give each group a home and consider labeling it. This way, others can return things to the proper place.

If you're using open shelving, take the time to display things attractively. Experts say to display items in odd numbered groupings — three vases, instead of two, for instance.

SUPER TIPS for organizing the dining zone

Make sure your dining area measures up. Remember that people need a bit of elbow room at the table as well as space to maneuver in and out of their chairs. That's why experts say you need to leave at least 12 to 18 inches between each typical dining room chair. In addition, leave at least 36 inches between the back of the chairs and the closest wall or door. These numbers will tell you right away if you can fit your table plus four dining chairs or if you have room for more.

Set table to stop clutter. Here is a simple way to prevent your dining room table from becoming a dumping ground for mail and other odds and ends. Just cover it with a fancy tablecloth, and set it with dishes and silverware as if you were expecting company. It will look too pretty to disturb.

SUPER TIPS for organizing china and glassware

Be creative with surplus items. You don't have to cram all of your dining room items into storage. Why not display a few of them? Here's one way to keep some glassware or crystal on display and make it useful at the same time. Just turn a few wine glasses into candle holders. Fill the bottom of the glass with some sand or pebbles, and put a votive candle inside. Then enjoy a romantic dinner by candlelight.

Find room on the wall. Don't forget about wall space. Use plate racks to showcase beautiful pieces of china. Display shelves can hold larger pieces like teapots or pitchers.

SUPER TIPS for organizing table linens

Halt creases with hangers. Tired of rooting around drawers for the right tablecloth, only to find it wrinkled and in need of ironing? Save yourself time and trouble by keeping your tablecloths on padded hangers in a closet. No more creases. You can even make your own padded hanger by cutting a lengthwise slit in a paper towel tube and placing it onto the straight edge of a wire clothes hanger.

Tie napkins together to save time. Togetherness is important for families — and for your family's napkins. Keep your linens organized by folding and stacking each set of napkins, then tying a ribbon around each set. That way, you can easily go through your collection and find the right set, without making a mess.

Pack linens in a picnic basket for easy access. When you have to search through several drawers, finding the right set of table linens is no picnic. Make things easier by keeping your table linens in a picnic basket. They'll be easy to find, and you'll be adding a decorative element to your dining room.

Step 4 Keep it clean

Now that your dining room is free of clutter, you'll find it's easy to keep it clean. Here's a chart that gives you a list of chores you can complete in 10 minutes. Add a few weekly, monthly, and occasional chores, and you've got one smart cleaning plan. Then keep reading to find plenty of quick and easy cleaning tips for your clutter-free dining room.

10-minute daily speed cleaning	Weekly chores	Monthly chores	Occasional chores
Remove items that belong somewhere else	Vacuum or sweep	Clean air and heating vents	Clean smudges off walls and light switches
Wipe table top	Dust chandelier	Wipe baseboards	Wash windows
Straighten chairs	Change or wash place mats or tablecloth	Check ceiling corners for cobwebs	Wash curtains
Lay out clean place mats or tablecloth	Dust furniture		Shampoo carpet
	Wipe windowsills		Wash crystal and china
			Clean inside of china cabinet

SUPER TIPS for cleaning your dining room

Tweak to keep room at its peak. A few cosmetic improvements can go a long way toward keeping your dining room clutter-free. Bring more light into the space with lighter curtains. Paint the walls a soothing color like green, blue, or white to make the space appear bigger or cleaner. Remove half the pictures on the walls for the same effect. Replace your old chandelier with a new one that helps set the mood better. Your "new" dining room will look too good to fill with clutter.

Clutter may not be your only problem. Maybe your dining room furniture has seen better days. In that case, it's tea time. Cold tea helps remove old furniture polish, dirt, and grime and restore the original look to wooden furniture.

Toss two tea bags in a quart of water, and boil until the water is a brownish color you like. Let it cool, then test the back of the piece or another unseen area with a soft rag soaked in the solution. The first pass should remove old polish and strip the wood. Then you can apply some as stain.

If you're pleased with the way it looks, finish the whole piece. But remember, tea is a permanent stain. When it's dry, buff it and follow up with polish if you want a finished look.

CHAPTER 4
The Home Office

To create a home office that meets your needs, you first have to define them. Will you just be paying a few bills here? Do you have a thriving, home-based business? Do you occasionally telecommute? Or do you plan to write the Great American Novel? Make a list of all the things you'd like to do from this space. Factor in how many people will work here, and if you will all be in it at the same time.

Remember, no matter what you do in your office, you'll be more productive if you're organized. Having a clean and orderly work area keeps you focused on your task.

Even though many people dump mail on a kitchen countertop, pile it on the dining room table, or let it build into a heap in the foyer, you're going to learn in this chapter how to purge, sort, and

Remember...

✓ make a wish list
✓ be realistic
✓ set priorities
✓ identify your clutter problems
✓ label your zones
✓ set a timeline

file mail. Keep in mind it doesn't really matter where you end up "handling" your mail — simply follow the organizing rules of purging, containing, and organizing.

Try to imagine how much time you waste right now looking for an important piece of paper. You could even be losing money because you can't find a client's phone number, the receipt for the stereo you want to return, or the documentation for a charitable donation. Ask the hard questions — do you need to downsize, containerize, organize, or all three?

Zones	Step 1: Cut the clutter	Step 2: Increase storage	Step 3: Get organized
Desk			
Filing			
Supplies			
Mail			
Additional zone			

You may have other zones for this space. If so, fill them into the table on the preceding page. Then take your best guess on how long it will take you to complete each task for each zone. You may need to factor in time to shop for new storage containers. Remember, this is just an estimate to help you plan your home office decluttering project. Don't let the prospect of several days of decluttering put you off.

Step 1 Cut the clutter

Before you can create order, you must create a little chaos. Get ready to clear every item out of your home office, making decisions as you go. Get bags, boxes, or floor space for your five categories: KEEP, TOSS, DONATE, SELL, and PASS ON. But wait. This could get confusing if you aren't careful.

Keep in mind

Make a decision:
- ✓ keep
- ✓ toss
- ✓ donate
- ✓ sell
- ✓ pass on

Follow purging rules:
- ✓ decide quickly
- ✓ handle items once
- ✓ set limits
- ✓ pass the "keep" test
- ✓ recognize garbage

You're sorting through a huge variety of items, everything from paper clips to computer manuals to tax records. You don't want your KEEP pile to become a huge mishmash of items you'll have to go through all over again. As you go through each zone and select things to keep, group similar items at the same time. Essentially, you'll be creating mini-piles within your KEEP pile. This will help you quickly see what size containers you'll need. You'll also be able to see at a glance that you have 500 rubber bands, probably 450 rubber bands too many.

Your paper items will be the most daunting, but don't get bogged down trying to attend to each piece now. Go through mail and anything that is not in your filing cabinet first. Create one stack for pieces of paper that need to be filed and another one for pieces that require some kind of action.

Save your filing stack and your filing cabinet for last. Sit down at your newly organized desk, and look at your files. You'll have to make some unique decisions in this area.

For one thing, you'll need a different "keep" test for your files. You won't save a document just because you love it. Come up with criteria like this — requires action, information would be difficult to replace, or save for tax or legal reasons. In addition, you'll pull out and archive anything over a year old. Generally, you keep only the current year's records in your active filing system. Later in this section, you'll find guidelines from experts on how long to keep documents or other pieces of information.

> Only 8 percent of American households had a personal computer 20 years ago. Now, you'll find one or more computers in over 60 percent of homes.

If you don't have a filing system that's working for you, you'll have to come up with a new method. See *Step 3 Get Organized* for some specific tips. Also, in *Step 4 Keep It Clean*, you'll learn how to prevent paper overload from ever happening again.

SUPER TIPS *for sorting out your desk*

Convert paper scraps to one-stop shop. Don't litter your desk with paper scraps and sticky notes filled with phone numbers and lists. Besides being messy, they can flutter their way into dark nooks and crannies where you may never find them. Prevent that paper chase. Turn a spiral notebook, personal planner, or calendar into your center for notes, phone numbers, and other useful facts. You'll gain a one-stop shop for information as well as a much neater desk.

Trade desktop displays for wall decor. Add family photographs, souvenirs, and even plants to personalize your office, but never let them touch your desk. Instead, hang them in a place of honor on the wall above your desk, or exhibit them on a shelf where you can enjoy them.

Purge publications by downloading. When you sort, add an extra pile for manuals, brochures, reference materials, and other publications that may be available online. For example, you might find the instruction manual for your fax machine on its manufacturer's "support" or "customer service" Web

Toss without a thought

Shred or toss these items the second you recognize them.

- ✓ articles or brochures you haven't needed in years
- ✓ old grocery receipts
- ✓ junk mail and advertisements
- ✓ expired insurance policies or related papers
- ✓ expired coupons
- ✓ warranties for items you no longer own

Jessica Duquette of In Perfect Order Organizing Solutions also advises tossing any papers you can easily and quickly get again.

pages. After you download, save, and open the online manual, you can toss the hard copy. Just remember to tear out and file any crucial pages like warranty forms, warranty information, serial numbers, registration codes, proof of ownership, or registration information.

SUPER TIPS for sorting your files

Sort "keep" files faster. Avoid covering up pile labels while sorting your "keep" papers into categories. Pull the bottom sheet of each pile halfway out, and attach a sticky note to the outermost end. Scribble a tentative file label name on the note and keep on sorting.

Fend off jam-packed files. You have to muscle files in or out of your filing cabinet. You catch yourself trying to get by without a file or keeping folders out on your desk. And just finding a particular file in the drawer is a battle. These are signs of jam-packed file syndrome. Cure it by leaving enough space in your file drawer to allow folders to lean noticeably. When they start getting packed, archive some files or transfer a few to an empty drawer. Your home office will run more efficiently, and everything will be easier.

Around 80 percent of papers that get filed are never referred to again, according to Harris Interactive.

Regain filing space with an archive. Create an "archive" — an out-of-your-way place for rarely used old files. To start, sort through your files and decide which papers are no longer active. For example, this

Are you holding on to papers from 20 years ago? This handy guide will help you know how long you should keep certain personal documents — and when it's OK to toss 'em.

Keep forever:
- ❏ Income tax returns and payment checks
- ❏ Retirement, IRA, and pension records
- ❏ Investment trade confirmations and investment records for stocks, bonds, and mutual funds
- ❏ Legal records
- ❏ Bills for big-ticket purchases — like furniture, jewelry, appliances, computers, cars, etc. (in case they're destroyed, stolen, or damaged)
- ❏ Home purchase and improvement records and receipts
- ❏ Important business correspondence
- ❏ CPA audit reports

Keep 7 years:
- ❏ Documents that support your tax return figures such as bills and canceled checks
- ❏ Tax-related medical bills
- ❏ Tax-related sales receipts, utility records, and other tax-related bills
- ❏ Property records/builder contracts
- ❏ Accident reports and claims (even if settled)

Keep 4 years:
- ❏ Credit card statements
- ❏ Medical bills (for insurance problems)
- ❏ Expired insurance policies

Keep until...
- ❏ Credit card receipts until you verify them on your statement
- ❏ ATM receipts until you verify them on your bank statement
- ❏ Car records until you no longer own the car
- ❏ Leases until seven years after they expire
- ❏ Pay stubs until you verify them on your W-2
- ❏ Sales receipts until the warranty expires
- ❏ Warranties and instructions until you no longer own the product
- ❏ W-2 forms until Social Security benefits begin

Both laws and IRS rules are subject to change, so check with your accountant or attorney before tossing any legal or financial papers.

According to the Washington State Office of the Attorney General, you should shred these items — preferably with a cross-cut shredder — once you no longer need them for your records.

- ❑ ATM receipts
- ❑ Bills for telephone, gas, electric, water, cable TV, Internet
- ❑ Bank statements
- ❑ Canceled or voided checks
- ❑ Receipts with checking account numbers
- ❑ Credit and charge card bills, carbon copies, summaries, and receipts
- ❑ Pre-approved credit card applications
- ❑ Credit reports and histories
- ❑ Investment, stock, and property transactions
- ❑ Magazine and junk mail address labels
- ❑ Birth certificate copies
- ❑ Employee pay stubs and employment records
- ❑ Legal documents and insurance documents
- ❑ Luggage tags, travel itineraries, used airline tickets, expired passports and visas
- ❑ Medical and dental records
- ❑ Papers with a Social Security number
- ❑ Report cards
- ❑ Transcripts
- ❑ Resumés or curriculum vitae
- ❑ Signatures (such as those on contracts or letters)
- ❑ Tax forms
- ❑ Expired credit and identification cards including driver's licenses, college IDs, military IDs, employee badges, medical insurance cards, etc. (Cut cards up if you can't shred them.)

year's tax-related papers are active, but tax folders from four years ago are not. If part of a folder is inactive, place those papers in a new archived version of the folder. Next, find a safe, dry space for "archive" file boxes or filing cabinets in another part of your home. It can even be in plain sight if you cover the filing cabinet with a tablecloth that matches your decor. Taking the time to archive files will give you extra file storage space in your office.

Get extra hard-working desk space. Set a table at a right angle beside your desk, and you'll rack up writing space, storage space, and an area for computer work. Use one "leg" of this L-shape as a writing workspace and the other "leg" for your computer. The hard-to-reach far corner of the L is ideal for a small file rack, computer disk holder, or other storage. This also works with L-shaped desks.

Put shredded paper to better use. As long as you use a crosscut shredder, you can use your shreds as packing material when shipping boxes or moving to a new home. You can also donate them to a local animal shelter where they'll be used for pet bedding.

SUPER TIPS for sorting supplies

Organize office supplies for convenience. Pull out all your office supplies and sort them into three piles — those you use daily or almost every day, those used less often, and those you never use. Store daily-use supplies at or near your work area so they're always convenient right when you need them. Store those you use less often in other parts of your office. Toss or donate anything you don't use.

Store space hogs in the right place. You keep the tape dispenser on your office desk, but it sees much more action in the kitchen. Review your office supplies, and put them where they're used most — even if that's outside your office.

SUPER TIPS for sorting your mail

Organize fantastic finds. You found a fabulous article in a newspaper, magazine, or your favorite journal. Instead of keeping the entire ad-infested publication, clip the article and start a folder or binder for that topic. For example, file articles about gardening tips in a "Gardening" folder or stories about marketing your business in a "Marketing" folder.

Fight back against junk mail. Write to the Direct Marketing Association and ask to be taken off their lists. Include your address, signature, and all versions of your name. Within a couple of months, you'll be removed from all their lists for five years — at no charge. The address is Mail Preference Service, Direct Marketing Association, P.O. Box 643, Carmel, NY 10512.

Beat catalog clutter for good. Do these two things, and you'll never need to keep another catalog again. First, write down the catalog's Web site. You can probably see and order all their products online. Next, call the toll-free number for any unwanted catalog, and ask to be removed from their mailing lists — including the ones they sell or rent to other businesses. Throw out the catalog after you hang up.

Give up unread subscriptions. If the new edition of a magazine often arrives before you've read even one page of the previous issue, let the subscription run out. You don't have to give up the magazine. Just limit your spending to the issues that grab your interest.

Step 2 Increase storage

Here are some of the space-eating items you may have or need in your home office:

- chair
- desk
- filing cabinets
- bookshelves
- telephone
- computer
- fax machine/copier/scanner
- small supplies, like pens, staples, and CDs
- bulky supplies, like reams of paper or extra folders

> **Remember...**
> ✓ map your space
> ✓ shop for containers

As you can see, you're already dealing with quite a bit of stuff, and you haven't even gotten down to the nitty-gritty. That's why, unless you have a Trump-size office, you really must plan your storage carefully. Otherwise you'll drown in clutter — big and little.

What's your clutter quotient? If you have a separate, dedicated home office, you may be able to shut the door on a bit of disorder. In that case, open shelving or storage containers will do just fine. However, if your office is part of another room, with another purpose, it may be vital you hide things away when not in use. Think closed storage containers, shelves with doors, roll-top desks, and shrewdly placed curtains.

SUPER TIPS for storing at your desk

Go to the wall for storage. You don't have space for a bookshelf, but you need storage for binders, phone books, reference materials, and the like. Consider wall-mounted shelves. You can even get vertical railed shelf systems that you can tailor to your needs. You choose how many shelves to mount and the height of each shelf — and you can adjust them anytime you like.

Double the value of tight space. Get more out of limited office space with all-in-one office equipment. A "multi-function" printer can act as printer, copier, fax machine, and perhaps even a scanner. Some phones have built-in answering machines, and cell phones often do far more than make phone calls. Do some checking to find out what's out there, how well it multi-tasks, whether it's good quality, and whether it's worth the cost.

Create a hideaway office. An under-used closet could become your home office. Install track shelves or a closet organizer along one wall. Tuck in a small desk or table and perhaps a rolling file cabinet. While you're at it, mount cork tiles to serve as a bulletin board, or nail little boxes to the wall to store stationery and writing supplies. If needed, get electric outlets and phone or cable jacks installed to make your office fully functional. While you may need to keep your chair outside, you can hide your office — and any financial paperwork — by simply closing the door when you're done working.

Solve the no-room-for-a-desk problem. Don't worry if you have no room for a permanent desk. Consider a temporary one, instead. After all, a folding table could easily be slipped behind the couch, under a bed, or into the garage after you're done using it. So check garage sales or discount stores for a sturdy table that can be folded flat. Then just reserve a nearby space to hold any work-in-progress materials you can't complete at one sitting.

Assemble a professional office on the cheap. Arm yourself with a list of office furniture, office supplies, and other needed items, and start bargain hunting. Take cash when you visit garage sales, yard sales, going-out-of-business sales, and flea markets. Inspect everything carefully before you buy, and make sure you have a way to get large items home. Move on to thrift stores, used-goods stores, dollar stores, and classified ads. And don't forget county surplus stores. These sell used government merchandise — like desks, chairs, and filing cabinets — at rock-bottom prices. Although you buy them "as is" without a warranty, you'll find plenty of sturdy furniture in good condition or in need of only minor refurbishing. You may have to check all these sources more than once, but you'll save money.

Improve a table with a rollout keyboard drawer. Check office supply stores, home improvement stores, and computer stores for a drawer — or tray — that comes with its own mounting hardware. You can also order online from *www.stacksandstacks.com*. But before you buy, be sure to measure your keyboard to make sure the tray will fit.

SUPER TIPS for storing files

Play the accordion file. Use a 12-pocket accordion file for items you organize by month — like receipts, coupons, birthday cards, and bills. Upgrade to accordion files with more pockets for owner's manuals and warranties.

Prevent paper mountains. Downsize your to-be-filed container, and set up a plan to get things filed. Otherwise, paper will accumulate into little mountain ranges, and your files will be almost worthless. Use these ideas to build a plan you can live with. File every paper as it comes into your office, or set up a to-be-filed repository you empty once a day or once a week. You can schedule a weekly appointment to file, or fit filing into gaps in your schedule. For example, you can file when you're waiting for something, when you need a short break, or when you're too tired to do more mentally demanding work.

Control business card clutter. Use ideas like these to change a scattered herd of business cards into a "contact management" system. "Laminate" each business card to the upper part of an index card with a short strip of clear packing tape. Keep the cards in an index-card file box or recipe box. Or buy a business-card binder that contains slotted plastic sleeves for business cards. The easiest thing is to just put the information on your computer. Chances are your operating system already has software designed for this.

Manage office equipment problems with less misery. Here's how. As you buy each item, add its manuals, warranties, and other documents to a three-ring binder. Use a three-hole-punch, or put small-sized documents into a zippered pocket designed for binders. Then, if your fax machine won't fax one day, you can just grab your manual and start working on the problem — without the frustrating misery of an endless search. Even if you have to call tech support or ask for warranty work, all the information will be easy to find right when you need it most.

Skip ahead with a pre-labeled filing system. Check your local office supply store for a ready-made filing system. These supply all kinds of subject labels or subject dividers ideal for home office filing — and they may even be color coded. Some filing systems also come with software to help you print labels and organize more effectively. Look for products tailored for households or for home-business use.

Pick a better file cabinet. Savvy file-cabinet shoppers always bring three tools — measurements of their space, a heavy book, and a measuring tape. At the store, measure the cabinet to see if it will fit your office. Next, test for quality. Place the heavy book in the file cabinet's bottom drawer, and open and close the drawer. If it screeches or doesn't open smoothly, don't buy the cabinet. And don't forget to check for bonuses like a rack that supports hanging files or the ability to switch between legal-size files and regular files.

Work anywhere with basket file boxes. You'll find surprising advantages in a wicker file-storage box. These lidded cubes make any pack of hanging folders so conveniently portable that you can work in any room of the house. Plus, a wicker file box lacks the industrial look of metal file cabinets and file boxes, so it fits just as nicely in the living room as it does in the office.

Whip up a cheap and easy desk. Scour yard sales and discount stores for two or more two-drawer metal file cabinets. Then buy a sheet of plywood at a home improvement store, cut to fit the size of the cabinets. Make sure the plywood sheet is long enough to give you a good amount of desktop space. Place the plywood on top of the filing cabinets, and voilà — you have a desk. If money and space permit, you may want to stain or paint it and add more filing cabinets for extra storage and desk stability.

SUPER TIPS for storing supplies

Clear your desk of the small stuff. Keep an eye out for hanging wall-pocket baskets — the kind designed to lay flat against a wall. Hang these above your desk to store lightweight office supplies that hog valuable desk space. If you already have storage for the supplies, use a group of these baskets to file mail by category.

"Fish" for easy storage. A fishing tackle box makes a perfectly good drawer substitute for storing small office supplies.

Convert a closet to office supply storage. Karen C. transformed her guest bedroom closet into an office supply closet, and you can, too. Rather than tear things out, Karen took advantage of the closet's coated-wire-rack organizer. She filled its wire-rack rollout drawers with drawer organizer trays full of small office supplies. Then she added square coated-wire basket sets designed to suspend under the closet organizer shelves. Although she was careful not to put too much weight in the baskets, they were still ideal for individual packs of printer paper and other office items. Finally, Karen lined one of the closet shelves with her 20-binder collection of bank statements and other financial records. Although Karen converted an entire bedroom closet, you may prefer to use half the closet for office supplies while leaving the other half as regular closet space.

SUPER TIPS for storing mail

Manage mail with a household post office. Prevent new paper piles from forming by setting up individual mailboxes for each member of your family. Choose from stacked bins or boxes, or use wall-mounted baskets. Label each container with the owner's name, and be sure to keep a trash can nearby so everyone can toss unwanted mail.

Keep bills in sight and on time. Manage your bills with a stair-stepped file organizer. Or use a dish rack as a handy organizer. As each bill arrives, put its due date on the envelope and "file" it in your dish rack or organizer. Keep the bills in order of due date so that the ones you must pay next are always in front.

Never misplace another bill. You won't once you've organized your desk like this. Number the slots of an accordion folder 1 through 31 — one for every day of the month. As each bill comes in, put it in a slot that's a few days ahead of its due date. Check this file daily. If you find a bill in the slot, write that check immediately, and send it on its way.

Create a collapsible bill-paying station. When you have so little office space that a large, permanent home for bill-paying isn't practical, try this suggestion from professional organizer Ramona Creel of *OnlineOrganizing.com*. Create a use-anywhere bill-paying kit in an accordion folder or portable file box. Tuck in envelopes filled with bill-paying supplies like stamps and pens. Next, transfer your filing system for bills into the accordion folder pockets or file-box folders. Take your kit to a table or other flat surface any time you need to handle bills. Pull out what you need to check deadlines, file bills, or pay bills on time — and just pack everything up when you're done.

Step 3 Get organized

Keep only the essentials out on your work surfaces. Set up everything else so the things you use most often are within easy reach when you're seated, including critical supplies and "action files."

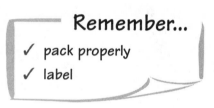

Remember...

✓ pack properly

✓ label

That leads to one of the most basic, but also most challenging, issues of a well-designed home office — the physical layout. Expert organizer Julie Morgenstern gives advice on arranging office furniture in her book *Organizing From the Inside Out*.

She recommends positioning your main desk first, taking into account view, access, and comfort. Then build an "L," "U," or "J" shape out of it using whatever other furniture pieces you need for your computer, paperwork, filing, or phone. These shapes maximize work surface and storage in a small space.

Don't be afraid to experiment with layout. Pull pieces away from walls, position them at angles, or place them back-to-back. There are lots of tips throughout this chapter that will help you maximize your home office space.

SUPER TIPS for organizing your desk

Iron out tangled cord problems. Straighten the tangled cords so they all run parallel. Then corral them with strips of Velcro, wide trashbag fasteners, or even some spare coiled telephone cord — the kind between the headset and phone. Your cord chaos will be cured.

Waste less effort and get more done. If you catch yourself repeatedly crisscrossing the room or stretching for that top shelf to fetch something, you're wasting time. Unless you're deliberately trying to get a workout, rearrange things so often-used items are nearby and easily reached. This includes office supplies, equipment, papers, folders, disks, and items you regularly check or use for reference.

Take a space-making break. When you need a quick break, spend five minutes taking inventory of every item sitting on your desk. Grab anything you haven't used in a while, and file it or find a new place for it to live. Do the same for items or papers you've finished working on or use rarely. "Take inventory" daily or weekly so you'll never get buried under desktop clutter.

Make office furniture fit perfectly. Before you buy furniture and equipment for your home office, measure the room and sketch its layout. Include windows, doorways, closets, and phone and electrical outlets. If you're furnishing an upstairs office, get the width of your staircase and landings. Also, take whatever measurements you need to ensure that a computer monitor, CPU unit, and any office equipment will fit into cubbies designed for them in furniture. And check that cubbies won't prevent cords and wires from reaching a connection on the CPU or power outlet.

Prevent miles of cords. When you lay out your home office, plan ways to cluster office equipment close to electrical outlets, cable outlets, and phone jacks. That's one way to keep unsightly — and potentially dangerous — cords from running all over your room.

SUPER TIPS *for organizing your files*

Organize files from general to detailed. Start with broad, general categories, and work your way down to the nitty-gritty details. See if you can group all your files under a few "parent" categories so that you can label each file drawer with one of those categories. For example, you could label one file drawer "Home" and the other "Work." To subdivide these, sort papers into subject piles, and award each one its own hanging file. In turn, each hanging file can contain manila folders labeled with sub-topics. For example, your Home drawer could have a hanging folder for "Insurance" that contains sub-folders for "Home insurance," "Car insurance," and "Life Insurance."

Label your way to more productive files. You can label your files by name, number, or topic. Arrange files by name to organize information by client or other contacts. Arrange files by number for security. Set this up like the library's Dewey decimal system. Make each number translate to a topic, but give only a few people the "secret decoder" list of topics. To arrange files by subject or topic, choose label names based on the words or phrases you use rather than what you think others would use. For example, instead of "mortgage," you may decide to use "house payment." If no single phrase fits the file, split the file into folders that fit the phrases that come to mind.

Add dates to file labels. Include the year on labels of folders used for tax records, annual expenses, and other single-year files. When labeling any file, consider adding the starting date, ending date, deadline, or other date-related information to the label.

Color your way to speedy, low-hassle filing. Speed up filing and retrieval with colored files or labels. If you file alphabetically, imagine how much easier it would be if all your As were red, your Bs — blue, Cs — red, Ds — blue, and so on. You'd immediately know where each letter ended and the next began. If you file by subject, you could color code broad categories instead. For example, you might choose green for your money-related folders, blue for health, and red for school and work. Or you could use plain manila folders and labels for most items but switch

Pendaflex recommends these rules for more productive files.

❑ Prevent protruding papers and smothered labels. Slap a strip of clear tape on tears in pages before you file.

❑ Prohibit paper clip pandemonium. They snag edges of folders and papers. Staple groups of papers instead.

❑ Pencil in the file heading on one of the page corners before you file — just in case that paper escapes.

❑ Put papers in the correct order before filing.

❑ Schedule a regular appointment for filing. Do it daily instead of weekly so it takes less time — and keeps piles from growing and multiplying when you're not looking.

❑ Create an archive for files you'll rarely use but must retain. Twice a year, determine which active files need to be archived, and transfer them.

to red for files that are urgent, important, or time-sensitive. Anything is possible if you have a "colorful" imagination.

File by month for easier decisions. You may hesitate to toss something out, fearing you may need it later. Here's a way to relieve your anxiety. Get an accordion folder, or use 12 files, so you have one folder or slot for each month. File items like bills, receipts, records, or other paperwork

Have your taxes done in February so you can receive your return by April. Set up a tax-oriented filing system during the first few days of every January to make it a cinch. Start with basic categories as recommended by the IRS — income, expenses, home, and investments. Each one can be a hanging folder with individual folders for subcategories. Your income hanging file would include folders for items like your W-2 and 1099 forms as well as bank and brokerage statements.

Expense records should contain items like sales slips, receipts, canceled checks, invoices, or other proof of payment. Don't forget insurance records in the home file along with items like closing statements, purchase and sales invoices, and proof of payment. Examples of records for investments folders include brokerage statements, form 1099, and form 2439.

You may need extra hanging folders for things like running a business from your home, contributing to charity, reporting losses, or receiving retirement payouts. To learn about other possible categories, and to get general information on which records to keep for tax purposes, read the short IRS Publication 552 *Recordkeeping for Individuals*. Download it from *www.irs.gov*, or order a hard copy by calling 800-829-3676. Once you set up your system, keep up with the filing all year long. If you do, you'll be ready to complete your taxes the following January.

by month. When you come back around to a month after a year has gone by, empty the pocket. Glance through the items to find those you must keep for taxes, insurance, or other long-term storage. Otherwise, if you haven't needed them by then, you can probably go ahead and toss them.

Convert from piles to files painlessly. Try long sticky notes or Pendaflex label clips to start labeling your piles — or even sections of them. After you've done this for a while, you'll know how you organize information. Then you can use folders and filing labels to create a filing system that matches the way you think. If you're afraid folders will bury your papers too far out of sight, use three-ring binders instead. Although this may take more money and time, it helps keep your information visible, available, and on your mental radar. You may want to list each binder's contents on the spine — just to make sure.

Establish a "to do" folder. You should have one or more "to do" folders for items you must act on. You may have one folder for tasks to complete today or several folders categorized by priority, type of work, project, or time remaining before a deadline. Choose folders that look different from your "regular" folders, and put them where you won't ignore them.

Corral receipts into ready-to-use categories. Label the pockets of an accordion file with different categories like "under warranty," "gift receipt," "tax records," "proof of value for insurance," and anything else you need. Then store your receipts in the appropriate pockets. If you'd rather not buy an accordion file, label shoe boxes or gallon-size freezer bags — or reuse large envelopes that show up in your mailbox.

Enjoy filing convenience. Choose a lateral file cabinet if you have extra floor space and want to reach files with

Find out what papers you should have in an emergency and exactly where you should keep them. The best place for these and other never-toss, hard-to-replace personal documents is in a safe deposit box at your bank.

- ❑ adoption papers
- ❑ citizenship papers
- ❑ divorce decrees
- ❑ household inventory
- ❑ income tax returns
- ❑ military records
- ❑ mortgage papers
- ❑ deeds, titles, and mortgage notes
- ❑ important contracts
- ❑ copy of school records
- ❑ car titles and registration
- ❑ passports
- ❑ bonds and stock certificates
- ❑ copies of insurance policies
- ❑ Social Security card
- ❑ copy of driver's license (both sides)
- ❑ copies of wills, advance directives, living wills, powers of attorney

In addition to a bank safety deposit box, prepare an evacuation box. This is a container you can grab on your way out the door if you must evacuate from your home. It may be a lockable box or a small safe — preferably fireproof and waterproof — but it must be portable. Keep the original of your will, advance directive, and power of attorney in your evacuation box. Add items like these — or copies of them.

- ❑ list of banks and account numbers
- ❑ copies of both sides of each credit card
- ❑ personal checks, check registers, latest bank statement
- ❑ family medical, dental and immunization records
- ❑ list of insurance companies with policy numbers
- ❑ ownership papers for car, home, real estate properties, etc.
- ❑ list of contact information for employer, bank, insurance company, and utilities

astonishing ease. Lateral cabinets have wide drawers to arrange letter-size folders from left to right. Buy a vertical file cabinet if you need a cabinet that takes up less floor space. Vertical cabinets usually order folders from the front of the drawer to the back.

Be prepared for the worst. In case of a citywide or countywide disaster, consider keeping additional copies of your safe deposit box and evacuation box papers outside your county with a lawyer or other person who can be trusted.

SUPER TIPS for organizing your supplies

Create departments to get things done. Just as businesses assign space for marketing and finance departments, you can set aside space for important, frequent, or ongoing tasks that happen in your home office. For example, if you write many letters and thank you notes, section off a "correspondence department" complete with stationery, note cards, stamps, pens, address labels, and appropriate envelopes. Another sectioned-off area — your bill paying department — can include your checkbook, security envelopes, a calculator, and a place to file bills. Feel free to create as many of these "departments" as you need.

Straighten out your office drawers. The same tricks that neatly arrange kitchen junk drawers can transform office desk drawers, too. Just make sure every item lives in some kind of partition. Try cutlery trays. They come in inexpensive plastic forms, pricier mesh models, or even upscale styles. Or partition frugally with egg cartons, film canisters, a muffin tin, small jars, old checkbook boxes, cleaned pill bottles, or plastic margarine tubs.

SUPER TIPS for organizing your mail

Make mail sorting task fly by. Treat each day's batch of mail like a plane full of passengers. Set aside an area for a "mailport" where you can put mail and sort it into categories. This gives mail a place to land and its "passenger" envelopes places to go. Make room to set up "terminals" for each of your mail categories, and don't forget to include a nearby trash can "terminal." Round it out with a "take-off" terminal of mailing supplies for outgoing mail.

Eliminate your pile of correspondence and still keep in touch with everyone you care about. Friends and relatives will simply love getting letters from you! Your time commitment? Just sit down at your computer for one or two minutes a week and write up the funniest, most interesting, or most important recent events.

After a few weeks, turn that text into a more monthly "personal letter" version of that holiday newsletter you see in Christmas cards each year. Pull up an online letter form in your word processor, type "Dear" followed by the person's name, and tailor one or two introductory sentences especially for that recipient.

Then copy in your newsletter text below. Print the page, and hand write your signature. Change the name and first paragraph to fit the next person before printing and signing again. Keep going until everyone on your list has a letter. Then just address, stamp, and send.

Tame the mail monster. Prevent mail from ever piling up again, with this super-simple three-step process. First, stand by the trash can to open junk mail and other mail. Drop junk mail in the can the moment you recognize it, and it will never pile up again! Next, set up an accordion file or a team of file folders or large envelopes for the rest of the mail. Reserve a place for bills and additional places for the four Ss — Start (to-do items), Standby (papers you can't process until something else happens), Send (stuff to pass along), and Store (items to be filed). You can also create other categories, if needed. These folders can fill up fast and overflow if you don't check them regularly. So eliminate potential paper piles in two minutes a week with a quick review of these files.

According to Harris Interactive, 23 percent of adults say they pay bills late because they lose them. The resulting late fees make clutter a pricey pack of piles.

Step 4 Keep it clean

Now that your home office is free of clutter, you'll find it's easy to keep it clean. The chart on the following page gives you a list of chores you can complete in 10 minutes. Add a few weekly, monthly, and occasional chores, and you've got one smart cleaning plan. Then you'll find plenty of quick and easy cleaning tips for your clutter-free home office.

10-minute daily speed cleaning	Weekly chores	Monthly chores	Occasional chores
Return all items to their homes	Toss old catalogs and magazines	Clean air and heating vents	Clean smudges off walls and light switches
Open and sort bills	Wipe computer monitor and clean keyboard	Check ceiling corners for cobwebs	Wash windows
Shred junk mail	Vacuum or sweep floor	Wipe baseboards	Wash curtains
Empty trash	Dust furniture and pictures		Shampoo carpet
Wipe desk surface	Dust light fixtures		
	Wipe windowsills		

SUPER TIPS for cleaning your home office

Never run out of office supplies. Take a 10-minute inventory of office supplies once a week for the next few months. Each time, write down the date and make a list showing how much of each item you have left. You'll soon determine exactly when and how often you need to reorder each thing. Then you won't need to take inventory as often.

Lower paper clutter with high tech. Keep paper out of your office with help from your computer and its buddies. Download brochures or instruction manuals, and try the online or e-mail versions of your favorite journals, newspapers, and newsletters. Keep addresses in your computer instead of an address book. You can even use a scanner to record your paper documents so you need fewer hard copies. Just remember to make backups of any important documents or information you keep online.

Subtract files to add space. Your file cabinets may be crammed so full that your filing space dwindles to nothing. So set aside one day each year to transfer papers that are no longer "active" to your archive file cabinet — the home of files you rarely need. Some people transfer folders in January while others would rather wait until after taxes are done. Pick a time that's right for you, but avoid those weeks when you expect to be swamped with other tasks.

Load the bottom drawers of file cabinets first, and never open more than one drawer at a time. This prevents that scary life-passes-before-your-eyes moment as the filing cabinet tips over. It also will prevent injuries.

Chapter 5
The Bedroom

Your bedroom should be a refuge — a place you can escape to, where you feel calm and rested. More than any other room, this space must nurture. Here you sleep and restore your physical and emotional reserves.

Stand at the door to your bedroom. What do you see? Are the surfaces clear? Can you walk from one end to the other without tripping over piles of dirty clothes? Is the bed made with comfy linens? Pick out your favorite items in this room. Try to remember why you placed them here and decide if they still make you feel good.

If you're like most people, your bedroom is the last room you decorate, the first spot you "hide" things from visitors, and the area you spend the least amount of time thinking about. But it's also the place for two very important

Remember...

✓ make a wish list

✓ be realistic

✓ set priorities

✓ identify your clutter problems

✓ label your zones

✓ set a timeline

tasks — sleeping and preparing for your day.

Many decluttering experts discuss the merits of feng shui, the Chinese philosophy of placing objects according to positive and negative energy patterns. You don't have to embrace all the feng shui principles to see its value. For instance, think about having a home office in a corner of your bedroom. The office space represents work and energy — the exact opposite of what you need to feel in your bedroom. Decide what is necessary and important in this space. Perhaps you'd like:

- your bed to be a comforting space to sleep and relax.

- a well-organized display of your jewelry.

- a small, cozy space to rest and read.

Zones	Step 1: Cut the clutter	Step 2: Increase storage	Step 3: Get organized
Sleep area			
Dressers			
Entertainment			
Additional zone			

It should be easy to identify what really belongs in a bedroom. Removing all the inappropriate items will make a significant difference in your space and frame of mind.

You may have other zones for this space. If so, fill them into the table on the preceding page. Then take your best guess on how long it will take you to complete each task for each zone. You may need to factor in time to shop for new storage containers. Remember, this is just an estimate to help you plan your bedroom decluttering project.

Step 1 Cut the clutter

Too much stuff in your bedroom translates into stress or stimulation, or both. Neither of these allow you to relax, unwind, or sleep. Your goal is to get rid of things that don't belong in this very personal space. If you can also purge items that don't help you feel soothed and calm, you're well on your way to creating an oasis in your home.

Keep in mind

Make a decision:

✓ keep
✓ toss
✓ donate
✓ sell
✓ pass on

Follow purging rules:

✓ decide quickly
✓ handle items once
✓ set limits
✓ pass the "keep" test
✓ recognize garbage

You probably have a few drawers and shelves in this space. You're going to empty them out, sorting into your designated piles as you go. Clear off all surfaces. Don't forget to look under your bed. It can be scary, but this is prime storage space. You don't want it wasted on the lost and forgotten.

SUPER TIPS for sorting out your sleep area

Get pumped up and show no mercy. Anger is a great motivator for cutting clutter. If there's a chip on your shoulder, take advantage of your fiery mood and sort through that freeloading mess in your bedroom. You'll be more likely to take control of your space and less likely to show mercy.

Shed some bedding and help others. Since you only need one or two sets of bedding, give those extra sheets and blankets to a women's shelter. They can always use donations, so they'd love to take them off your hands. Got any other linens or fabrics you've been meaning to use? The local senior citizen's center may also lighten your load.

Create a haven from work. There's a time for work and a time for rest. If you're in your bedroom, it's time to rest. So leave your work outside. Your bedroom should be a place where you can relax and retreat from the outside world. With office materials in

DON'T STORE...

Bedrooms mean different things to different people. But some stuff doesn't belong there no matter who you are. Mark your bedroom "off limits" to these dormitory violations.

✓ food

✓ dirty dishes

✓ paperwork

another room, you'll find it easier to let your mind settle into sleep mode.

Fill your night stand with only bare necessities. No two night stands are exactly alike. Only you know what really needs to go on your bedside table. Just remember to put only the things you'll need to reach when you're in bed. Books, your cell phone, reading glasses, and a glass of water are good examples, but you decide what's necessary. You can also leave room for a photograph or a pitcher of flowers to dress it up, but everything else has to go.

SUPER TIPS *for sorting dressers*

Give yourself breathing room. You don't have to cover every inch of wall space with furniture and photographs. Take a look around your bedroom. Are there pieces of furniture or piles of books you could do without? Removing them will make the room seem bigger and less crowded. You may be surprised at the difference it makes when you move your exercise bike to another location and take down a few posters. You'll have a whole new room.

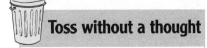
Toss without a thought

✓ worn-out underwear

✓ single earrings without matches

✓ socks without matches

✓ accessories you haven't worn in two years

Take it one drawer at a time. Rome wasn't built in a day. If cleaning out your dresser seems daunting, spread the task over several days. Every night sort through one drawer. Take everything out and only put back items you still use and like. Give away or trash everything else. At the end of the week, your dresser will be free of clutter.

Ditch duplicates to free up space. The advantage to sorting your dresser contents into categories is that you can see how many duplicates you have. You may decide eight pairs of brown socks is a bit much, and you can get by with two. Pull out the extras and donate them to charity. You'll be doing yourself a service by freeing up new space.

Pare down your jewelry collection. When you sort your jewelry, take it all out at once and remove any broken pieces. Then go through and take out the ones you don't wear anymore because they're out of style. They're not doing you any good in your jewelry box. Give them to someone who can use them, like a charitable organization or kids who like to play with grown-up jewelry.

SUPER TIPS for sorting entertainment items

Keep your book collection up to date. Every time you buy a new book, take an old one — or even two — off the shelf and donate it. Libraries always accept used books, and this will ensure your own collection stays up to date.

Stick with your decision to toss. As you collect things to donate, put them in paper bags or boxes and tape or staple them shut. Write "Donate" on the side so you know what they're for. Don't open them again! You'll just second-guess your decisions. Leave the boxes sealed and remove them from your home as soon as you can so they don't find a way back into your bedroom.

Catch up on your reading. Make room on your bookshelf. Donate any books you've already read. Then get cracking on the ones you still have to read so you can donate those, too. Carry a book around with you in a purse or briefcase, and pull it out when you're on a plane or in a doctor's waiting room.

Develop new decluttering habits. Keep a box in your bedroom closet or under your bed where you can put clothes, jewelry, or anything else you want to donate. When the box is full, take it to the secondhand store or women's shelter. Make this a habit to ward off clutter in the future.

Step 2 Increase storage

More and more often, bedrooms are called upon to do double, even triple, duty. This is where you fold your laundry, pay your bills, jot a note to a friend, check your e-mail, watch TV, or even exercise.

Remember...

✓ map your space

✓ shop for containers

All this varied activity inevitably leads to clutter. If you can simplify this space, do it. Limit the number of activities you do here. Choose those most important to you that fit your goals for this space.

Now think about your furniture. Do the pieces accommodate how you use this room? Start thinking outside the traditional bedroom box. Perhaps the matching night stands just aren't cutting it. Replace them with something more functional. This is your private sanctuary, and you need to make it work for you.

SUPER TIPS for storing in your sleep area

Hide clothes during the off-season. It's easy to conceal seasonal clothes. Put them inside suitcases or storage containers and place those under your bed. No matter what storage you use, remember to put in a bug repellant. Cedar blocks and mothballs work fine, but your best bet is to pour a cup of cedar chips into an old pair of pantyhose, tie it shut, and place it with your clothes. They'll be just as you left them when you pull them out in the spring.

Break the rules with two clutter tricks. Double the storage space in your bedroom with two items — bed risers and space bags. They work to increase storage in different ways. Bed risers actually give you more space. You put them under the feet of your bed to raise the bed higher, which gives you more under-bed storage space to work with. Remember to get a longer bed skirt to conceal your new storage. Space Bags, on the other hand, help you fit more stuff into a smaller space by compacting clothes and linens. Put bulky clothes into the Space Bag and vacuum the air out. It will shrink to a fraction of the size. Together these inexpensive tricks clear clutter for good.

Find furniture in unexpected places. The next time you wander through the farmer's market, keep an eye out for empty produce crates. They make great night stands and will add a rustic touch to your decor. Use them to store everything from books and magazines to hobby supplies — or even fruit.

Maximize space with clever beds. Some beds are so smart they can perform more than one job. That means less furniture and more space in your bedrooms. See if these multifunctional beds could work for you.

- futon — smaller than a regular bed and turns into a couch

- day bed — doubles as a bed and sofa

- air mattress — inflates for guests, deflates for storage

- Murphy bed — folds up into the wall or a cabinet during the day

- trundle bed — rolls under your regular bed when not in use

- captain's bed — drawers beneath the bed provide extra storage

Hide your dirty laundry. Put a hamper in your bedroom where you can hide all your dirty clothes. Having a specific place for it will keep you from leaving dirty clothes on your bed or piled on the floor. You can even have more than one so you can sort the clothes as they go in.

Do away with your box spring. Increase your under-bed storage with a platform bed. These popular bed frames are built higher and sturdier to support a mattress without the need for a box spring underneath. You can then use the foot of space where the box spring used to be for storage.

SUPER TIPS *for storing in dressers*

Gain control of drawers with shoe boxes. Put your socks in one shoe box, your pantyhose in another, and so on with all the tiny clothes items in your dresser drawers. Then slide the boxes into your drawers. Voila! Without spending any money, you've installed an organizational system that keeps small things from mixing together.

Show off your earrings with style. Dust off your arts and crafts skills to make a unique display for your earrings. Start with an attractive picture frame that can stand on its own. Remove the glass and backing until you're left with the empty framed space. Take some flexible window screening — you can buy some at your local hardware store — and cut it to fit the frame's opening. Hot glue the screen into place on the back. Hang your post or wire earrings on the screen. You now have a charming way to find them easily.

Sort dirty clothes as you go. Save the time you would spend sorting your dirty clothes. Put two laundry bags in every hamper — one for darks and one for lights. When a bag is full, take it straight to the washer. The sorting is already done.

Track down free jewelry storage containers. Your refrigerator is a great place to look for cheap jewelry organizers. An empty egg carton fits nicely in a dresser drawer and has a dozen little compartments perfect for rings, pins, earrings, and other small items. They're made to cradle something as gentle as eggs, so they'll be safe for your jewelry. Now open your freezer. That plastic ice cube tray will work well, too — when you're not using it for ice, that is.

Bag up dirty socks to maintain order. Buy one small mesh bag — the kind used for lingerie will do nicely — for each person in your house. Identify whose is whose with an indelible marker or a knotted colored ribbon. Then hang them discreetly in bedrooms, closets, near laundry hampers, or wherever is most convenient. Dirty socks go in throughout the week, and when it's laundry day, close the bags and toss them into the washer, then the dryer. Each person gets back his bag of clean socks. No more sorting.

Straighten out your necklaces with a tie rack. A jewelry box is great, but sometimes necklaces get tangled up inside the little drawers. Prevent those tangles by hanging your necklaces on the knobs of a tie rack. They'll hang straight and orderly instead of in a clumpy mess. You can make your own rack by attaching cup hooks or nails to a strip of wood. Mount the rack on the wall near your dresser for convenience.

SUPER TIPS for storing entertainment items

Put your TV behind closed doors. If your television is surrounded with piles of wires and more electronic equipment, you may need an entertainment center. These storage units have cabinets and drawers to hold your VCR, DVD player, CD player, as well as videos, CDs, and DVDs. There's also a place to put your television so you can close the doors and hide it when you're not watching it.

Start your own library. If you've got enough books in your bedroom to start a library, install shelving for your nighttime reading material. Some shelves above your bed or beside it will make sure you always have access to a good book.

Turn a shoe box into a CD caddy. Turn an empty shoe box into a CD caddy. These containers are the perfect fit for compact discs. Put them in with their titles facing up so you can easily find the album you want. For a touch of style, decorate the outside of the box with some paint or contact paper so it goes with your decor.

Conquer TV clutter. A television can take up valuable space on your dresser. Get your TV up and off the ground by mounting it on the wall. You can install a wall-hung unit yourself, but be sure to mount it securely.

Step 3 Get organized

Make sure the furniture in your bedroom is placed sensibly and comfortably. Take natural and artificial light, views, and air flow from fans and vents into consideration. Think about how easy it is to access pieces of fur-

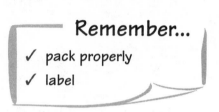

Remember...

✓ pack properly
✓ label

niture and maneuver around in the dark or in a sleepy daze. Make it easy and comfortable to do what you need to do here.

Remember, proximity is your new favorite word. Place items close to where they are used. You shouldn't have to race around between dressers to get dressed or get out of bed to grab your favorite book.

SUPER TIPS for organizing your sleep area

Slide it under your bed. Under-bed storage isn't limited to just bedroom belongings. You can hide all sorts of stuff under there as long as it's organized. That space is perfect for tucking away photo albums, office supplies, tool kits, and extra light bulbs. If you're strapped for space in other areas of your house, put sports equipment or even rarely used dining ware under there, too.

Restore order with a quilt rack. Picking comforters and blankets off the floor is an easy way to make your bedroom look less cluttered. Keep them neat and organized with a freestanding quilt rack near the foot of your bed. It's attractive and handy for tidying bulky bedding.

Your night stand should only contain things you'll need when you're in bed — books, reading glasses, cell phone, memo pad. But all of it can't go on top or it would get crowded. The surface is just for things you use all the time, like a lamp or clock. The rest can go in the drawers.

Screen out essential eyesores. Divide up your bedroom with a folding fabric screen. These attractive dividers can create a dressing room out of nowhere. They're also perfect for hiding things — like an exercise bike or television — while they're not in use. Since fabric screens don't weigh much, they're easy to rearrange whenever you have the whim.

SUPER TIPS *for organizing dressers*

Revitalize your room plan. There's no rule that says you have to scatter your furniture evenly about your bedroom walls. For a more convenient arrangement, put your dressers close together near your closet. It will take less time to get dressed and put away clean laundry if you don't have to run from one side of the room to the other.

Turn your dresser into an organizer. Create an organizational system for your dresser drawers. First, group like items together. Then put each group in its own drawer. You can sort by type of clothing — underwear, socks, pajamas, or by occasion — casual attire versus work clothes. Put the things you use most in the drawer that's easiest to access, usually the top one. If you have two dressers, you have the option of putting seasonal clothing in one dresser and year-round threads in the other. Or if you share a room with someone, you should both have a dresser so your clothes never get mixed up. Whatever works best for you is your new system. To stick with it, put labels inside each drawer so you'll know what goes where until you have your system down pat.

Get your socks in order. If you open your sock drawer to find a mess of random socks, put them in order with a diamond drawer organizer. The plastic strips interlock diagonally to form a diamond pattern, and you can cut it to fit your drawer. You'll never have to search for a match again after you put each pair in its own diamond-shaped slot.

Fine tune your sock drawer. Once you've organized your sock drawer, keep it organized. When you put laundry away, remember to roll or fold your socks instead of balling them up since it breaks down the elastic. As you place them in the drawer, sort them according to color and style. If you make this a habit, you'll always be able to find the pair you want.

Clamp down on wasted drawer space. Jewelry goes better in shallow drawers than deep drawers. It's easier to find the necklace you need, and you won't waste space in deeper drawers that could hold bulkier items, like clothes. The same goes for belts and other smaller items.

SUPER TIPS *for organizing an entertainment area*

Customize your space to meet your needs. Do you watch television every night in bed? Position your TV across from you in your direct line of sight. Absolutely need music playing to fall asleep? Keep your CD collection and stereo close at hand. When you organize your bedroom, consider your daily habits and needs so you have the most comfortable bedroom possible.

Cast aside unread books. Only keep books on your night stand if you're currently reading them. Your bedside table isn't a bookcase. Move any other books to their rightful shelf and free up that space for something you'll actually need in bed.

Teach your CDs their ABCs. Store your CDs in alphabetical order so you'll know exactly where to look for the album you want to hear. It will take a little time at first, but you'll save even more time later searching through your collection.

Evict unloved movies and music. Designate a shelf or compartment to store your DVDs and limit your entire collection to that space. Every time you get a new movie, get rid of one of your least favorites. Donate any overflow that doesn't fit in that space to a library, senior center, or other organization. Eventually, your collection will be nothing but new releases and absolute favorites.

Have Hollywood at your fingertips. Sometimes you're in the mood for a comedy, and sometimes a tear-jerker is in order. Organize your DVD collection into genres, like drama, romantic comedy, westerns, science fiction, foreign, and family films. Then alphabetize them within their genre.

Step 4 Keep it clean

Now that your bedroom is free of clutter, you'll find it's easy to keep it clean. The chart on the following page gives you a list of chores you can complete in 10 minutes. Add a few weekly, monthly, and occasional chores, and you've got one smart cleaning plan. Try these quick and easy cleaning tips for your clutter-free bedroom.

SUPER TIPS for cleaning your bedroom

Fluff up tired pillows. To freshen up your pillows, throw them in the dryer with a fabric softener sheet and two white towels, slightly damp. Run them on the air fluff cycle for half an hour. When they come out, they'll be like new.

Beat allergies in your bedroom. Make your bedroom a safe haven from allergens. Wash your bedding frequently. If you don't have time, put them through the air fluff cycle in your dryer. That'll do in a pinch. Run an air purifier to get allergens out of the air so you can breathe easy. And if you can bear it, don't let pets in your bedroom.

Transform your room by making your bed. If you do only one thing to keep your bedroom clean and tidy, make your bed. No matter what else is going on in your room, it will look much cleaner and more organized if your bed is made. Do it every morning when you wake up, even if all you do is pull the covers up.

Save time putting clean sheets on your bed. Instead of walking around the bed to tuck in corners every time you put on another layer, lay out the top sheet and any

10-minute daily speed cleaning	Weekly chores	Monthly chores	Occasional chores
Remove items that belong somewhere else	Dust furniture	Clean air and heating vents	Clean smudges off walls and light switches
Return clean clothes to closet or drawers	Dust knick-knacks, lampshades, and artwork	Wipe baseboards	Wash windows
Put dirty laundry in hamper	Vacuum or sweep floor	Check ceiling corners for cobwebs	Wash curtains
Return shoes to closet	Clean mirrors	Clean light fixtures and ceiling fan	Shampoo carpet
Make bed	Wipe windowsills	Flip mattress	Machine wash or dry-clean comforter or bedspread
	Change sheets	Wash mattress pad	Wash blankets
			Wash or fluff pillows in the dryer

blankets all at one time. Then walk around once and tuck in all the corners together.

Decimate dust mites and reclaim your home from these tiny, allergy-causing critters. According to the American Academy of Allergy, Asthma and Immunology, following these tips will give those bugs the boot.

- ❑ Use a dehumidifier to keep humidity below 50 percent.
- ❑ Have as little carpeting as possible.
- ❑ Seal mattresses, box springs, and pillows in allergen-proof fabric covers.
- ❑ Wash bedding once a week in hot water at 130 degrees Fahrenheit.
- ❑ Dry linens in a hot dryer.
- ❑ Vacuum weekly with a HEPA, or high-efficiency particulate filter.

Take your mattress for a spin. Flip your mattress once every three months so it wears evenly — just like you rotate your tires. Remember to turn it side-to-side half the time, and end-over-end every other time.

Dust with a gentle touch. Delicate pieces, like knickknacks and lampshades, require a more delicate touch when it comes to dusting. Use a brand new paintbrush to get the dust off these dainty items without damaging them.

Sign up for Shirt Folding 101. Folding shirts neatly is easy if you know how. Simply lay the shirt face down and smooth it out. Fold each sleeve across the back so they

make an "X."
Fold each
side of the
shirt inward
so they meet
in the center,
like in the diagram.
Fold the bottom half
up and turn the shirt
over. You've got a
neat and tidy shirt. If
you need a template,
place a magazine on
the shirt and fold
around that until you
get the hang of it.

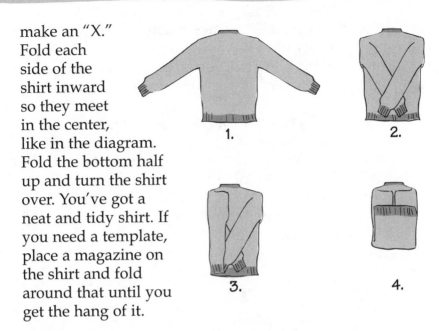

Line your drawers with place mats. Cleaning out your
dresser drawers is a cinch when you line the bottom with
place mats. Whenever one gets dirty, just pop the place
mat in your washing machine and slip it back into the
drawer when it's clean.

Let pantyhose help you vacuum. You want to vacuum
inside your dresser drawers, but don't feel like taking
everything out first. Not a problem. Just slip an old pair of
pantyhose over the nozzle of your vacuum. Now you can
vacuum around your things without watching them get
sucked up.

Freshen the air while you vacuum. Just drop a single cin-
namon stick into your vacuum cleaner bag. This spice will
deodorize your home naturally with no extra effort on
your part.

Remove sticky labels easily. You just bought a new CD.
The album sounds great, but you can't get that annoying

price sticker off. Luckily, many household products you might already have will help remove the label. Dab on some cooking oil or rubbing alcohol, and it should come right off. Laundry pre-wash treatments will also work.

Restore CDs to their former glory. CDs stay pretty clean most of the time. But if they get dusty or need a gentle scrub, mix a few tablespoons of baking soda into a spray bottle filled with a pint of water. Shake it up and spray the solution on your compact disc. Use a soft cloth to wipe in a smooth motion from the center to the outer edge. Then admire the shine.

CHAPTER 6
The Clothes Closet

Closets. We love them, and we hate them. They could be so perfect if they would just behave. But somehow the hangers tangle, shoes become scattered, sweaters wrinkle, and that perfect blue blouse is MIA.

There is a way out of the closet jungle but simply purging items won't get you there. Even if you cut your wardrobe in half, shoving everything back onto that one wooden rod won't solve your closet confusion. You must evaluate and measure your space, categorize your clothing, and assign every item a home.

Hang in there — it's not as hard as it sounds. Fix the image of a streamlined storage space firmly in your mind, take a deep breath, and open your closet door.

Remember...

✓ make a wish list

✓ be realistic

✓ set priorities

✓ identify your clutter problems

✓ label your zones

✓ set a timeline

Experts agree that besides simply having too much stuff, the root of most closet disorganization is the basic design. If you take a look at magazines or brochures of custom closets, none of them feature just a single hanging rod. They usually have multiple rods, shelves at varying heights, bins, baskets, dividers, and cubbies.

But you don't have to spend a lot of money on a professional closet system to achieve a similar result. There are lots of free and inexpensive ways to get creative, functional storage. When you are through with this project:

- you'll be able to find every article of clothing quickly and easily.

Zones	Step 1: Cut the clutter	Step 2: Increase storage	Step 3: Get organized
Folded clothes			
Hanging clothes			
Shoes			
Accessories			

- you'll feel confident nothing will fall on you when you open your closet.

- you'll save money because you won't buy duplicate items.

Look at the chart on the preceding page. Take your best guess on how long it will take you to complete each task for each zone. You may need to factor in time to shop for new storage containers. Remember, this is just an estimate to help you plan your clothes closet decluttering project.

Step 1 Cut the clutter

There's no way around it. You're going to have to try things on. So make some room, set up a full-length mirror, and strip down. Be brutal. Check out the *Toss Without a Thought* suggestions on page 146 because you're going to have to lay down some hard and fast rules here. Anything that goes in your KEEP

Keep in mind

Make a decision:

✓ keep

✓ toss

✓ donate

✓ sell

✓ pass on

Follow purging rules:

✓ decide quickly

✓ handle items once

✓ set limits

✓ pass the "keep" test

✓ recognize garbage

pile must be something that fits, looks good on you, and you'll wear often.

SUPER TIPS *for sorting folded clothes*

Ask these five questions to decide what to keep. Is your closet bursting at the seams? Then it's time to toss the old and make room for the new. Start by pulling all the clothes out of your closet. Hold each item up, take a good look, and ask yourself these five questions to decide what to keep and what to toss. If you answer "no" to any of them, send that garment packing.

- Have I worn this in the last two years?

- Does it still fit? Will it ever fit?

- Does it even belong to me?

- Can it be mended, or is it beyond repair?

- Do I use it, or am I only keeping this for emotional reasons?

Divvy up closet space wisely. Your closet should reflect who you are and what you do, not who you used to be or wish you were. Decide how much of your life you spend doing various things. Maybe you spend 60 percent of your time at work. In that case, dedicate 60 percent of your closet space to work clothes. Allot the rest of the space the same way to avoid filling up your closet with clothes you rarely wear.

Create separate piles for "keep" and "toss." As you begin cleaning out your closet, set up four boxes. Label the first one "keep," the second "donate," the third "mending,"

Set rules for keeping clothes. Separate the best from the rest by keeping only those garments, shoes, and accessories that:

❑ fit well

❑ are ready to wear (no mending or stains)

❑ flatter your figure

❑ make you feel good

❑ you absolutely love

and the fourth "rags." Place clothes in the appropriate box as you go through the closet trying them on.

Set the mood. Try on clothes in front of a full-length mirror, and make sure you have good — but not harsh — lighting. The right lights make a difference in how colors and style complement you. Add a lamp or two if necessary. Put on music that makes you want to boogie and the task will go faster.

Toss clothes that don't fit. Don't keep clothes that no longer fit. They waste space and energy and do nothing for your self-esteem. You can keep one skinny outfit if it motivates you to get fit, but no more. On the other hand, some people's weight fluctuates slightly over the course of a year. In that case, storing a few clothes of different sizes makes sense, but be discriminating.

Give clothes to a good cause. Take the sting out of decluttering your closet. Get rid of that outfit you never wear and feel good about it by donating it to a worthy cause. Women and men who have fallen on hard times desperately need warm clothes, good shoes, and a helping hand. These charitable organizations aim to help. Contact one and ask about donating gently used clothing, or check your Yellow Pages for "Social Service Organizations" or "Human Services Organizations." Many will pick up items from your home.

- The Salvation Army 800-95-TRUCK (to schedule pick-up) or *www.salvationarmyusa.org*

- Excess Access *www.excessaccess.org*

- AmVets 800-810-7148 or *www.amvets.org*

- Goodwill Industries 800-664-6577 or *www.goodwill.org*

- American Kidney Fund *www.kidneyfund.org* or check your local telephone book

- Society of St. Vincent de Paul *www.svdpusa.org* or check your local telephone book

- Dress for Success (for women's suits and professional clothing) *www.dressforsuccess.org*

- Career Gear (for men's suits and professional clothing) *www.careergear.org*

Toss without a thought

It's hard to feel good about yourself when your closet is full of clothes you can't or don't wear. Stop suffering! Liberate yourself and your closet by tossing anything that:

✓ doesn't fit

✓ is uncomfortable (itchy, too tight, hurts your feet)

✓ is stained or torn beyond repair, including stockings with snags and runs

✓ fails to make you feel wonderful when you wear it

✓ you bought on impulse and never wear

✓ does not flatter your figure

✓ you have not worn in two years

Stock a clothing play chest for kids. Know any kids who love to play dress-up? Collect some clothes for them while you clean out your closet. Silky scarves, sparkly belts, feathered hats, and brightly colored clothes are perennial favorites. Put them in a toy chest or vintage suit-case and give as a gift to the children in your life.

Remove clothes that need repair. In your "mending" box, place garments that need a little repair — loose or missing buttons, tears, unraveled hems, broken zippers, or alterations. Write the date on the box. Now carry it to the place you do your mending, or put it in the trunk of your car to take to a seamstress. Do not put these clothes back in your closet until you have fixed them. Keeping them in the closet gives you the false impression they are ready to wear. Set a time limit — if you haven't repaired them in a month, get rid of them.

Pack away a "maybe" box. If you have trouble letting go of some items, create a box labeled "maybe." In it, place clothes you haven't worn in a year or more but you aren't ready to give away. Seal up the box, write today's date on it, and store it in a spare closet or dry basement. Open it again this time next year. If you haven't needed anything in it all year, donate the items to charity.

SUPER TIPS *for sorting hanging clothes*

Hunt down clothes you never wear. Try this trick at the start of each season when you swap the clothes in your closet. Turn the hangers the "wrong" way, with the hook

Next time you're clearing out clothes, consider this — experts say most people only wear 20 percent of their clothes on a regular basis. The other 80 percent hangs in their closet, just in case.

pointing toward you. Each time you wear an item, hang it up as you normally would, with the hook pointing away from you. By season's end, you'll be able to see at a glance which outfits you never wore. Give these to friends or charity.

Shop without guilt. Cutting closet clutter doesn't mean you have to go on a clothing diet. You can still shop. But each time you bring home a new outfit, take one from your closet you no longer wear and donate it to charity.

Consolidate empty hangers. Sometimes you can't see the forest for the trees, or the clothes for the hangers. Open up space by consolidating empty hangers. Either move them to your laundry room, ready to hang clean clothing, or keep them together in your closet. Hang a short rod just for empty hangers, or hang them all together at one end of a regular clothing rod.

SUPER TIPS *for sorting shoes and accessories*

Give unwanted shoes the boot. Go through your shoes at least once a year the way you do clothes, using some of the same keep-or-toss criteria. Give away shoes you don't like, no longer fit, hurt your feet, or you haven't worn for two years. It's OK to keep a few special pairs for parties or just-in-case events. Still have shoes you rarely wear but want to keep? Place them where you can easily see them, and maybe you'll wear them more often. Give them a year, then let them go.

Stock first-rate stockings. Always have two good pairs of hosiery on hand. Throw away stockings once they develop a run, hole, or snag. You'll save yourself the headache of searching frantically at the last minute for one without flaws.

Step 2 Increase storage

If you haven't done this already, sort everything in your Keep pile into categories — long-sleeved shirts, T-shirts, pants, skirts, dresses, etc. You get the idea. Now count the number of items in each catego-ry. Count shoes, belts, and other accessories, too. Write everything down.

Remember...
✓ map your space
✓ shop for containers

Next, measure the inside of your closet. This is critical. You'll have to match containers to your clothing and to your closet space. Sketch out a diagram of your closet and start thinking about new ways of using this space.

You have a few options for reorganizing. You can essentially leave your closet design as it is and integrate individual storage pieces into it by either purchasing new items, like shoe trees or specialty hangers, or recycling things you have around the house, like baskets or plastic bins. This way, there's no demoli-tion or major construction. You may not end up with the "perfect" closet, but you won't spend a lot of money. Plus, you get the chance to be creative.

You could remove most or all of the "guts" of your existing closet and build a custom system yourself. This can be time-consuming and will require a bit of construction know-how. Done well, this option gives you the exact storage system you need.

Or you could replace most or all of your existing closet with a closet organizing system. You can purchase pieces or entire kits at most home and hardware superstores. These are fairly easy to assemble, vary widely in price depending on the style and size you need, and require exact closet measurements.

SUPER TIPS for storing folded clothes

Squeeze in more shelves. Keep stacks of items under 12-inches tall and move shelves closer together, leaving a few extra inches in between. By carefully managing shelf spacing, you may be able to squeeze in one or even two additional shelves, creating lots more stackable storage. If your shelves are stationary, invest in cheap wire organizers that sit on shelves and create another shelf within a shelf.

Move bookcases into closet. Old spare bookcases are ready-made shelves for shoes, sweaters, baskets of accessories, and other stackable items. Place a short bookcase underneath a high hanging rod, and hang short garments, like blouses, above it. Or dedicate one closet wall to a tall, narrow bookcase. You get instant storage without spending a penny.

Put unused furniture to work. Dressers come in many shapes and sizes — some short and long, some tall and narrow. Buy the size that fits into your spare closet space, or move an old, unused dresser from another part of your house into the closet. An extra bedside table can fit into especially small closet spaces and store extra items.

Invest in movable sweater shelves. Short on shelves? Create more instantly with hanging sweater shelves. These come in plastic, wire, or cotton canvas varieties, hang from your main clothes rod, and give you six shelves to stack foldable clothes, like sweaters and T-shirts. Best of all, you can easily remove them when the seasons change or you need more hanging space.

Shrink bulky items with a vacuum. You know food comes in vacuum-sealed packages, but clothes? Special plastic garment bags are perfect for storing seldom-worn suits, out-of-season sweaters, and bulky blankets. Place your clothes in the right size bag, then hook the hose of your vacuum cleaner to the special valve on the bag. The vacuum sucks out the air, shrinking the item to around one-third its original size.

Find free inspiration and advice. For quick ideas and inspiration, jump on the Internet and surf the Web sites of professional closet organizers and container stores. You can see photographs of products and finished projects and

Organize on a budget with these tools. Who says you need expensive closet systems when these cheap substitutes can do the job? Check out these super-simple storage solutions.

❑ Old bookcases house folded clothes and shoes.

❑ Milk crates turned on their sides hold purses and scarves. Stack them to create even more storage space.

❑ Old dressers can find a new home in a closet for storing folded items and accessories.

❑ Woven baskets on shelves charmingly organize belts, T-shirts, and socks.

❑ Extra shower rings clipped onto a clothes rod holds handbags.

❑ Cheap multi-hangers hold several garments at a time.

gather ideas on how best to arrange your own closet. Some sites even offer free tools to help you design the closet of your dreams. Start with these:

- California Closets — *www.californiaclosets.com*

- The Container Store — *www.containerstore.com*

- ClosetMaid — *www.closetmaid.com*

- EasyClosets.com — *www.easyclosets.com*

- Mill's Pride Cabinetry — *www.millspride.com*

- Organize-It — *www.organizes-it.com*

Create space with closet kits. Superstores, home stores, and professional organizing companies sell whole closet kits to help you organize your clothes, complete with rods, racks, cubbies, and shelves. Specialty companies, like California Closets, will custom design a closet system for you based on your closet dimensions and the number of hanging and folded garments and shoes you need to store. Superstores and home stores offer more general kits you can custom fit yourself. You can also buy closet systems piece-by-piece from these same stores.

Turn unused room into walk-in closet. Consider converting a small, spare bedroom into a walk-in closet if you desperately need a bigger closet. You can then design a closet specifically for the number of hanging clothes, shoes, and folded garments you have. Add full-length mirrors, good lighting, and an island ottoman in the center to sit on while dressing.

SUPER TIPS for storing hanging clothes

Redesign your closet to maximize space. Now that you've whittled down your clothes, you should know exactly what you plan to put back in your closet. That's important, because you need to count how many hanging garments you have in order to redesign and maximize the space. Do that now. Count the number of:

- long dresses
- short dresses
- skirts
- suits

- hanging pants
- hanging shirts
- jackets

Hang rods to meet your needs. Once you know how many hanging garments you have, it's time to decide where to put the rods. Take a look at your closet dimensions and start mapping out how much room they'll need. First, gauge the width of your hanging clothes. This tells you how far from the wall you need to hang the rod — for most clothes, that's 21 inches away from the wall. If you plan to hang bulky coats in the closet, add a couple of extra inches.

Measure the space. Next, grab a tape measure and measure the closet from front to back, side to side, and floor to ceiling. Measure the height and width of the doorway, too, and write it all down.

Hang 'em high. How high you hang clothes rods depends on the length of the garments you plan to hang. Group your clothes together by type — skirts, blouses, pants, dresses, and so on. Then measure the longest garment in each group from the top of the hanger to the hem. Add another six inches, and that's how much hanging space each group of clothes needs.

Double your closet space in just 10 minutes. Make your bedroom closet twice as roomy just by hanging double rods. Hang one rod high to hold shirts, blouses, and other short garments. Add another rod below it for pants folded over a hanger. Measure the length of clothes you plan to hang from the bottom rod, add another six inches for clearance, and hang the lower rod at that height. Next, measure the longest garment you plan to hang from the upper rod, add six inches, and hang the upper rod that much higher than the lower one. Attach rods to wall studs, not just drywall. Otherwise, they may collapse under the weight of clothing.

Estimate how long the rod should be. While you have your garments grouped by type, count the number of hanging items in each group. Julie Morgenstern, author of *Organizing from the Inside Out*, says each item will need about one-half to one inch of space on the clothes rod. Multiply this number by the number of garments in each group of clothes. This tells you how long a rod you need for long items, like dresses, and short ones, like blouses.

Group items by length to stretch space. If you're stuck with just one clothes rod, make the best of it. Hang all the

When redesigning closet space, remember to plan plenty of space for shoes and folded clothing. Count the pairs of shoes you own and how many stacks of clothes you have. Limit stacks to less than 12 inches tall. Based on these numbers, build shelf space, racks, or other storage into your closet design.

long garments at one end, and the short ones at the other. Then place a small dresser, several shelves, or a large shoe rack under the short end.

Multiply closet space instantly. Buy hangers that let you hang multiple shirts, pants, or skirts. These vertical hangers often hold up to five garments. They're perfect for small closets and limit the wrinkling you normally get from cramming too many hanging items together on one rod.

Make your own multi-hanger. Buy an 18-inch brass chain, like the kind used to hang flowerpots. Make sure the links are wide enough to slide the head of a hanger through. Wrap one end around the closet rod, tie the links together with a piece of wire or sturdy twist-tie, and let the rest dangle. Hang clothes along the length of the chain by hooking hangers through the links.

Streamline slacks with trouser racks. Outfit your closet with trouser racks. These attach to the wall or closet door, hold up to 20 pairs of pants, and take up very little space. The slacks hang on dowels that swing out from the wall. To see the trousers, you simply flip through the dowels.

Go long to save space. Most closets have more vertical than horizontal space. Take advantage of that. Instead of folding pants in half over a hanger, hang them lengthwise. Clip the cuffs to a hanger and hang the pants upside down, with the bulky waist near the floor.

Hang whole outfits together. Combine matching pants, jackets, or shirts on one strong hanger. You'll create more space, keep outfits together and ready to wear, and end hanger clutter.

Stash specialty clothing in spare closets. Store seldom-worn clothing, like formal wear and out-of-season items, in a spare closet. Delicate items are less likely to get crushed if they have their own roomy home. Plus, you wear them much less often than your everyday clothes, so you don't need easy access to them.

SUPER TIPS for sorting shoes and accessories

Store shoes on eye-level shelves. Storing shoes on the floor is not convenient for many people, especially if you have trouble bending to reach them. Keep them at eye level instead. Raise the upper rod in your closet and lower the lower rod. Add a shelf or two between them about eye level to hold shoe boxes, shoe racks, or baskets for accessories.

Organize shoes on floor racks. Under all those rods and shelves you could have floor space going to waste. Floor shoe racks make the most of space between hanging clothes and the floor and can neatly organize many pairs of shoes in a small space.

Install sliding shelves for hidden storage. Put sliding shelves in your closet to hold shoes, sweaters, or accessories. Pull them out for a better look at the items stored on them, and slide them back into place to save valuable closet space.

Hide shoes in attractive cabinet. Shoe cabinets look like a regular piece of furniture, but the drawers open to reveal slots for storing shoes. These cabinets cost more than inexpensive wire racks, but they're a good option if you want tasteful storage that resembles real furniture.

Buy baskets for display and shelf storage. Place attractive baskets on closet shelves to hold sweaters, socks, T-shirts, rolled belts, or assorted winter items, like gloves and scarves. These containers stop clothes from spilling all over shelves and keep small items together. Woven baskets cost little but lend an air of calm elegance to any closet.

Organize accessories in clever bags. Clear, over-the-door shoe bags are sometimes too flimsy to house shoes, but they're just right for holding scarves, ties, bangles, hosiery, and other accessories. They're clear, so you can quickly spot what you want without rummaging. You can also buy clear bags that hang from your clothing rod with pouches made specifically for accessories.

Get hooked on specialty hangers. Container stores, like *www.containerstore.com*, sell special hangers and racks just for belts, scarves, and neck ties. Racks screw easily onto the back of a closet door, while the hangers hook onto regular clothes rods. They all keep accessories wrinkle-free and easy to see.

Open the door for more valuable space. The inside of closet doors often goes unused. Hang hooks for robes, purses, belts, ties, or hats, or install miniature clothing rods and shelves on the back of the door.

Show your style with hat boxes. Some good ideas never go out of fashion — like hat boxes. Now that these containers have come back in style, you can find them in a wide variety of colors and patterns. Large hat boxes safely store your favorite hats, while smaller ones can hold gloves, hosiery, jewelry, and other accessories. Stack them on a shelf in your closet, or display them on a bedroom dresser or atop an armoire.

View accessories while picking out clothes. Store accessories in stackable, clear plastic boxes on your closet shelves. These containers let you see your accessories while you decide what to wear.

Make the most of high ceilings. Don't let high ceilings go to waste. Install an extra shelf above the clothes rod, closer to the ceiling, and use it to store out-of-season shoes, sweaters, and even extra blankets.

Step 3 Get organized

There are many ways to arrange the items you plan to put back into your closet — by type, color, frequency of use, or even by assembling complete outfits. Pick a method that makes sense to you and suits your lifestyle.

Remember...

✓ pack properly
✓ label

However, unless you have the grand ballroom of closets, experts recommend you store off-season clothes somewhere else. You'll find an entire section on sorting, storing, and organizing out-of-season clothes in *Chapter 13 The Attic or Basement*.

SUPER TIPS *for organizing folded clothes*

Fold shirts like the pros. Ever wonder how clothing stores keep their shirts stacked so neatly? The secret is out. Take an old cardboard box and cut out a rectangle the size you want your folded shirts to be. Lay the shirts front-down on a flat surface, and place the rectangle in the center of the back, just under the shoulders. Fold the shirt over the rectangle, starting with the bottom hem, then both sides. Slide the cardboard out the top, and you have a perfectly folded shirt. Use the rectangle to fold the rest, and stack them neatly in your closet.

Tidy up folded stacks easily. Plastic and wire shelf dividers create instant order to keep folded clothes stacked neatly. No more towers of sweaters spilling into your sweats or, worse yet, onto the floor.

Give out-of-season clothes the heave-ho. Don't keep out-of-season clothes in your main closet unless you have loads of space. Protect them from dust and must by storing them in cheap plastic bins. Stack them in a spare closet, dry basement, or attic, or buy bins made to fit under your bed. Simply unpack the bins and swap out clothing when the weather changes.

Protect delicates with separate hampers. Set up separate hampers or baskets for clothes that need dry cleaning versus those you can wash. You may want to add a third basket for garments you have to hand wash. You'll never ruin another delicate item by accidentally tossing it in the washer.

DON'T STORE...

✓ other people's clothing, unless your spouse shares the closet

✓ mending

✓ stained garments

✓ anything that isn't ready to wear

✓ clothing, shoes, or accessories you plan to get rid of

✓ items that no longer fit

✓ things you don't wear, for whatever reason

SUPER TIPS for organizing hanging clothes

Trade in tired wire hangers. Get rid of your wire hangers without a second thought. They tangle too easily, lose their shape and sag, stretch out knit fabrics, and generally wrinkle everything. Now fill your closet with:

- padded hangers for sweaters

- hangers with clips for slacks, skirts, and slips

- heavy-duty plastic or wooden hangers for shirts, jackets, and suits

- plastic hangers with notched shoulders for sleeveless or spaghetti-strap dresses and blouses

Color-code hanging clothes. The National Cleaners Association warns against hanging light-colored fabrics next to dark ones. Over time, the dark dyes vaporize and stain nearby light garments. Group hanging clothes by color in your closet. You'll have an easier time finding and returning garments, and you'll keep colors from bleeding on each other.

Locate confusing dark-colored clothes with ease. It's hard to tell navy blue from black, even in good light. In dark closets, it can be impossible. Here's a quick solution — simply hang colors you have trouble distinguishing on differently colored plastic hangers.

Recycle your wire hangers. Call your local dry cleaner and ask if they accept donations of wire hangers. Some cleaners will take them off your hands, especially if the hangers came from them in the first place.

Hang those navy slacks on a bright blue hanger, and the black slacks on white hangers. You'll never have trouble telling them apart again. Now if you could just do the same with your socks ...

Group clothes by style or type. Categorize your clothes to spot items in a snap. Group them in whatever way makes sense to you. You might hang work clothes on one rod and casual clothes on another. Or hang skirts, pants, shirts, and jackets in separate groups. You can even create categories within categories, like grouping turtlenecks together in the shirt section.

SUPER TIPS *for sorting shoes and accessories*

Photograph shoes for easy finding. Many people keep shoes in their original boxes or in plastic shoe boxes to protect them from dust and damage. But opening every box to find the right pair can be a real hassle. Try this instead — snap a photograph of each pair of shoes and tape it to the front of the box. When you want certain shoes, just look for the picture.

Save shoe boxes for off-season storage. Save at least some of the original shoe boxes when you buy a new pair. When the seasons change, store the off-season shoes in their boxes in the top of your closet, or in a spare closet with other out-of-season clothes. Keep the in-season shoes on easily accessible racks in your closet. Simply swap them all out when seasons change.

Round up belts and purses. Hanging handbags and belts is a cinch if you know this nifty trick. Attach shower curtain rings to your regular clothing rod, and hang a purse or belt from each. Voila! No more lost belts or messy piles of purses.

Pair up accessories with outfits. Do you always wear certain belts, bracelets, or scarves with a particular outfit? Then hang them together. Hook the belt and bracelets over the top of the hanger, and drape the scarf or tie around the hanger's neck. You'll have a whole outfit ready to go, and no more last-minute searching for missing accessories.

Hang up handbags. Hang a brass chain from a hook on the inside of your closet door. Attach S-hooks along the chain about 6 inches apart and hang handbags or belts from them.

Divide drawers to keep belts neat. Buy inexpensive dividers for shallow drawers or plastic storage bins, and use them to store belts. Simply roll up each belt and place in its cubby.

Roll your socks to store. You can use the same drawer dividers to neatly store socks and stockings in shallow drawers. Be sure to roll or fold your socks. Balling them together stretches out the elastic.

Make your own shelf dividers. Cut the bottoms off milk jugs and small boxes and use these to organize accessories on closet shelves or in drawers. You can make these containers as deep or shallow as you need. Clean them thoroughly, then cover them with decorative fabric, contact paper, wallpaper, heavy wrapping paper, or paint them — whatever you like. You can even add ribbons and buttons for flair.

Protect delicate hosiery. Save the original bag or box your hosiery comes in. After you've worn and laundered it, gently roll it up and pop it back in the container. Store these neatly in a drawer or over-the-door organizer. Or, you can hang stockings by the waist from hangers with plastic clips. Just be certain to hang them together and away from anything that might snag them.

Step 4 Keep it clean

Congratulations! Clearing out and cleaning up your closet is the hard part — keeping it that way will be a breeze. Start with these tips to maintain order and protect your clothing.

SUPER TIPS for cleaning your clothes closet

Tidy up as you take things off. Once everything in your closet has a proper place, keeping things neat should be easy. As you change clothes, automatically return all items to their rightful spots. Drop dirty laundry in your new hamper, and hang shoes on the attractive racks you installed. Put it all back as you take it off, and you won't have to wade through a pile of stuff on the floor next time you open your closet door.

Clean out closet at start of each season. The beginning of each season is a great time to clean out your closet. You haven't seen those clothes in several months, so you'll have a fresh perspective on them. As you unpack the new season's clothes, eye them carefully. Check for moth or storage damage and toss items you can't repair. Reconsider which outfits you want to keep and which you'd like to donate. Maybe your size has changed, or perhaps a new style has caught your eye. Weed out clothes, shoes, and accessories at the beginning and end of each season to keep your closet updated.

Move unwanted items to a "give away" box. Keep a separate hamper or box as your "give away" box. Every time you pull something out of your closet that doesn't fit or you no longer want, drop it in the special hamper. At the end of the season, donate all the items to charity or give them to a friend.

Shed light on a dark closet. Beautiful, organized closets are little help if the light inside is too dim to see by. At the same time, the light from bare-bulbs can be too harsh. Get creative and stylish by installing track lights or recessed lights in the ceiling of walk-in closets. Too much trouble? Simply hang a small shelf, even a corner shelf just inside the door, and set a lamp on it. Simply flip the lamp on when you open the closet. For very small spaces, consider hanging a battery-powered light on the wall inside the closet. Just press the light to turn it on and off.

Trash plastic dry cleaning bags. Those thin plastic bags can protect your clothes temporarily, but they should not be left on long-term. They trap moisture, which can stain fabric. Instead, drape an old sheet over leather, furs, evening wear, or other delicate garments to keep off dust. Cut a hole in the sheet's center and slide it over the hanger's hook. Hang several items together under larger sheets.

Shelter shoes from dust. To keep shoes clean, especially between seasons, store them in regular or clear plastic shoe boxes. You can help them retain their shape by stuffing them lightly with tissue paper or newspaper.

CHAPTER 7
The Bathroom

Some days your goal is to get in and out of the bathroom as fast as possible. And then there are days when you have lots of time to soak, steam, savor, and pamper.

This means your bathroom needs to be streamlined, yet well-stocked — practical, yet self-indulgent. After all, if you walk out of this space sparkling and spiffy, can a perfect day be far behind?

But first, you must turn the array of bottles, spritzers, cans, gadgets, and paper into something a bit more shipshape.

The average American spends over $500 a year on personal care products and services. That's a lot of shampoo and mouthwash. Multiply that by the number of people sharing your bathroom, and you could be looking at constant bedlam.

Remember...

✓ make a wish list

✓ be realistic

✓ set priorities

✓ identify your clutter problems

✓ label your zones

✓ set a timeline

Even though the scale of your bathroom space can vary, the basics stay the same. You essentially have the tub or shower area and then everything else. And even though you can probably get the job done in your existing bathroom, think about how you'd like this space to function.

Is a candlelit bath in your future? Or would you simply love a spot to sit and fix your hair? Don't give up on these things until you clear out the clutter and see what you have to work with.

You may have other zones for this space. If so, fill them into the following table. Then take your best guess on how long it will take you to complete each task for each zone. Keep in mind, you may need time to shop for new storage containers. Remember, this is just an estimate to help you plan your bathroom decluttering project.

Zones	Step 1: Cut the clutter	Step 2: Increase storage	Step 3: Get organized
Vanity			
Tub and shower			
Additional zone			

Step 1 Cut the clutter

Although most bathroom items tend to be small, you probably have a lot of them. Combine that with the typically limited bathroom storage, and you have a recipe for clutter.

Be careful trying to DONATE, SELL, or PASS ON bathroom items. Unless you're talking about unopened products or working appliances, most things you don't want will go in the trash. Pay special attention to expiration dates.

Keep in mind

Make a decision:

✓ keep

✓ toss

✓ donate

✓ sell

✓ pass on

Follow purging rules:

✓ decide quickly

✓ handle items once

✓ set limits

✓ pass the "keep" test

✓ recognize garbage

SUPER TIPS for sorting through your vanity

Think before you sort. Don't be hasty! Before you dump the entire contents of your bathroom vanity on the floor, take a second to look at the system you've got now. Take out one group of objects at a time and make sure they're sorted like-with-like. If you remove everything at once, it will take a lot longer to get through. And putting things in sorted piles as they come out will give you a better idea of how many duplicate items you have.

Show no mercy. Be ruthless when sorting through toiletries. Take every item out of your cabinets and off your counters and divide it all into two groups — "Must Keep" and "Undecided." "Must Keep" means stuff you absolutely need or use on a regular basis. The rest goes in the "Undecided" pile, which goes in the trash. If you have trouble letting go, remember that those little bottles of shampoo and conditioner from every hotel you ever stayed in aren't as valuable as the space they take up in your cabinets.

DON'T STORE...

It turns out the worst place to store medicine is where you're most likely to keep it. Before you fill your next prescription, relocate the contents of your medicine cabinet. Because of moisture and heat, a bathroom cabinet is not a good place for prescription and over-the-counter medicines. Keep these items together in a cooler, drier place, like a bedroom or your linen closet. Just be sure they are safe from children and pets. Medicines that require cooling should go in a sealed plastic bag in your refrigerator.

Clean as you go. Wipe off each item as you pull it out to sort. Once you've emptied the drawers and shelves, give those a good wiping, too. It's a lot easier to clean surfaces when they're cleared off, and after you replace everything, it will look twice as nice.

Excavate your cabinets. You may feel like Indiana Jones when you sift through the depths of your bathroom cabinets and find artifacts from a bygone era. Pull out the things you don't have a use for anymore, like that package of hair color that was so fashionable a few years ago, and throw them away.

Take charge of antibiotics. No matter what, you should not have extra antibiotics lying around. Always finish your antibiotics when they're prescribed. If for some reason you do have leftovers, throw them out. Antibiotics become less effective over time, and you should never self-medicate with leftover prescription drugs.

Think before you toss. Before you throw out any medications, take a couple of precautions. Don't flush them down the toilet — that's not good for the environment. Instead, put them in a childproof container. Then put that inside another container that's completely sealed, and throw it in the garbage. Taking those extra steps helps keep children and pets safe.

Be picky about your blow dryer. How many blow dryers does a person really need? Since you've only got one head, you should only need one blow dryer. If you have more than one, try them all out and decide which one works best. Donate the others.

Learn to let go. Some things are worth fixing — others aren't, so throw them out. Take all the broken and malfunctioning items from your bathroom and toss them in the trash. This includes hair bands whose elastic has broken, barrettes whose clasps have snapped off, and combs missing half their teeth.

Keep first aid supplies together. As you sort through your medicine cabinet, hang on to anything that might go well in a first-aid kit. Bandages, antibiotic ointment, gauze, alcohol, and small scissors can come in handy during an emergency. Store all the items in a sturdy container, like an old lunch box, and put it in a safe place. Just remember to label it "First-aid kit."

Give away gift bags. You'll feel better about getting rid of unwanted cosmetics if you know they're going to someone who will appreciate them. Whether you've got two of something or you just don't like that new color as much as you did at the store, your castoff beauty products can still do some good. Put all those extras into gift bags and give them to girls and young women you know who like trying new products. They're excited. You're popular. Everyone wins.

Pare down your Band-Aid collection. You may have a habit of accumulating adhesive bandage boxes in your bathroom cupboard. If so, consolidate them. Take all the bandages out of the unfinished boxes and combine them in just one box. Same bandages, less space.

 Toss without a thought

Look around your bathroom for things that obviously need to go in the trash, like rusty razor blades, old toothbrushes, expired medications, and used-up cosmetics. Those are an easy call. But you may be hesitant to throw away some of your personal hygiene products, even if they have been around forever. Use this list as a guide.

✓ body wash — 3 years

✓ facial cleanser — 6 months

✓ moisturizer — 1 year

✓ sunscreen — 1 year

✓ mouthwash — 3 years

✓ nail polish — 2 years

✓ shampoo — 2 to 3 years

✓ conditioner — 2 to 3 years

✓ hair gel — 2 to 3 years

✓ hair spray — 2 to 3 years

✓ rubbing alcohol — 2 years

✓ mascara — 3 months

✓ lipstick — 1 year

✓ eye makeup — 3 months

✓ blush — 6 months

Make scents of old perfume. Most fragrances, such as colognes, after-shave, and perfumes, have a shelf-life of one year. At the end of the year, they start to oxidize. If you wear a fragrance past its expiration date, you may not smell like a bed of roses anymore. And isn't smelling good the whole point? Your best bet is to toss any scents that have been opened longer than a year. If you need a new bottle to last longer than that, put it in your fridge unopened. The cool temperatures will preserve it for an extra year or two.

Start with a clean slate. Clear all the clutter off the top of your sink and leave it that way. Remember that sinks have many purposes, but storage is not one of them.

Polish off that bottle of polish. Don't leave that old bottle of nail polish in your bathroom drawer. If it's almost empty or the color is out of style, pull it out and put it to good use. Paint numbers, words, or designs onto items that need labeling. Store clear nail polish with your hosiery so it's right there in case of a run. Dab colored nail polish onto your garbage disposal's switch, and you'll never confuse it with the sink light again. It will be useful almost anywhere except your bathroom.

SUPER TIPS *for sorting the tub and shower*

Restore order to your bathtub. Your bathtub is not a storage unit. Take all the shampoo bottles and other toiletries off the ledge of the tub and put them in a cabinet or shower caddy.

Use it or lose it. If you don't use it, there's no point storing it. Toss any toiletries you haven't used in several months. A good rule of thumb is to throw away anything covered in dust. It can't be too important to you if it's been left alone long enough to accumulate dust.

Transform old towels into something new. When you remove old towels from your stack of linens, it leaves room for nicer, newer ones. But don't throw the old ones away just yet. They could come in handy. Use old towels for jobs around the house, like washing your car. Or recycle them by turning them into washcloths. Just cut the towels into smaller squares and hem them along the edges.

Update your reading material. Go through the stack of magazines next to your commode and purge all but the newer issues. Time is precious. It should only be spent reading the latest news and gossip.

Step 2 Increase storage

Your goal is to make bathroom upkeep as easy as possible. Give every item a home and even the worst clutter offender can follow the new rules. And who says a bathroom has to be conventional? Use unusual items in new ways. Flea markets, the garden store, or even your attic or garage are great places to find creative storage containers.

Remember...

✓ map your space

✓ shop for containers

SUPER TIPS *for storing in your vanity*

Shape up your makeup. Transform an ordinary tooth-brush holder into a makeup caddy. Get all those makeup brushes and eye pencils in order by plopping them in the slots of a toothbrush holder. You may even be able to fit in a mascara or two.

Turn your bathroom door into storage space. Think you're out of space in the bathroom? Think again! Add an over-the-door shoe organizer to your bathroom, and clear off the counters completely! Just hang it over your bath-room door to take advantage of that unused wall space. Then take any items lying around your sink or counters and place them in the organizer. This $5 item will give you a more spacious bathroom in two minutes!

Double your storage space. When it comes to storage, remember to think vertically as well as horizontally. Don't limit yourself to the floor and countertops. Look up at your bare walls. That's where shelving comes in. A few glass shelves installed on your bathroom wall make an attractive and convenient space to put some of the things now crowding your countertops.

Whip untidy drawers into shape. Turn that messy draw-er into the picture of organization. Place a silverware tray in the drawer and sort your toiletries into the slots. You'll have no problem finding exactly what you need from now on.

Get help from a magnet. You probably use magnets to organize things on your refrigerator. Now apply that idea to your bathroom. Keep track of nail clippers, tweezers, and other little metal gadgets by mounting a magnetic strip to the back of your medicine cabinet. Stick the gadgets on the magnet and you'll never have to search for them again.

Display fragrances on a silver platter. Perfume should make you feel elegant, not disheveled. If you can't seem to make heads or tails of your fragrance collection, maybe it's time you reined things in. Group all your perfumes and colognes on a single tray. For a touch of class, use a silver tray and arrange the bottles in an attractive formation.

Keep cords under control. Hair dryers, curling irons, and electric toothbrushes all have cords that can get out of control. Tame those wild wires without bothering with hard-to-handle twisty ties. Wind up excess cords and insert them into a cardboard toilet paper tube to keep them out of the way. It's a quick fix, it reduces waste, and it's easy on arthritic fingers.

Display extra toilet paper creatively. You don't have to hide your toilet paper so no one can see it. Bring it out into the open so guests can easily retrieve a roll if need be. There are lots of unique and convenient ways to store your supply.

- arrange toilet paper rolls in a wicker basket

- place rolls one on top of the other in an unused flower vase

- stack rolls on a vertical paper-towel caddy.

Pull out your picnic caddy. If you have a utensil caddy you use to separate knives, forks, and spoons at a picnic, try using it in your bathroom, as well. Whether it's made of wicker or plastic, a caddy's dividers make it perfect for sorting and storing toiletries. And so much the better if it has a handle to make it easy to carry.

Rein in unruly cosmetics. One of the best storage units for your makeup collection may be the most unlikely. Savvy gals on the go use a fishing tackle box to store their cosmetics. The nooks are perfect for holding lipstick, eye shadow, and blush, while the larger compartment in the bottom is good for bigger items, like hair accessories. Want a more feminine look? Decorate the outside of your tote with shiny and glittery crafts materials so it will be fashionable as well as functional.

Hang up your blow dryer. If you can't find a place to put your bulky blow dryer, hang it up. Install a hook on the wall next to your vanity, or mount a blow dryer caddy. It will be right there for you to grab whenever you need it.

Multiply your cabinet space. Make use of the cabinet space beneath your sink. Don't let things pile up in a haphazard heap. Slip in a set of pullout drawers or stackable baskets. Not only will your stuff be more organized, you'll increase your storage capacity by using vertical space, instead of just the bottom of your cabinet.

Round up clutter in a drawstring bag. Here's a great way to take advantage of unused cabinet space. Hang drawstring bags from nails or hooks installed on the inside of your bathroom cabinet or on its doors. Fill the bags with toiletries, cosmetics, hair accessories, or anything you want. You can label the bags so you know what's inside or choose different colored bags so you can tell them apart. Drawstring bags are great because you can pull out things as needed or just take the whole bag out of the cabinet. And if you go on a trip, your toiletries are already packed and ready to go.

Put extra shelves in your corner. If you're running short on counter space, remember to utilize the corners. Install corner shelves near your vanity where you can put things that once crowded your counter, like lotions, colognes, or toothbrush holders.

SUPER TIPS for storing in the tub and shower

Go above and beyond your toilet. Solve the shortage of shelving in your bathroom with an over-the-toilet storage unit. It creates shelves where once there were none, and it's perfect for storing towels, toilet paper, and anything else that requires extra space. Plus, it's cheaper and less time-consuming than actually installing shelves.

Get wet towels off the floor. Turn your bathroom door into something more than an entrance. Install a hook to hang up your bathrobe. Or invest in an over-the-door towel holder that easily hooks over the top of your door. These are perfect for hanging up wet towels. You'll find that keeping towels tidy and off the floor will bring you leaps and bounds closer to a neater bathroom.

Bring on the bubbles. Everyone loves a relaxing bubble bath. But all those bath and body products can result in a jumble of bottles under your sink. Bring them out of the dark and into an attractive basket placed near your tub. They'll be more accessible, and you'll be more likely to pour in the bubble bath next time you need a stress reliever.

Corral your conditioner in a caddy. A shower caddy can be your best friend when it comes to storing bottles of shampoo, conditioner, body wash, and whatever else you have stacked around the edge of your tub. These inexpensive organizers come in a variety of styles. Get one that hangs from your shower head to make the most of your space.

Hide dirty towels. Make that mountain of dirty towels disappear. Place a small hamper or laundry basket in your bathroom and use it to hide your used towels.

Install a mini-library. Reading in the bathroom is an American pastime. Keep your reading materials from getting out of hand. Mount a magazine file to the wall next to the toilet and fill it with your favorite newspapers and magazines. They'll be an arm's reach away when you feel like reading. And best of all, they'll be up and out of your way.

Step 3 Get organized

If this is your private family space, make it work for your family's routine and habits. If they simply can't clean up without using two bath towels each every day, you better make space for hooks, racks, hampers, and a reserve supply.

Don't forget to think about your guest bathroom when it comes to decluttering and organizing. Family and friends will really appreciate the thoughtfulness of a plush towel or handy supply of toiletries.

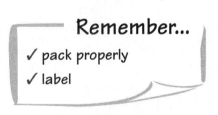

Remember...
✓ pack properly
✓ label

SUPER TIPS for organizing your vanity

Find what you need in an instant. It will always be easier to navigate through your bathroom stuff if it's sorted into groups that make sense. Try putting like with like. For instance, keep your hair care products in one spot and your shaving supplies in another. Your morning routine will run more smoothly when you don't have to search for a razor in a drawer full of hodgepodge.

Get creative with a sink skirt. Most sinks have a cabinet beneath them for storage space. If you have a freestanding sink, you'll need to get creative. Make a cabinet appear out of nowhere by putting a fabric skirt around your sink. You can store supplies under there or hide away a laundry basket for towels.

Take extras on the road. You've sorted through your toiletries and cosmetics, you've thrown out the ones you don't need, and you've still got extras you can't part with. Not a problem. Put all the extras in a travel bag to take on trips. This kills two birds with one stone. You get rid of clutter, and it won't take as long to pack for your next vacation.

Hang onto info, not trash. Don't hesitate to throw away expired medications, but do jot down some notes beforehand. Keeping a list of your past prescriptions can come in handy later when you're discussing health issues with your doctor. Take all the expired medications from your medicine cabinet. Copy down information like the prescription name, the date, the dose, what it was for, the doctor's name, the pharmacy, and the prescription number. If you want, include whether it worked and how much it cost. File this information with your other health papers. Now comes the best part — chuck all those old medicines and bottles into the waste basket. Just remember to keep them away from children and pets.

Play spin the bottle with toiletries. If you've got a lot of bottled toiletries in your cabinet, put them on a turntable, like the ones used in kitchens. The bottles will be easier to reach, and you won't have to stretch toward the back of the cabinet.

Make clutter control a family affair. Sharing a bathroom just got easier for big families. Clear your vanity of all your family's toiletries. Sort each family member's things into a separate group and put them into a corresponding container. You can use buckets, baskets, storage containers, or travel cases. Anything goes so long as each container is a different color so you can tell whose is whose. Each family member keeps their container in their bedroom and then brings it with them to the bathroom when they need it. No more cluttered mess!

Keep track of backups. Put extra toiletries in a separate place, like a basket, shelf, or drawer, so you can keep track of them. Whenever you run out of something, just go to this section and pull out the backup. Keep a list of the items and how many there are. Replace them when supplies get low. You'll never run out of toiletries again.

Turn trash into something special. Make a cup holder that coordinates with your decor. Cover a potato chip can with wallpaper to match your bathroom. These cans fit 5-ounce paper cups perfectly, and with the matching wallpaper, the holder will fit your bathroom perfectly, too.

Keep nail polish in line. Keep those bottles of nail polish in your bathroom drawer from tipping and sliding every time the drawer opens and shuts. Take a piece of sewing elastic and tack it across the inside of the drawer. You can choose the height and width that suits your needs. Slip the nail polish bottles into their new home and they'll never misbehave again.

Restore order to a messy drawer. Sort the contents of your vanity drawer into an adjustable drawer insert. Put

Be prepared for anything. You never know what minor emergencies will pop up. Keep a first-aid kit in your bathroom for the occasional crisis. Here are some essentials every first-aid kit should have.

- ❏ triangular bandage
- ❏ adhesive tape
- ❏ scissors
- ❏ elastic wraps for sprains
- ❏ pain reliever
- ❏ antihistamine
- ❏ adhesive bandages
- ❏ rubbing alcohol
- ❏ cotton balls

your hair accessories, makeup, tweezers, clippers, and other little items in it so they'll stay organized and not slide all over whenever you open the drawer. You can buy inexpensive drawer inserts at most home improvement stores.

Take charge of your electric toothbrush charger. If you're technologically savvy enough to use an electric toothbrush, keep the charger stored away when you're not using it. You only need to charge your toothbrush once a month, and leaving it in the charger will destroy the battery. So keep the charger in a cabinet to leave more space on your counter.

SUPER TIPS *for organizing the tub and shower*

Roll up towels for smart storage. If you want an easy way to manage your towels, try rolling them instead of folding. Rolled towels are easier to handle, store, and display than folded ones. And they stack nicely in a pyramid shape or in a basket.

Put a cap on rust. There's an easy way to keep your shaving cream can from leaving a rust ring on the side of your tub. Save the lid from a potato chip can. The lids fit snugly on the bottoms of some shaving cream cans. Snap them on to prevent the rust stains that are hard to remove from bathroom counter tops and bathtubs. Painting the bottom of the can with clear nail polish is another simple way to prevent rust rings.

Mobilize your cleaning supplies. Having more than one bathroom doesn't mean you need more than one set of cleaning supplies. Save space by keeping a whole set in a bucket or other movable container and then carrying it to whichever bathroom needs cleaning. When you're not using it, store the bucket in one of your bathrooms so you'll always know where it is.

Do away with bathroom trash with ease. Taking out the bathroom trash doesn't have to be a chore. Line the trash can with a plastic grocery bag, letting the top drape neatly over the sides. When it gets full, just pull up the top by the handles and tie them in a neat bundle. Pop another bag into place and your chore is practically done. Store extra grocery bags in the bottom of your trash can. They'll all be in one place so you can grab one when you need it.

Ponder while you potty. Inspiration strikes in the most unlikely of places — including the bathroom. Keep a pad of paper and a pencil near your throne so you can jot down ideas as they come to you. You can even mount a memo pad on the wall or place it next to your magazine stash.

Step 4 Keep it clean

Now that your bathroom is free of clutter, you'll find it's easy to keep it clean. The chart on the following page gives you a list of chores you can complete in 10 minutes. Add a few weekly, monthly, and occasional chores, and you've got one smart cleaning plan. Keep reading to find plenty of quick and easy cleaning tips for your clutter-free bathroom.

SUPER TIPS for cleaning your bathroom

Erase dirt from grout. Wipe away a dingy bathroom with a common circular typewriter eraser. Simply roll it along the grout to rub it clean. Many typewriter erasers even come with a fine-bristled brush on the handle end to help whisk the eraser crumbs out of the corners.

Clean your faucet in one step. Pare your cleaning process down to one easy step. Use rubbing alcohol to polish chrome bathroom fixtures. They'll be clean as a whistle. And since alcohol evaporates, you don't even have to rinse.

Apply car wax to your faucet. Car wax is not just for cars anymore. The stuff you use to buff your auto works just as well on bathroom fixtures, tile, sinks, and shower doors. Because it offers protection from soap and water, car wax leaves your fixtures looking shiny longer. You'll see your reflection in your sink as well as your mirror.

Give an old toothbrush a new life. Now that you've sorted all the old toothbrushes out of your collection, put them to use. Soak them in cold water and a bit of bleach for

10-minute daily speed cleaning	Weekly chores	Monthly chores	Occasional chores
Return vanity items to their homes	Clean mirror	Wash shower curtain	Unclog shower head, if needed
Wipe sink, fixtures, and counter	Pour cleaner into toilet and swish	Clean air, heating, and exhaust fan vents	Clean smudges off walls and light switches
Close shower curtain or door	Shake out rugs and wash them	Wipe baseboards	Wash windows
Check the toilet paper supply	Mop or vacuum floors	Check ceiling corners for cobwebs	Wash curtains
Wipe hair up off floor	Clean sink	Clean light fixtures	
Straighten towels on racks	Scrub tub and shower		
Spritz air freshener	Change towels		
	Empty trash		

about 20 minutes to remove any odors or dried-on tooth-paste. Rinse them off and use them to clean your bathroom in places a sponge can't get to easily. Toothbrushes are good at getting in between tiles, around fixtures, and into anything with tiny, hard-to-reach grooves. These handy tools will make lots of cleaning jobs quicker and easier.

Break down soap scum with vinegar. If your sink fixtures are covered with an unsightly film, don't waste time scrubbing. Soak a cloth rag with vinegar and lay it over your faucet for several minutes. The vinegar should loosen up the gross film. Dampen another rag and use it to wipe off the fixture. When you're done, it will shine like new.

Guard against soap sludge. Don't put up with the soapy sludge that builds up in your soap dish. Place a small sponge in the dish and lay the soap on top of it. If you like, you can cut the sponge to fit the dish. When it starts to get soapy, just rinse it out with warm water and put it back in the dish. No more soap sludge.

Keep your mirror crystal clear. In the rush to get ready for the day, you may get a little hairspray on your mirror, or it may accumulate over time. To keep it from sticking to the mirror like it sticks to your locks, wipe it off with rubbing alcohol. It'll take the murky buildup right off.

Make your own mildew remover. No need for expensive mildew cleaning solutions for your bathroom. Add liquid bleach to a spray bottle, label the bottle "bleach," and spray away the fungus. Be careful not to spray bleach in your eyes or on fabrics.

Speed up cleaning with paper towels. If you want to give your vanity a quick once-over but don't have a lot of time, grab a paper towel and some spray cleaner. Give your counters a fast swipe and throw the paper towel away. For easy access, install a paper towel rack on the inside of your vanity door where it'll be hidden. Using paper towels means you don't need a damp sponge sitting under your sink causing mildew.

Wipe away fingerprints and germs. Don't forget the spots that really need cleaning. The germs on hands get passed around when people touch faucets, doorknobs, and flusher handles, but most people hardly ever think to clean those. Spray high-contact areas with disinfectant and wipe them down to prevent infections.

Brush away unsightly buildup. If you want to get that grimy buildup off your shower head, but the usual sponge just won't cut it, grab an old toothbrush. The course bristles will take that grime right off. This will save you time and elbow grease.

Put power back in your shower. Mineral deposits can build up on your shower head and block the flow of water. To get rid of them without taking apart your fixture, fill a plastic sandwich bag with vinegar. Pull the bag up so the shower head is completely immersed in the vinegar. Use a rubber band to attach the bag. Let it soak for several hours or overnight. Remove the bag and, if necessary, use an old toothbrush and toothpicks to clean all the holes. Then you'll be back in business.

Outwit mildew with fresh air. Prevent mildew growth in your shower and you'll have less to clean. Leave your shower doors, or shower curtain, open for a while after you've bathed so they'll have time to dry. If mildew shows up anyway, use bleach or a cleaner containing bleach to clean it off.

Check the label on your cleaning products to guarantee you're killing disease-causing germs when you clean. If a product has an EPA registration number, it meets government requirements for getting rid of germs. If it doesn't, maybe you should use another product.

Save time when you clean your shower. Multi-task during bath time, and cleaning your shower will be a breeze. One option is to clean your shower stall first and then yourself. Get in like you're going to shower, then scrub the shower surfaces. Just be careful with those harsh cleansers. Rinse everything and then clean yourself in your sparkling clean shower. Like to take baths instead? Clean yourself first and then use your soapy washcloth to wipe off the ring around the tub. Just chuck the washcloth in the laundry afterward. Either way, you save time.

Triumph over toilet brush germs. You may wonder how well a toilet brush can clean a toilet if the brush is loaded with germs to begin with. Worry no longer. Pour about a cup of water and bleach solution into the toilet brush caddy and then close it. Water and a disinfecting cleaner work well, too. The brush will be disinfected and ready to go every time you clean.

Clean your toilet without even trying. Keep your toilet clean between scrubbings. Enlist the help of an in-tank cleaner. Just drop it in the tank and it will freshen your toilet bowl every time you flush. You don't have to lift a finger. In-tank cleaners don't substitute for good, old-fashioned scrubbing with a toilet brush, but they may put more time between cleanings.

Baby your shower to keep it clean. If you want your shower to stay clean and mildew free, give it a good once-over every time you shower. Make it part of your after-shower ritual. Just rinse it off and wipe it down. It won't take long. Use a squeegee to make the task even quicker.

Spray once a day to keep soap scum away. Spray your shower and tub with a daily shower cleaner to keep them cleaner longer. Give them a good misting after you shower before those surfaces become dry again, and it will cut down on soap scum and mildew stains. This way, you won't have to supply as much elbow grease later on. To make your own daily shower cleaner, pour 8 ounces of rubbing alcohol into a 32-ounce spray bottle and top it off with water. Spray all surfaces. You don't even have to rinse.

Give your shower curtain a bath. Get the mildew off your shower curtain without even trying. Fill your bathtub with cold water and bleach. Then submerge the curtain in the water. Weigh the curtain down with something heavy if it won't stay under the water. Let it soak overnight. The bleach should get most of the mildew off without your having to lift a finger. Rinse off the curtain and hang it back up to dry. As a bonus, the bleach will clean your tub at the same time.

Sprinkle Tang in your toilet. Freshen up your toilet by giving it a drink — an orange drink. Sprinkle about half a cup of Tang drink mix into your toilet bowl. Leave it for a couple of hours and then flush. Your toilet will be cleaner and have a fresh, citrus scent.

Chapter 8
The Linen Closet

A well-organized linen closet can be one of the little joys in life. Imagine the thrill every time you open the door and find neat stacks of clean, fragrant linens.

Even though this is probably a tiny space, it is full of possibilities. Just think outside the box. What changes can you make that will not only increase your storage but increase your efficiency, too?

And simply because this is such a small space, you can get almost instant gratification decluttering it.

Some organizing experts recommend storing bed linens in the room in which they are used, instead of in a communal linen closet. That means setting up space in that room for at least one full set — perhaps in a dresser, chest, or bedroom closet. This follows the golden rule of proximity because your linens will be closer to where you need them.

Remember...

✓ make a wish list

✓ be realistic

✓ set priorities

✓ identify your clutter problems

✓ label your zones

✓ set a timeline

Moving bed linens out of the linen closet will free up space for bath towels, medical items, table linens, or extra paper supplies.

Consider shuffling some things around. You may come up with a better storage plan after all these years.

Take your best guess on how long it will take you to complete each task for each zone. Keep in mind you may need time to shop for new storage containers. Remember, this is just an estimate to help you plan your linen closet decluttering project.

Zones	Step 1: Cut the clutter	Step 2: Increase storage	Step 3: Get organized
Linens			
Medical items			
Extra bath supplies			

Step 1 Cut the clutter

Once you decide how you'd like to use your linen closet, pull everything out and start making your piles. Stick to the rules, evaluating each item.

Surprised by how many bedsheets you have? This could be a major cause of linen closet confusion. Many clutter experts suggest keeping two sets for each bed. You'll always have a clean set available, and you'll cut down on storage woes. Don't forget one set for the futon or sofa bed.

The same goes for bath towels. Be ruthless here. Ratty, torn, faded, and stained towels can find a perfectly good second life drying the dog or washing the car. Just keep them in the garage, not the linen closet.

Keep in mind

Make a decision:

✓ keep

✓ toss

✓ donate

✓ sell

✓ pass on

Follow purging rules:

✓ decide quickly

✓ handle items once

✓ set limits

✓ pass the "keep" test

✓ recognize garbage

SUPER TIPS for sorting linens

Give worn-out towels to a worthy cause. You want to donate your old towels, but you're not sure where to take them. Some of them may still be intact, but maybe they're too ratty to give to charity. In that case, offer your towels to local animal shelters. These organizations can use donated towels and blankets regardless of whether or not they're in mint condition.

Shake the "pack rat" habit. Since the space in your linen closet is so precious, there's no room to spare for stuff you can't use. Force yourself to part with sheet sets that don't fit your bed; frayed, torn, stained, faded, or worn out bath linens; ripped or misshapen pillows; and medicines past their expiration date.

SUPER TIPS for sorting medical items

Keep track of expiration dates. Whenever you buy an over-the-counter medication, check to see if it has a printed expiration date. If not, mark it with the purchase date, and discard it after a year.

Ditch almost-empty bottles. Think twice about saving that last little bit of cough syrup for next winter's colds. You may not have enough medicine left to help, and the nearly empty bottle will add to your clutter.

SUPER TIPS for sorting extra bath supplies

Send toiletries back to the bathroom. Leave your over-flow of extra toilet paper, bags of cotton balls, and other bulky bathroom supplies in your linen closet. But don't go overboard. Toiletries belong in your bathroom. If you can't fit them in their rightful home, you may need to give them away.

Say goodbye to products you'll never use. Powders, lotions, bubble bath, shampoo. Somehow you've acquired a collection of bath products you neither need nor want. Instead of trying to find a place for them, consider donating these items to a women's shelter or other organization. They'll give someone else a much-needed lift, while giving you some much-needed space.

Step 2 Increase storage

Now that everything is out of the space, stand back and give it a good, long look. Is it still configured exactly as the builder left it? If so, you probably don't have enough shelves, and the ones you have are probably too deep for convenience.

Remember...

✓ map your space
✓ shop for containers

This is the time to reconfigure, rebuild, or replace. You can shift things around yourself or hire some handyman help. You can build shelving from scrap lumber or use the same kind of closet organizing products and systems marketed for clothes closets and kitchen or pantry cabinets.

Or simply indulge in a few baskets, dividers, and bags. Just take careful measurements before you buy anything.

SUPER TIPS for storing linens

Hide linens in plain sight. Free up more space in your linen closet by hiding your linens in the middle of the room. Put extra sheets on an unused bed or put more than one set on each bed — one inside the other. Next time you change your sheets, just pull off the old set and another will be waiting underneath. For storage right under your guests' noses, hide linens under the seat cushions of your couch.

Give your shelves some space. When installing your own shelving, remember this rule of thumb. Leave just under a foot between shelves for sheets and other thin linens. Towels need a foot or more of distance. And the top shelf should be at least a foot and a half away from the ceiling to store blankets or sleeping bags. Knowing this ahead of time gives you an idea of how many shelves you need.

Vacuum pack blankets and comforters. You can triple your storage without tripling your space. Put bulky linens in vacuum sealable bags, and more will fit in a smaller area. With your vacuum's help, these bags condense blankets and comforters into smaller, stackable bundles. The bags also protect linens from pests and moisture. To make your own, remove the air from a garbage bag with a vacuum and close it up with rubber bands. Place a towel underneath the bags, so wire shelves won't puncture one when you pull it out.

SUPER TIPS for storing medical items

Make a cramped linen closet twice as roomy. Put a wire shelving unit on the back of the door. It's perfect for storing medical items, and it will free up room on the other shelves for more linens.

Provide a safe haven for medications. First-aid kits and bulky medical supplies find a natural home in the linen closet, but prescription medicines may belong there, too. Your bathroom's hot and humid environment makes a medicine cabinet the last place you want to store your medications. Keep them in your linen closet instead.

SUPER TIPS for storing extra bath supplies

Put your toilet paper on wheels. Store your extra toilet paper and other supplies in a cart with wheels at the bottom of your linen closet. Most of the time it stays out of the way. When it's time for replacements, pull out the cart and take what you need. You can also roll it into the bathroom for easy refills.

Send toilet paper packing. You don't have to hide all your supplies in the linen closet, especially toilet paper. Many stores sell decorative spindles, similar to paper towel holders, that hold a number of toilet paper rolls. Just find something that matches your bathroom decor, and place it in a convenient spot. An added bonus — your guests will never have to guess where to find the next roll.

Create space in your closet easily. If your linen closet is short on space, don't be afraid to take items out and put them on display. Even toilet paper looks good arranged in an attractive basket. And rolled-up washcloths or hand towels can look positively decorative. By finding other storage solutions for small items and supplies, you'll have more room for your linens.

Add space and style with a window box. Attach a window box or planter to your bathroom wall for storage with a bit of personality. This unlikely shelving unit is great for towel storage. Place towels, washcloths, and various toiletries in it for extra space on your counters and in your linen closet. While you're at it, get creative and paint the box to go with your decor.

Step 3 Get organized

The key to organizing your linen closet is to fold, stack, or roll everything — from oversized bath towels to tiny fingertip towels — so they fit the space.

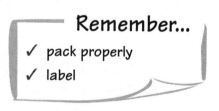

Remember...

✓ pack properly

✓ label

That's it. There's no one right way. If your shelves are deep, but narrow, you'll want long, thin stacks of towels. Other than that, you can use a variety of organizing tools to keep things separated, stacked, and orderly.

SUPER TIPS for organizing linens

Match up your sheet sets before storing. Save time looking for matching bed sheets and pillowcases. Fold up the entire set and put it inside one of the matching pillowcases so it will all be together. No more searching through stacks of random pieces.

Keep your bedsheets close at hand. Store linens in the room where they're used. Put sheet sets on a shelf in your closet or in a drawer next to your bed so they're right there next time you change the sheets. You'll have more room in your linen closet, and you won't have to search for the right sheets.

SUPER TIPS for organizing medical items

Prioritize your shelves. It makes sense to store things you use every day — like bedsheets and towels — in easy-to-find and easy-to-reach places. That means shelves that are no higher than your shoulder and no lower than the middle of your thigh. Keep your first-aid kit there, too. Guest sheets, spare pillows, and anything else you don't need very often can be stored on out-of-the-way shelves.

Gather together your first-aid supplies. Organize all your important medicines and first-aid supplies, and keep them in a central location so your family will know where to go in an emergency. A hall linen closet fits the bill perfectly. It's easily accessible, and unlike the bathroom, you don't have to worry about someone occupying it when you need emergency supplies.

SUPER TIPS *for organizing extra bath supplies*

Make a mental note to stock up. When you open your last pack of toilet paper, bag of cotton balls, or other bathroom supply, save the label from the packaging. Put it with your coupons or in your purse. Next time you go shopping, you'll remember to buy more.

Stack your extra stock. Your favorite shampoo and toothpaste were on sale so you just had to buy extra. Now you need to make sure they don't get lost in the back of your closet. Buy a plastic bin with a cover to keep all your extra bathroom supplies in one place. Or buy two if you're a warehouse shopper who likes to stock up. Just place the bins on the floor, or stack them if they're small. Your supplies will stay in perfect order until you need them.

Step 4 Keep it clean

Your linen closet should be the easiest space in your house to clean. Not only is it small, it doesn't get very dirty. If you keep the contents of the closet clean, you're halfway done. Beyond that, it's just a matter of simple maintenance. Set aside a few minutes regularly, and you'll have this space spick-and-span in no time. Here are some tips to get you started.

SUPER TIPS *for cleaning your linen closet*

Make a quick stop at the closet. Cleaning your linen closet is an easy task. When you vacuum the rest of your house, just open the linen closet door as you pass by and give the inside a quick once-over. A small handheld vacuum may be easiest to maneuver within the small space and under any shelves.

Come home to fresh linens. When you pull a towel out of the linen closet, you expect it to be clean. Make sure your linens are always clean and dry before you put them away. Moisture may cause them to mildew or start to smell, and stains will set if they're left on linens.

Toss in tennis balls for a comfy comforter. Anyone for a game of tennis? Throw a few white tennis balls into your dryer when you run your comforter or mattress pad through a cycle. This unconventional addition will prevent clumps in the filling and help the comforter maintain its shape. If you don't have white tennis balls, clean towels will also do the trick. Either way, you can go practice your forehand without worrying about the shape of your comforter.

Breathe in that fresh scent. Give your linen closet a clean aroma. Put a dryer fabric softener sheet inside. It will get rid of any stale odors and leave your closet smelling as fresh and airy as a field of daisies.

The Hobby Room

Not everyone has a room devoted strictly to hobbies or leisure-time activities. You may have carved a tiny corner out of another space for your fun. Just remember, there are clutter dangers in both situations.

It's easy to fill a hobby room to the brim with all the stuff that makes your hobby so entertaining. And if you don't have a dedicated space, you may find hobby paraphernalia drifting throughout your entire house.

The definition of hobby is "an activity engaged in for pleasure and relaxation during spare time." Just how pleasurable and relaxing is it when your embroidery thread is a snarl the size of Texas and no one knows precisely who spilled the beads?

Remember...

✓ make a wish list

✓ be realistic

✓ set priorities

✓ identify your clutter problems

✓ label your zones

✓ set a timeline

One thing's for sure — there can be a hobby heaven. And you can find it in your home.

There are no suggested zones for this space simply because the range of possible hobbies is enormous — everything from quilting to scrapbooking. You'll need to evaluate the items in your space and identify those that represent your true hobbies of passion. Only these will be the pursuits you will keep and organize around.

Write the zones that apply to you, your family, and your space into the following table. Then take your best guess on how long it will take you to complete each task for each zone. Keep in mind you may need time to shop for new storage containers. Remember, this is just an estimate to help you plan your hobby room decluttering project.

Zones	Step 1: Cut the clutter	Step 2: Increase storage	Step 3: Get organized

Step 1 *Cut the clutter*

Remember to set limits. Half-finished projects and hobby fads that came and went can reproduce like dust bunnies. Keep your goal fixed firmly in your mind as you honestly assess how you want to spend your free time.

Keep in mind

Make a decision:

✓ keep

✓ toss

✓ donate

✓ sell

✓ pass on

Follow purging rules:

✓ decide quickly

✓ handle items once

✓ set limits

✓ pass the "keep" test

✓ recognize garbage

SUPER TIPS for sorting your hobby items

Donate excess to a good cause. Use these two heart-warming ideas, and you may smile when you thin out your excess hobby supplies. Turn some of your supplies into a "starter kit." For example, scrapbooker Judy P. suggests, "Go through some of your stuff, and make a kit for somebody that's never scrapbooked." This idea can work for any hobby — not just scrapbooking — and it makes a great gift. Don't forget that you can also pare down your hobby supplies in the name of a good cause. Donate them

DON'T STORE...

Just a few simple mistakes could damage your pictures forever. Protect your photographs from these errors so you'll have the chance to enjoy them for years.

✓ Don't store photos in shoe boxes, cardboard boxes, or magnetic albums.

✓ Don't label photos with just any old pen. Use a special pen that's photo-safe, or avoid writing on the back of the photograph.

✓ Use only those albums, photo boxes, scrapbooks, or other storage that feature label phrases such as "acid-free," "non-magnetic," "non-PVC," "photo safe," or "archival."

✓ Don't keep photographs in the attic, basement, garage, or any other place that may have high moisture, high heat, or too much light.

to a senior center, scout troop, nursing home, daycare center, or elementary school.

Let go with less pain. Your storage space has overflowed, but you can't bring yourself to toss any hobby supplies. Try this. First, figure out how much time a medium-sized project takes from start to finish — on average. For example, if you love embroidery, about how many days or weeks usually pass between the beginning and end of a project? Use that number to calculate how many projects you can get done in the next three years. Remember that number because that's your limit. Next, sort your project-specific supplies into project piles. If you end up with more project piles than your limit, donate, pass on, or toss your least favorite piles until you're down to your three-year number.

Get your photos organized at last. You're overwhelmed by a huge photo collection, and some of them are so ancient you can't imagine how to label them. Take the easy way out. Sort and label your most recent photos first. Then move to the next-newest batch. Keep working your way backward. You'll not only get more photos organized, but you'll also get it done faster than you would if you tried to slog through those difficult older batches first.

Transfer photos to your computer without extra equipment. You can put your photos on your computer even if you don't have a scanner or digital camera. Ask your favorite photo developer how much it costs to get a CD of your photos along with your prints. If the price is reasonable, copy your pictures to your hard drive, and keep the CD as a backup. Next, get free software to help organize and edit your photos. Windows users can visit *http://picasa.google.com*, while Mac users can use iPhoto — which comes free on new Macs. You can even find inexpensive software to help you create scrapbooks on your computer.

Separate the good from the gaffes. If you have digital photos, you can turn your bad pictures into good ones with computer software. Find out what these programs can do by visiting a software store, reading up on the Internet, or checking scrapbooking magazines. Decide whether you'll spend the time and money to rescue faulty photos, and then go through your photo collection. Delete any photos you find embarrassing, and get rid of pictures that can't be repaired. Be sure to ditch the ones with chopped-off heads or closed eyes as well as those that are blurry, dark, overexposed, or just

Toss without a thought

✓ sewing patterns with pieces missing

✓ glues or markers that are dried out

✓ fabrics that are obviously out-of-date

✓ fabrics that are mildewed, moth-eaten, stained, or frayed

✓ projects for fads whose five minutes of fame are over

✓ anything broken or worn out beyond repair

✓ anything you can't identify

plain lousy. That's a good idea even when you're organizing your non-digital prints.

Step 2 Increase storage

Storing all the things you need, to do the things you love, is key to getting this space decluttered. So get creative with your storage containers, and find new ways to use old things. You'll save money and add a personal touch to your hobby space.

Remember...

✓ map your space

✓ shop for containers

SUPER TIPS for storing your hobby items

"Tackle" your small-stuff problem. Whether it's sewing notions, scrapbook supplies, crochet needles, or other small necessities, a container that holds them all is what every hobbyist needs. Look no further than your local sporting goods store. A fishing tackle box is the ideal solution to organizing, storing, and transporting a multitude of hobby supplies.

Recycle baby containers for small items. Clean baby-food jars are great for holding small items such as sewing notions, beads, and small craft supplies. Use the sturdy lid from a box of printer or copier paper to keep the jars together. Label their lids with strips of masking tape, and place fabric or folded paper between the jars to protect and stabilize them. You can also clean rectangular baby-wipe containers to store more hobby supplies. They'll hold larger items than baby-food jars, and they're stackable.

No matter what your favorite hobby, you'll love these tips from Claudia B. Wood — a designer, quiltmaker, textile artist, teacher, and author in Senoia, Ga.

- ❏ **Store works-in-progress** in a plastic or rattan tray such as a dinner tray. Or store them in empty shoe boxes, shirt boxes, or gift boxes. Stack them and label the box ends so you can find a particular one easily.

- ❏ **Save the zippered plastic bags** that hold tablecloths, bedspreads, and comforters. These are great for storing works-in-progress, too. Also consider large shopping bags with handles. Store them standing up, or hang them from a doorknob or clothing hanger.

- ❏ **Use tool boxes for small items** like embroidery floss, needles, pins, thimbles.

- ❏ **Keep scissors,** pliers, or other small tools in old or mis-matched clear glasses.

- ❏ **Use baskets to store like items.** Get them at garage sales for a dollar or less.

Although Wood uses coffee mugs to hold paintbrushes, markers, pens, and pencils, she has a more stylish container, too. "I also have an old teapot that I always liked but never had a lid," she explains. "I have all of my colored pencils standing up in the teapot, so it looks cute — but it's also very useful."

Transform free storage boxes into pretty decor. Store sewing notions, craft supplies, crocheting yarn, and more in shoe boxes. Decorate them with wrapping paper, contact paper, fabric, or even shiny or metallic spray paint. Then label them on at least two sides so you'll always know exactly what is in them.

Find fabrics and yarns easily. "I store my skeins of yarn in big plastic crates in the top of the closet," says crocheter Penny B. She suggests turning the crates on their sides so you can stack them before loading them up with yarn. "That way you can see what color yarn you have," she explains. If you quilt, sew, or craft with fabrics, you can fill stacked crates with folded fabrics to get similar find-at-a-glance storage.

Make a tools-in-use kit. The same pencil box children use in school can conveniently hold hobby supplies. "Those are very good for carrying any kind of tools," says professional quiltmaker and textile artist Claudia B. Wood. "They snap shut securely, and you can just stick them in a bag and go." But these little gems are great for home use, too. Wood keeps a sewing kit in a pencil box. "I always keep it accessible on the counter so that I have a pair of scissors, some thread, needles, thimble, ruler, pins, a seam ripper, and tweezers," she says. "I also put a pair of reading glasses in it now." Check your local office-supply store for this handy holder. "It keeps items neat, but it also keeps them easily at hand," says Wood.

Wheel in extra storage. If space is tight, or you don't have a permanent place for hobby work, tuck your hobby supplies in "stealth" storage — a container that can be hidden under or behind something else. Look around your house, check garage sales, or even go shopping for storage with wheels or casters. Consider rolling file cabinets, drawer towers on casters, carts with racks or shelves, rolling storage boxes, or even rolling luggage. If needed, stock these portable storage wonders with tackle boxes, baby-food jars, shoe boxes, baskets, coffee cans, plastic trays, and other small-item storage containers.

Clean up with deli and fast-food containers. Visit a supermarket, deli, or fast-food restaurant, and you may come home with cubed fruit in clear, thick plastic containers or salads in "clamshell" plastic containers that snap shut. Once you've used and cleaned them, give them a second career like crafter and quiltmaker Claudia Wood. "Those things are fabulous, and I use them a lot to store small items in," she says. Wood recommends flat plastic containers for storing plastic quilting templates. "The little bowls are great for spools of thread or thimbles or any kind of small things you have," she adds. Wood also uses deli-style Styrofoam soup containers for storing small tubes of beads. "It'll hold quite a few of those little tubes of beads standing upright," she says.

Get creative with a tie rack. Scrapper Judy P. hangs her decorative scrapbooking scissors from a nearby tie rack. No more wasting precious time tracking down supplies.

You may have a lot more free or cheap storage available than you think. Imagine what you could store in these.

❑ Styrofoam bowls

❑ cleaned prescription pill bottles

❑ compote dish

❑ plastic resealable envelopes that hold new jewelry

❑ laundry detergent box

❑ wine rack

❑ magazine rack

❑ old dressers or night stands

Keep tiny scrapbooking stamps from getting lost. You can buy individual alphabet letter rubber stamps for scrapbooking, but these tiny tools are barely the size of a gun bullet. Perhaps that's why some people store them in ammunition cases.

Customize storage when space is tight. You don't have extra storage or even floor space, so look to the walls. The same white Pegboard you've seen on store walls can work for you. Pegboard is a great place to put scissors and printed instructions no matter what hobby you love. But it's also super for sewing notions, scrapbooking supplies, or small craft supplies. Make a list of the supplies that will live on your Pegboard. Then buy the size of white Pegboard that will fit your wall, along with the right hooks, shelves, containers, and so on to store exactly what's on your list.

Step 3 Get organized

Sort by color, pattern, texture, style, size, manufacturer, person, or project — anything that will make it easier to find exactly what you need in the shortest amount of time. This will also keep you from buying duplicate items because you will know at a glance exactly what you have.

Remember...

✓ pack properly

✓ label

SUPER TIPS *for organizing your hobby items*

Make a tips and troubleshooters library. Start filing all the creative ideas, hobby tips, and problem solvers you find. Some people like to clip or print out pages from magazines or Web sites and file them in file folders or three-ring binders. This saves storage space and gives you the opportunity to organize information your way — so you can find it quickly and easily. For example, if you use binders, you could have one binder for problem-solvers, another for tips to make things easier or faster, and a third for project ideas or inspirations. Use labeled tabs to subdivide each binder so you'll never get stuck hunting through a whole binder.

Store works-in-progress for easy access. Use big tote bags, and store each project in them like Penny B. does. "All I have to do is pick up that bag when I am ready to work on that project," she says.

Arrange fabrics cleverly. Colorful fabrics fill inexpensive bookshelves in the studio of professional designer, quilt-maker, and textile artist Claudia Wood. "I roll up each piece of fabric to the depth of the bookshelf and close it with a rubber band so that when they are all stacked, you see the end of each fabric roll." Wood groups them by color for added convenience. "You can see the color and the print of the fabric so you don't forget what you have," she explains. "It looks decorative, neat, and tidy." She also recommends writing down the fabric measurements and tucking the note in the roll. When you pull out the fabric roll to use it, the note will show how much you have left.

De-tangle your thread spools. Professional Claudia Wood groups her thread spools by color and stores each group in its own resealable plastic bag. And she has a neat trick for keeping the threads from tangling. She buys child-sized ponytail holders that resemble narrow scrunchies. "I got 42 of them for less than $1.50, and they fit around the spools of thread," says Wood. "You can still see the color of the thread. It doesn't cover it up. But it's enough to hold it in place so it doesn't unravel and get messed up with the other threads."

File patterns to find them quickly. Drop patterns into quart- or gallon-size resealable bags. Organize them by category, size, or alphabetically, as needed. Then just store them in wicker file boxes, flat-bottomed baskets, shoe boxes, or even a filing cabinet.

Seal success with a project kit. Use resealable plastic baggies to keep all the notions for a sewing project together — including things like buttons, thread, elastic, and zippers. For even better organization, drop a smaller notions bag into a gallon-size bag that holds the pattern for the project. This will save you from going on an unnecessary scavenger hunt when it's time to gather project supplies.

Cure photo madness. Choose one of these popular techniques to group photos for albums or scrapbooking. If you want one photo album per family member, make one pile per person. Otherwise, consider annual piles — one pile for each year. Some scrapbookers even recommend sorting by event or theme. For example, they may dedicate a single book to last year's Christmas pictures or a larger book to several years of Christmas celebrations. Choose the organization that works best for you. Then store your photos in photo albums, binders, accordion folders, photo boxes with tabbed dividers, or scrapbooks. Make sure your photo storage is acid-free, PVC-free, and non-magnetic.

Group card stock for speedier access. Separate your scrapbooking card stock by color. Store all the greens together, all the blacks, all the reds, and so on. Keep each group in its own file tray, rack, or hanging folder so you can quickly find the color you want whenever you need it.

Solve the 12x12 problem. You'd like to get containers that fit the 12x12-inch sizes scrapbooking pages often come in, but who wants to spend all that money. Try these instead. The next time you pick up a pizza from a restaurant, ask for a spare box. Or purchase two-gallon resealable bags or oversized hanging folders.

Find scrapbook stickers pronto. Combine three-ring binders with sheet protectors or business card sheets to store and organize your scrapbooking stickers — or just use old photo albums. Throw in a few labeled dividers, and you can even subdivide sticker collections by category.

Rev up your photo organizing with themes. The key to organizing your photos may simply be finding the right themes for your photo albums or scrapbooks. Check scrapbook stores, catalogs, and online catalogs to find the best theme or try one of these — baby firsts, holidays, family pets, birthdays, anniversaries, wedding, family heritage, Little League, recitals, scouting, summer vacation, vacation trip, graduation, or family events this year. Once you've chosen your scrapbook themes, it's just a matter of sorting your photos into individual theme piles.

Make messy hobby supplies disappear. That jumble of hobby supplies on your open shelving could look as neat as a pin. Simply hide it behind a lovely curtain. Choose a fabric or curtain that matches your decor, and mount it on a tension curtain rod, or use Velcro. The new Velcro Decor product is made so that one side attaches to hard products — like shelves — while the other side is designed to be sewn on to curtains, fabric, or other cloth items.

"Plant" scrapbooking pens in pretty pots. Your old flowerpots may not be fit to use for plants anymore, so clean them up and take them inside. Store your scrapbooking scissors in one and your scrapbooking pens in another.

Be creative with small supplies. These tips work for crocheter Penny B.

- Wrap crochet hooks with a washcloth, and tie with a rubber band — or keep your hooks in a plastic travel toothbrush holder.

- Use a travel plastic soap holder or any small plastic container with a lid to store small crocheting supplies.

- Keep scissors and tapestry needles in a zippered pouch.

Step 4 Keep it clean

If you're lucky enough to have a room devoted to your hobbies, you can shut the door on your mess during the day, and no one will be the wiser. But be sure to follow your usual weekly cleaning schedule of vacuuming, dusting, and tidying up. If your craft area is out in the open, you'll need to straighten things up daily to keep the area looking neat. When you do your weekly room cleaning, include this area as well. These tips can help.

SUPER TIPS for cleaning your hobby items

Keep crochet needles clean. "Wipe your crochet hooks with a dry, soft cloth," suggests crocheter Penny

B. This will help keep your crochet tools in good working order.

Neaten up with a scrap container. Keep a broad, shallow container near your scrapbooking work area for scrap paper. This will help keep your work area neat, but your scrap paper will be readily available the moment you have a use for it.

Have a "no-clutter" zone in your work area, and you're more apt to complete your projects, advises professional designer and quiltmaker Claudia Wood. "I always try to have one surface in my sewing room completely uncovered and ready for me to go and work on it," she says. "If you come in there and there's stuff all over it, you will not do it. And when you're finished with whatever the project is — or even just at the end of the day — clean up the messy part and leave it all neat and ready to go."

Chapter 10
The Laundry Room

Not everyone has a beautifully finished laundry room with gleaming cabinets and enough space to do the rumba. Many people have to tromp down the basement stairs or squeeze into a hallway just to clean their clothes. But that doesn't mean your laundry space can't be tidy and efficient. After all, doing laundry is chore enough. Don't make it harder by being cluttered and disorganized.

Of course, it doesn't help that you have several stain removers, a special detergent for delicate items, a regular detergent for everything else, a whitener, a brightener, and don't forget that special something to make every load smell like sunshine.

Add in the fact that most people generate over a quarter ton of dirty clothes each year. Multiply that by the number of people in your home, and you've got the recipe for one messy laundry room.

Remember...

✓ make a wish list

✓ be realistic

✓ set priorities

✓ identify your clutter problems

✓ label your zones

✓ set a timeline

It will be easy to focus on the goals for your laundry room. All you need to do in this space is get clothes clean and ready to wear. That may involve some soaking, hanging, folding, and ironing, in addition to the usual washing and drying.

Take your best guess on how long it will take you to complete each task for each zone. Keep in mind you may need time to shop for new storage containers. Remember, this is just an estimate to help you plan your laundry room decluttering project.

Zones	Step 1: Cut the clutter	Step 2: Increase storage	Step 3: Get organized
Laundry			
Laundry supplies			

Step 1 Cut the clutter

Now that you have the function of your laundry area firmly fixed in your mind, it should be easy to purge the items that don't belong.

Keep in mind

Make a decision:

✓ keep

✓ toss

✓ donate

✓ sell

✓ pass on

Follow purging rules:

✓ decide quickly

✓ handle items once

✓ set limits

✓ pass the "keep" test

✓ recognize garbage

SUPER TIPS for sorting your laundry

Use the laundromat to catch up. If you can't clean your laundry room because it's too full of dirty clothes, gather them all up and take them to the laundromat. Go when it's not busy so there are plenty of machines available and you can do five or 10 or more loads in the time it

Toss without a thought

✓ bent or broken hangers

✓ dried-up or moldy boxes, cans, and bottles

✓ ineffective laundry products

takes to do one. Then you can go home with a clean slate to start decluttering.

Sort laundry as you go. Take a cue from commercial cleaners, and put multiple hampers in your laundry room. Then when anyone brings in soiled clothes, they can sort them on the spot. This system works best when you have plenty of space. Get a rack that holds large, open bags or hampers, or see if you can find a few rolling carts like they use in laundromats.

Put baskets in bedrooms. That's where dirty clothes come from, so put a laundry basket in each closet and bathroom. Even better, give each person in the house two wide-mesh bags — one for white clothes and one for darks. Toss the bags in the washer, and you save sorting both before and after you do the laundry. Just make sure they're not stuffed too full so the clothes have room to move around.

DON'T STORE...

✓ clean clothes

✓ non-laundry items you don't have a place for

✓ wire hangers — use plastic or wooden hangers instead

Don't let clean laundry pile up. It creates just as much clutter as dirty laundry. If it's still there after supper, fold it while you're watching TV. Put each folded piece in a pile according to where it belongs — linen closet, kitchen, husband — and during the commercials take each stack to its home. Save yourself some steps by placing each person's stack on their bed. That way, they'll have to put it away before they go to sleep.

SUPER TIPS for sorting laundry supplies

Keep only what you need. Different types of laundry products have special ways of getting your clothes clean. Think about these differences when you sort through your collection of liquids and powders. Eliminate duplicates and those you don't use or need.

- True soap, made from fats and oils, is less effective in hard water and more likely to form a film or scum that is hard to rinse away. Some soap products claim to clean delicate fabrics and woolens better.

- Detergents are synthetic cleaning products and are used for most laundry needs. Liquid detergents are best in cold water and for washing out grease and oil. Powdered detergents are better for heavily soiled articles.

- Bleaches brighten, whiten, and help with stubborn stains. Chlorine bleach has the most power and also disinfects and deodorizes, but should only be used on white fabrics. Oxygen bleach is gentler and is safe for almost all fabrics.

Save old detergent boxes. Cut off the tops, and turn them into trays and carrying cases for laundry and cleaning supplies. Use a 3-inch high tray to keep stain removers and additives together on the shelf instead of scattered all over the laundry room. Cut off just the top so the handles are still intact and you have a carrying case for taller cans and bottles, which you can also use in the bathroom and kitchen.

Recycle used dryer sheets. Reserve an old tissue box to save used fabric softener dryer sheets. Their antistatic and fragrance powers have a myriad of uses. Wipe off your

dryer lint filter with one. Use them also for cleaning —
and keeping clean — horizontal blinds, TV and computer
screens, and car dashboards. They're also good for a fresh
scent in luggage, drawers, closets, and under car seats.
When traveling, tuck a sheet into your shoes before packing. They'll smell fresh, and you can use it to dust off and
buff up your shoes before you put them on.

Step 2 Increase storage

Now you need somewhere to
put all this laundry and all
those cleaning products. When
you're designing storage, think
hard about efficiency. After all,
you don't want to spend any
more time doing your laundry
than you have to. There's less wasted effort if you keep things
close to where you use them. That means you're out of the
laundry room and on to yoga class that much faster.

Remember...

✓ map your space
✓ shop for containers

SUPER TIPS for storing your laundry

Pick a machine that saves space. A traditional side-by-
side top-loading washer and dryer may not be the right
answer if your laundry room is small. There are many
varieties of very efficient stackable units that only take up
half the floor space. A front-loading washing machine
may also be the answer. You can use the top for permanent work space, or stack your dryer on it. Front-loaders
are also considered better machines because of their wash
action and energy conservation.

Use a wastebasket for your laundry. A dirty clothes basket just looks messy, especially when items overflow onto the floor. Clean up that clutter by hiding it in one of those round, steel step cans made for holding trash. They have a lid and usually blend in nicely with the decor.

Set up an easy sorting system. You can sort your laundry into multiple categories even if you don't have enough space for large hampers. Several standard laundry baskets on a shelf above your washer and dryer will do. Label them so everyone knows which bin to drop their clothes in. Along with the normal "whites" and "colors," you can also have a place for hand washables, dry cleaning, and clothes that are worn out or outgrown.

Plan plenty of folding space. You need a wide, flat area for folding clean laundry. If there is not enough space, you end up with clutter again when you can't fold each load as it comes out of the dryer. A countertop in front of a window is an ideal place. It should be far enough away from the dryer to keep your clean clothes from picking up loose lint.

Make a movable folding table. Attach casters to a cabinet, and you have a table you can fold clean clothes on and also use as a cart to put them away. Plus you have storage underneath. This only works, of course, if your laundry is on the same level as your bedrooms. You can use an old, short dresser or a bathroom vanity cabinet. If it doesn't have legs, screw a wood block to each corner on the bottom, and attach the casters to the blocks. Be sure the wheels on the casters are large enough to maneuver over your particular type of carpet or other floor covering.

Solve the single-sock syndrome. The missing mates to single socks usually reappear in the next wash or two.

Keep a small box or basket in your laundry room to hang on to unmatched items until their lost mates show up.

SUPER TIPS for storing laundry supplies

Include plenty of space-saving shelves. Laundry rooms often end up as a collection point for a variety of household items, so it's nice to have enough storage. This can be floor-to-ceiling enclosed cabinets, simple open shelves, or something in between. A shelf or cabinet above the washer and dryer is the handiest place for soap, bleach, and other washday supplies. Along with your shelves, install hooks or a rod to hold clothes that are drip drying or freshly ironed.

Dress up concrete walls with shelving. Wire shelving in your basement laundry room not only gives you needed storage space, it also makes those cold cement walls more attractive. It's a little more trouble to attach things to concrete, but you don't have to worry about finding the studs. You'll need a masonry drill bit and concrete screws or some kind of an anchor for conventional screws. Check with your hardware store for the right supplies.

Shelves above your washer and dryer are sometimes too high to reach safely. Keep a small folding step stool in the laundry room to make high shelves easy to get to.

Raise appliances for more storage. Bending over to load and unload clothes from front-loading washers and dryers is a definite pain in the back. You can buy a pedestal stand to get them up to an easier working height. If you do, be sure and get one with a door or drawer that lets you store things underneath.

Pretreat soil with an easy squeeze. Fill a plastic ketchup or mustard dispenser with liquid laundry detergent, and keep it next to the washing machine. Then you can just squirt detergent directly on soiled collars and other extra-dirty spots before washing.

Step 3 Get organized

Devising a no-nonsense system for getting your clothes and linens into the laundry room, through the washing and drying process, and back to their respective homes will make your life so much easier.

Remember...

✓ pack properly

✓ label

SUPER TIPS for organizing your laundry

Cut the laundry pile with a schedule. It doesn't take long to get buried in dirty laundry — especially if you're washing for a large family — so make it easier on yourself by doing a load or two every day. You'll cut down the mess in the laundry room as well as the whining when someone is looking for a favorite shirt that's still dirty. You could even have a routine where you do each family member's laundry on a certain day. Then they would know when to have laundry in the hamper and when to expect it to be done. The next logical step is to have older

225

children do their own laundry. Then they can't whine when their favorite shirts are not clean.

Build a chute to save steps. When your bedrooms and bathrooms are upstairs and your washing machine is downstairs, a laundry chute is a tidy and efficient way of getting dirty clothes to the laundry. If you don't have one, try to figure out a way to build a shaft you can toss laundry into so it drops all the way to a basket near the washer. You eliminate the clutter of dirty clothes upstairs and the task of carrying them downstairs for cleaning.

It's possible the reason you struggle with laundry is not because it's so hard to do, but because you do so much of it. A lot of clothes end up in the washing machine when they're not really dirty. It's just easier to wad them up and throw them in the hamper than it is to put them away properly. Train yourself and your family to take care of unsoiled clothes so they can be worn again. They'll have to be hung up or folded no matter what you do. You don't always have to wash them first.

Never sort (or lose) socks again. To avoid the aggravation of missing or mismatched socks, try this little tool. It's a patented ring that holds pairs of socks together. Slip the toe of each sock through the ring, and they stay together from the washer to the dryer and back into the drawer. Have the wearer put them back in the ring before washing again, and your sock-sorting days are over. Order them online from *www.sockpro.com*, or call 800-762-5776. They come in packs of 20 with a choice of five colors. For an easy, homemade solution, use a safety pin to keep socks paired up in the wash.

Post laundry aids on a bulletin board. Bulletin boards are not just for the office. Hanging one near your washing machine can be a big help, too. It's a good place to keep the care tags for garments that need special attention as well as spare buttons that come with new shirts and slacks. You can also stick up threaded needles, iron-on patches, long pins with extra buttons on them, and other supplies. Then you can easily repair clothing before it goes into the wash or back into the closet.

Drip-dry the smart way. Your laundry room may only be a closet just big enough for your washer and dryer. That probably means you use the bathroom to hang clothes that need to drip-dry. Hanging them on the normal shower rod still leaves puddles on the floor. The solution? Install another shower rod over the middle of your bathtub, and they can drip completely into the tub.

Find ways to air-dry. Laying sweaters flat or hanging sheets outside aren't the only ways you can air-dry your laundry. Take shirts and blouses out of the dryer early, and hang them on plastic hangers — they'll have fewer wrinkles and are less likely to shrink. The dryer is also hard on delicate items. If you have room, install a long rod or even an inside clothesline. If not, collapsible drying racks are easy to fold up and store after use, or hang a retractable clothesline on the wall.

Cut down on your ironing — and clothes waiting to be ironed — by taking clothes out of the dryer right away and hanging or folding them. If a load of dry clothes has been left in the dryer, add a damp towel and run it again for five or 10 minutes to remove the wrinkles.

Make a removable drying rack. Turn a window screen into a hanging drying rack for sweaters and other clothing that needs to be laid out to air dry. Just punch holes in the four corners and insert shower curtain rings. Hang it on chains hanging from the ceiling. When you're not using it, take it down and store it between the washer and the dryer. Even easier, if the screen is wide enough, just lay it over your bathtub.

SUPER TIPS for organizing laundry supplies

Mount your ironing board to save space. It won't stay put when it's folded up and leaning against the wall, and it takes up valuable space when set up. It can also become a clutter magnet when not in use. Give your board a home when you're not ironing with a hook to hang it on the wall or back of the door. You can also get a surface-mount ironing board cabinet that keeps it hidden and out of your way until you're ready for it.

Keep stain remover handy. An excellent place for your can of pre-wash spray is right in the laundry hamper. Then it's available to treat nasty spots as you put clothes in the basket. There are many products for this task, so try different ones and see what works best for you. For oily or greasy stains, try the waterless hand cleaner used by auto repair shops and industrial workplaces.

Keep clothespins within reach. An outdoor clothesline is wonderful for saving energy and giving your sheets and towels that fresh-air smell. If you're lucky enough to have one of these old-fashioned conveniences, put your clothespins in a waterproof bag, and hang it on the line. Then the pins will be right where you need to use them.

Step 4 Keep it clean

Now that your laundry room is free of clutter, you'll find it's easy to keep it clean. Here's a chart that gives you a list of chores you can complete in 10 minutes. Add a few weekly, monthly, and occasional chores, and you've got one smart cleaning plan. Then keep reading to find plenty of quick and easy cleaning tips for your clutter-free laundry room.

10-minute daily speed cleaning	Weekly chores	Monthly chores	Occasional chores
Return clean clothes to their homes	Wipe tops of washer and dryer	Clean light fixtures	Clean inside of washer
Empty lint trap in dryer	Empty trash		Clean out dryer duct
	Mop floor		
	Wipe cabinets, shelves, or counters		

SUPER TIPS for cleaning the laundry room

Avoid mess by containing lint. Your dryer works better when you clean the lint filter every time you use it. But what do you do with the messy lint? Keep an empty tissue box near your dryer, and stuff the lint into it each time. Other former pop-up containers work just as well, or use a magnet to hold a plastic bag to the side of your dryer.

Clean out vent for safer drying. This is the pipe or flex hose that exhausts air through the back of your dryer to the outside. If lint clogs this area, your clothes won't dry properly. That means wasted time and energy running the dryer longer as well as increased risk of the lint catching fire. Remove the venting, and shake or vacuum out the dirt and lint. Use your vacuum attachments to get the buildup around the outside vent, too. Then go to the front of the dryer and vacuum out the slot the lint filter fits into.

Make your machine sparkle like new. The buildup of scum on your washing machine parts and hoses comes from the reaction of detergent with hard water. The harder your water, the more scum is created. Get rid of this crusty coating by running a solution of warm water and a gallon of white vinegar through a machine cycle.

Your laundry area should be clean and sparkling. You don't want dust, sticky spills, or little pieces of dried-up paper left lying about. Keep a sponge handy to wipe up the dirty stuff around your washer and dryer.

CHAPTER 11
The Garage

The typical garage presents a thorny organizational problem. It's supposed to "store" your cars, but you also need a place for tools, garden hoses, fertilizer, golf bags, car wax, paint, lumber, and don't forget the dog food.

No wonder most garages become overstuffed and underutilized. In fact, one survey showed that 38 percent of homeowners cited the garage as the messiest room in the house.

Add to that the public display of your disorganization every time your neighbors cruise by your driveway, and you've got a project begging to be conquered.

Or maybe you don't have a garage, and you need to organize your storage shed. You can use the same decluttering techniques.

Remember...

✓ make a wish list

✓ be realistic

✓ set priorities

✓ identify your clutter problems

✓ label your zones

✓ set a timeline

But unlike many other spaces in your home, the garage — or storage shed — is one great big box you can outfit to your specific needs. In addition, you can choose from an almost endless variety of shelves, hooks, bins, cabinets, drawers, pegs, slots, grids, and hoists. Dream big.

If you're downsizing, don't plan zones around everything you have. Instead, consider only the things you'll keep.

Zones	Step 1: Cut the clutter	Step 2: Increase storage	Step 3: Get organized
Lawn and garden			
Tools			
Sports and leisure			
Auto care			
Home care			
Pet care			
Additional zone			

You may have other zones for this space. If so, fill them into the table on the previous page. Then take your best guess on how long it will take you to complete each task for each zone.

Keep in mind you may need time to shop for new storage containers. Remember, this is just an estimate to help you plan your garage decluttering project.

Step 1 Cut the clutter

It's going to be a big, dirty job. That said, wait for good weather, pull on your grubby clothes, clear the cars out of the driveway, and turn up some finger-snapping, be-bopping music. Stash water within easy reach and plan on fast food for lunch.

It's easiest if you can designate driveway space for your piles and zones. If you think there's going to be a lot of trash for your Toss pile, perhaps you can load everything directly into your son's pickup truck and haul it to the landfill. Or contact your sanitation company. For a fee, they'll drop off and pick up a special collection container.

Keep in mind

Make a decision:	Follow purging rules:
✓ keep	✓ decide quickly
✓ toss	✓ handle items once
✓ donate	✓ set limits
✓ sell	✓ pass the "keep" test
✓ pass on	✓ recognize garbage

SUPER TIPS *for sorting lawn and garden items*

Take charge of your belongings. The hardest thing in organizing your garage is choosing what to keep and what not to keep. Only you can make the final decision, but here are some questions that may help you decide.

- When was the last time you used it? A good rule of thumb is that two years is too long.

- Is it in good working condition? If you can't use it because it needs repair, why keep it? And why haven't you fixed it already?

- Do you still need it? You may have bought new hedge clippers and kept the old ones, or you may have had a hedge to trim at your old house but not at your new one.

- Do you have a place to keep it? Sometimes you keep things just because you can, but if you want the space for something else — like parking your car inside — don't hang on to it.

DON'T STORE...

- ✓ furniture you don't have room for
- ✓ equipment you no longer use or need
- ✓ newspapers, cans, and bottles not being recycled
- ✓ large amounts of gasoline or other flammables

Look out for duplicates. You really have two issues in the lawn and garden zone. The first is all the equipment you've accumulated. It's likely over the years you've bought a better rake or sidewalk edger, but you still have the old one — or two or three. And how many old gloves, tomato cages, and clay flower pots will you ever actually use? The other issue is whether you're going to continue doing yard work yourself. Retirement may mean more time to enjoy working outside, but it may also mean you're ready to turn it all over to a lawn service. If so, you'll need a lot less equipment, and your "keep" pile will be much smaller.

Set aside pesticides and other poisons. Get all your garden chemicals together in one place away from food, pet food, and medical supplies. Store them separately out of reach of children and animals. Keep pesticides and fertilizers in their original containers so you don't mistake them for something else. If you can't identify the contents of a container, dispose of it safely.

Toss without a thought

✓ unidentified or out-of-date chemicals

✓ paint that has dried out or is in rusty cans

✓ damaged or unsafe tools and equipment

✓ worn-out sports gear

✓ instruction manuals and warranties for tools you no longer have

How do you use your garage? More than half of all two-car garage owners use theirs for something other than cars. The U.S. Department of Energy reports 25 percent of these garage owners don't park any cars in their garages and 32 percent park only one. It doesn't say, however, how many cars are parked outside because there's too much clutter inside the garage.

SUPER TIPS for sorting tools

Group similar items together. It's likely your hand tools are scattered not only all through your garage, but throughout the rest of your house and your cars, too. Before you start sorting, go around and gather up everything so you know exactly what you have. Lay everything out where you can see it all, grouping like items — hammers, screwdrivers, wrenches, and so on — together. Then you can eliminate broken or unsafe items, duplicates, and tools you aren't likely to ever use. A good rule of thumb is to consider the worst possible consequence if you get rid of it.

Set up a working workbench. Even if you have a low handyman rating, you still need a workbench. Most everyone needs a place for messy tasks and simple repairs — things you don't want to do on the dining room table. The exact size and complexity of your workbench depends on how you use it and how often. If you're only at your workbench several times a year, a small portable one will do. Otherwise, it's just a horizontal clutter magnet. If you're always working on — and completing — projects, you may want to spend from $100 to $1,000 for a better one. You can make a workbench out of an old dresser or cabinet, or a piece of countertop. Keep in mind the bigger your bench, the less floor space you have for other things.

Stop short of sorting nuts and bolts. Everyone has a coffee can or mayonnaise jar full of leftover nuts, bolts, screws, nails, and other assorted pieces just in case you need them sometime. You may think sorting the contents of that can is essential to cleaning out the garage, but it's not really necessary. You probably don't need them very often and dividing them up into many little drawers makes it harder to find the right screw. Instead, throw everything into the can. Then when you need something, dump the can onto an old cookie sheet or pizza pan. When everything is all spread out, you can find what you're looking for quickly and easily.

Discard out-of-date warranties. If you're lucky, you have one big pile of warranties, parts lists, and instruction manuals. If not, they're spread all through your garage. The first thing to do is throw away those that are for equipment you no longer have, and then ditch the ones that are out of date. Next, get a three-ring binder, punch holes in the sides of the paperwork or put it into sheet protectors with pre-punched holes, and consolidate it all in one neat book. You can even include tabbed divider sheets for quick reference.

SUPER TIPS for sorting sports and leisure items

List current sports to minimize gear. Before you start sorting sports and recreational equipment, take a few minutes and write down all the activities members of your household currently take part in. Don't include things you used to do or want to do but never have. There's not much sense in keeping gear for games you don't play.

Sort according to sport. Group recreational equipment by specific sports when you're doing your initial sort. It's a smart way to uncover duplicates and see what shape your gear is in. You may find you don't have enough usable gear to warrant keeping anything for a particular sport. It's also easier later on to organize and store things so you can find everything at once — golf clubs, shoes, balls — all in the same place.

Set floor space priorities. Does it make sense to park your cars in the driveway because less-valuable bicycles are taking up the floor space in your garage? Extra lawnmowers are also frequent offenders. People often have bikes or mowers they don't use but can't bear to throw them away because there's still some good in them. Consider giving this equipment away or selling it cheap to someone who will use it. Then it won't be wasted, and you can use your garage for more important storage.

Use it or lose it. If you can't remember digging through the piles in your garage looking for your roller blades, old baseball gloves, or discarded golf clubs, you'll probably never use them again. Sort through everything and quickly decide if an item is usable. If it is, take it to your Salvation Army store, Boys and Girls Club, or some other charity where it can do someone some good. If not, throw it away.

Sometimes there are discards in your garage that would be difficult to sell, but they're too good to throw away. The Freecycle Network can help you find a new home for a couch that got replaced, your old kitchen cabinets, or other things taking up space because you can't figure out how to get rid of them. Freecycle is a series of local groups that match up people who want to give or get free stuff so landfills don't get filled up with things that are still good. It's all on the Internet. Go to *www.freecycle.org* to find a group near you and list whatever you have to give away.

Give deteriorating gear the boot. The longer you store sports equipment, the more likely you'll find it in poor condition. Examples are broken-down shoes and boots,

If you wonder how so many golf clubs and tennis rackets found their way onto a pile in your garage, consider this — the National Sporting Goods Association says Americans spent almost $23 million on sporting goods in 2004. That doesn't include bikes, boats, shoes, or clothing, either. Think about how often you'll use that fancy, new racket the next time you're tempted to buy one. Sounds like a good opportunity to save both money and space in your garage.

cracked baseball gloves, and balls and tires with air leaks that can't be fixed. Camping equipment — such as sleeping bags, packs, and tents — begin to mildew and smell bad after being packed away too long.

SUPER TIPS   for sorting auto care items

Watch out for old car batteries. One easy decision when you're throwing things away is old car batteries. Leaking battery acid will eat through just about anything and, over time, batteries can also explode. Check with your mechanic or auto supply store for proper disposal.

Steer clear of toxic chemicals. The second-leading cause of injury-related death in the home is poisoning. Some of the most dangerous toxic items are often stored in the garage — like automotive fluids and pesticides. Dispose of as many of these as possible, following manufacturers guidelines for proper disposal. Definitely throw out anything that is unlabeled, obsolete, inadequately sealed, or too small a quantity to do the job. Garage poisons besides antifreeze, brake fluid, and oil include lighter fluids, paint thinners and removers, and many household cleansers.

SUPER TIPS *for sorting home care items*

Replace paint cans with a simple list. You save old paint because you want to remember the exact shade you painted the living room, but after awhile it dries up and the markings on the can fade away. A better way is to write down the brand, type, and name of the shade, along with the place you bought it. If you have the exact formula the paint store used, include that, too. Then you can always go back to the store and get the right color.

Get rid of leftover latex paint easily. Latex paint can be thrown out in the regular trash if you dry it out first. Just leave the lid off the can overnight, and it'll be dried up in the morning. For larger amounts, pour the paint onto old newspapers or cardboard, and let it dry. Take oil-based paint and primers to a toxic waste center.

Call for help when throwing away large items. After you've finished sorting and have given away, sold, or

Be extra careful when you get rid of hazardous material, such as toxic substances or anything that will burn, explode, or corrode metal. Hazardous waste you might find in your garage includes old car batteries, used oil, antifreeze, brake and transmission fluids, paint, paint thinner, strippers, herbicides, fungicides, and insecticides. Don't put things like this in the trash where they can end up contaminating a landfill. Take them to a licensed hazardous waste operator who will dispose of them properly. There are also recycling centers for things like batteries, used oil, and old tires.

donated everything you can, you need to throw away the rest. You might put smaller items in heavy-duty trash bags and include them in your regular garbage pick up, depending on your hauler's rules for volume and content. You could also take the trash to the landfill yourself, especially if you own or can borrow a vehicle to haul it in. For larger items, check with your trash service about bulk pickups — either on special days or through special arrangements. In most places, there are people who will haul away junk for a fee. Find someone locally by looking in the Yellow Pages and classified ads, or asking friends and neighbors. You could also try 1-800-GOT-JUNK. Call that number to see if there's a franchise in your area. They charge according to how much space your stuff takes up in their truck, and they take care of all the loading, hauling, and cleaning up after themselves.

It doesn't usually pay to buy the giant economy size of paint, paint stripper, and other hazardous liquids. Leftovers of these products, along with garden chemicals and automobile fluids, generally just waste space in your garage. They get contaminated, dry up, or leak all over everything and can't be used again. You're money ahead when buying only the amount you need, instead of paying for extra that only ends up as dangerous clutter.

SUPER TIPS *for sorting pet care items*

Separate pets and poisons. Curiosity can kill your cat, or any of your other pets, if it tastes harmful products. Watch for poisonous material when you're sorting your things, and keep it away from pet supplies or areas of your garage where your pet roams. Fertilizers, plant foods, insecticides, and many automotive products can be fatal if your pet ingests them. Surprisingly, another common source of pet poisoning is spoiled garbage.

The Pet Food Institute reports that more than 70 percent of American households include either a dog or a cat, and about 25 percent have both. That means there's a good chance you store pet food or pet supplies in your garage.

Step 2 Increase storage

What a beautiful thing this great big, empty garage is. Now you can really see how it is shaped — all the angles and niches, the placement of outlets, and the immovables, like the water heater and fuse box.

Remember...

✓ map your space
✓ shop for containers

Measure it all, just like you would for any other room, drawing it out on graph paper.

Now you must decide your budget. You could easily spend $1,000 or more on custom cabinets — and lots of people are doing just that. Marketing manager for Whirlpool's Gladiator GarageWorks, Christopher Hubbuch, claims he's in a $700 million industry. But you could also spend next to nothing on recycled and build-it-yourself organizers.

Remember some storage pieces or systems are not designed for a garage. You want items that are strong, adjustable, and impervious to water, dirt, mold, and swings in temperature and humidity. If possible, check the load-bearing capacity of shelves and hooks. Know where your wall studs and ceiling joists are.

Get everything off the floor. Not only will it be easier to clean, you'll eliminate nesting spaces for unwelcome critters and the possibility of water damage.

SUPER TIPS for storing lawn and garden items

Get cabinets for a fraction of the cost. You don't need to spend hundreds of dollars for fancy garage storage systems. Recycle old kitchen cabinets instead. If you're planning to remodel your kitchen, install the old cabinets and countertops in your garage. You can also ask friends who might be remodeling, visit a used-construction supply store, ask a kitchen installer about his throwaways, or look for returns and scratch-and-dent sales at home improvement retailers.

Find a few five-gallon buckets. They're the gardener's equivalent of baby food jars for storing stuff. Clean them out and use them for fertilizer, grass seed, birdseed, potting soil, and anything else you want to keep dry and safe from bugs and rodents. Original contents of these great containers include paint, joint compound, and swimming pool chemicals. If you don't know anyone who uses these things, you can also buy brand new buckets at Home Depot, Lowes, and other home improvement stores. Don't forget lids to keep the contents airtight. Lids also let you stack your buckets to save floor space — just be sure to label the outside. It's also a good idea to put the part of the original sack that has handling and application instructions inside the bucket.

Keep that worn-out golf bag. You bought a newer, nicer golf bag, but you can't bear to throw out the old one. Move it from the sports equipment pile over to the lawn and garden section and hang it securely to the wall. Now you have a place to store your rakes, hoes, and other long-handled items.

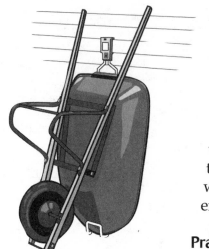

Hang up your wheelbarrow. A wheelbarrow is one of your most important tools when you need it, but it takes up a lot of floor space when you're not using it. For just $5 to $15, you can buy a holder especially for hanging wheelbarrows on the wall. The front lip fits into the bottom bracket, then you swing the wheelbarrow up until the other end snaps into the top bracket.

Practice proper gasoline storage. Keep gas for your mowers, blowers, and trimmers only in small amounts and only in tightly sealed containers. Never keep gasoline inside your house, and don't store it in your garage if there are any pilot lights or appliances around that might ignite the fumes. Always use an approved, properly identified container for gasoline. Don't ever put it in milk jugs, antifreeze cans, or glass containers.

SUPER TIPS for storing tools

Hang tools on Pegboard. It's a time-honored technique. Cut a piece of Pegboard — or have your store or lumberyard cut it for you — to fit the wall space you want to use. Locate your wall studs, attach furring strips to the studs, and screw in the Pegboard on top of the furring strips. Now there's room behind the Pegboard for the hooks, and it's attached solidly to the wall. Plan the location of your tools before putting in the hooks to get the best use of the space available.

Get creative with Pegboard. Don't limit your Pegboard storage to hammers, wrenches, and other small hand tools. It's also a good place for rolls of tape or wire, pieces of chain, saw blades, and other items you need in your workshop.

Do away with Pegboard hooks. One of the newer Pegboard fasteners is called Bunjipeg. It's an elastic cord held tight with slotted pegs. Slip just about anything behind the cord and it stays there without any special hooks, hangers, or adapters. You can make each pocket whatever length you want. You probably won't find Bunjipeg in stores, but you can order it online from *www.bunjipeg.com* or telephone 919-571-1283.

Save space with baby food jars. They're the staple of workshop storage. Some people say putting baby food in these little jars was only an afterthought. Their real purpose is to keep small items, like nuts, bolts, and washers, where you can see them and find them. Attach the lids to a board mounted above your workspace and then screw the jars to the lids for better organization.

Recycle common household containers. It may be an odd-sized tin can, the flat dish from a microwave meal, or a versatile plastic baby-wipe box, but you can usually find the container you need to keep nails, drill bits, and small tools separate and organized. Plastic food containers for keeping leftovers in the refrigerator are also good for small parts. You can recycle your old Tupperware or buy the inexpensive, disposable kind.

Buy a magnetic toolbar. They're usually used to hang knives in the kitchen, but these magnetic racks are also good for storing tools. Hang anything metal — from screwdrivers and drill bits to chisels, pliers, and garden tools.

Hang clamps from towel bar. Mount an old towel bar on the wall next to your workbench to hold your C-clamps. Arrange them according to size and you'll always know where they are and how many you really have.

File your sandpaper. Get an accordion file from an office supply store to keep the loose sheets of sandpaper you can never find. They stay clean and flat in the file, and you can sort them by type and grit. Label the tabs so you can quickly find the exact sheet you need.

SUPER TIPS for storing sports and leisure items

Hang seasonal items from the ceiling. Hang bicycles, lawn chairs, and sleds from ceiling hooks to keep them up off the floor during the times of the year when you're not using them. Make sure you screw the hooks into a ceiling joist so they don't pull out when you put weight on them. Most garage ceilings are high enough to provide lots of overhead space for these items.

Utilize space with a storage loft. Hanging things from the ceiling isn't the only way to take advantage of vertical space in a tall garage. If your ceilings are 10 or more feet high, you can build a loft high enough to walk under and park your cars under. You'll have two or more feet upstairs to store boxes and other items you can't hang. Get plans from home improvement stores, like Lowe's and Home Depot, or on the Internet.

Install shelves above your garage doors. Another way to utilize the empty space near the ceiling is to put shelves high up on the walls. An often-overlooked area is the space above your garage doors. Make sure these shelves are strong enough to hold the things you want to store there. One trick is to support one or more edges of the shelf from the ceiling instead of the wall. You can buy ready-made hanging brackets or fashion them yourself from metal strapping material.

Transform empty space into an attic. If your garage has open rafters, lay a sheet or two of plywood across them, and you've got an instant attic. Store coolers, camping equipment, Christmas decorations, and other seasonal items there. Make sure your plywood is thick enough for the weight it's supporting and be careful on the ladder when you put things up and take them down.

SUPER TIPS *for storing auto care items*

Build one-of-a-kind shelves. You can make shelves from new or used lumber that are just as good, if not better, than ready-made shelves. As a matter-of-fact, the narrow shelves you can make from 4- or 6-inch boards are perfect for storing cans of wax, oil, and other car-care products.

Keep track of your WD-40. Is your can of WD-40 nowhere to be found? Maybe it's some other important workshop helper you can never find when you need it. Keep track of it with a plastic drink holder. Get a sturdy one and mount it where you always want that can to be — then make sure you put it back when you're done.

SUPER TIPS for storing home care items

Eliminate clutter with plastic bins. These containers — 10 to 20 inches wide, 18 to 30 inches long, and up to 8 inches deep — keep your shelves neat and your home-care items together. Put spare light bulbs in one, electrical supplies in another, and so on. The lids let you stack them for good use of space. If they're clear plastic, you can see the contents, but you should still label the outside. This will help you find things easier and get them back to their proper place.

Pour paint into peanut butter jars. Instead of saving a pint of paint in a gallon bucket, transfer it to an empty, clean plastic peanut butter jar. It takes up less space and is easier to organize. You still have the leftover paint for touchup work, but now it's in a container that can't rust and won't be full of air to dry out the contents. The mouth is wide enough for a paintbrush, and you can hold the jar in one hand. Don't forget to label it so you know exactly what type of paint you have.

SUPER TIPS for storing pet care items

Tame unruly pet equipment. Once you've gathered up all your pet's food, toys, and other gear, store it all in a sturdy plastic container. It will hold up much better than

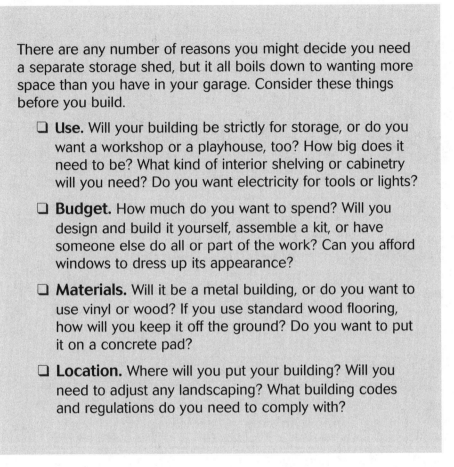

There are any number of reasons you might decide you need a separate storage shed, but it all boils down to wanting more space than you have in your garage. Consider these things before you build.

❑ **Use.** Will your building be strictly for storage, or do you want a workshop or a playhouse, too? How big does it need to be? What kind of interior shelving or cabinetry will you need? Do you want electricity for tools or lights?

❑ **Budget.** How much do you want to spend? Will you design and build it yourself, assemble a kit, or have someone else do all or part of the work? Can you afford windows to dress up its appearance?

❑ **Materials.** Will it be a metal building, or do you want to use vinyl or wood? If you use standard wood flooring, how will you keep it off the ground? Do you want to put it on a concrete pad?

❑ **Location.** Where will you put your building? Will you need to adjust any landscaping? What building codes and regulations do you need to comply with?

cardboard, and it's waterproof. Mice can't gnaw through it looking for a better meal, either. Label it so you can find it easily.

Grab hold of pet grooming supplies. Find a tool caddy and store all your soap, flea treatment, brushes, and other pet grooming supplies. When your dog needs a brush or a bath, just grab the caddy and you're ready to go.

Put the bite on contaminated pet food. Pet food stored in a paper bag on the floor of your garage is a disaster waiting to happen. The bag can become wet or torn, which leads to insects, mildew, and rodents. Consider buying an airtight plastic food storage bin, or simply set the sack inside an empty 5-gallon paint bucket.

Step 3 Get organized

Your garage is the biggest storage facility in your house. But today, most families think of it as an extension of their home, like a multi-purpose room. That means you have to be smart about where you put things.

Remember...

✓ pack properly
✓ label

SUPER TIPS for organizing lawn and garden items

Divide zones with floor paint. While everything is out of your garage, it's a good time to paint the floor. Mask off the place where the cars go and paint it a different color — that area needs higher-quality paint anyway — to emphasize that it's a no-clutter zone. You can do the same with other zones, too, using colors, stripes, and unique designs to keep your garden tools separate from your lumber and your camping equipment.

Organize lawn equipment with bicycle hooks. Most garage clutter is caused by equipment stored on the floor. Take advantage of vertical space in your garage by hanging fertilizer spreaders, trimmers, and blowers from bicycle hooks anchored firmly into ceiling rafters or high up on the wall.

Keep sharp tools out of the way. Shovels, rakes, and other sharp tools can be real safety hazards, especially when they're propped against a wall. Hang them up with the sharp edges toward the wall, away from high-traffic areas, and out of children's reach.

Make your own tool hanger. You can search the stores for a ready-made hanger that works for your garage, or you can make an adjustable peg hanger you can adapt as your needs change. Drill a line of holes a couple of inches apart in a long board and mount it on the wall. Then cut pegs from dowels the same diameter as your holes. Insert the pegs into the holes that let you hang your rakes and shovels in just the right places.

Stow away garden hoses on your patio. Get garden hoses out of your garage and closer to where they're needed by coiling them up inside those large planter pots you have sitting on your patio. They'll be neat, tidy, and out of the way, and you won't have to haul them back and forth. When cold weather approaches, make sure you drain them as you coil them if you plan to leave them outside through the winter.

SUPER TIPS *for organizing tools*

Build a workbench organizer. Bill Morris of Wichita, Kan., keeps his tools together with a homemade rack that hangs on chains above his workbench. "I got the idea from seeing overhead racks in kitchens that were used for pots and pans," he says. The rack is a simple rectangle made from 2x8 lumber, with the side boards extended about 18 inches from the short ends. It is hollow in the middle so light can shine through to the bench, and the corners are strengthened with angle iron.

Morris uses 16d nails for hooks and hangs all his commonly used equipment on it — from extension cords to a box of drill bits. "Gone are the days when I have to search for my tools," Morris brags. "There are a lot of surfaces to hang things on."

Stay organized by drawing around your tools. Before you mount the Pegboard to hold your small tools, lay it flat on the floor and decide on the most efficient arrangement for your tools. Then install the hooks and mount the board. After you hang your tools, draw an outline around them so you'll always know where to put things back.

Make your own worktable. If you have two rolling toolboxes, but not enough worktable surface, lay a piece of 3/4-inch plywood on top of them to make a table that fits the available space. If you only have one toolbox, make legs out of 2x4 lumber or attach a 2x4 to the wall at the

How many times have you bought a new tool because you couldn't find the one you already have? You end up with a mini-hardware store in your garage, but you can't put your hands on all the inventory. When your tools are sorted and organized, you can always find the one you need. Then you can spend your money for tools you don't have.

right height. Make sure the wall support is fastened into studs, and put a screw through the table into the support to keep it from sliding.

Find a place for a first-aid kit. When you're putting your workshop area back together, be sure and reserve a prominent place for a first-aid kit. It's important to be prepared to handle minor emergencies. Many stores and the Red Cross sell pre-assembled kits, or you can put one together yourself. The most important item to have in your first-aid kit is information — emergency phone numbers and contacts, and a booklet or guide on how to deal with different emergencies.

The garage is one of the most important amenities home buyers look for, so make sure yours is clean and well-organized before you put your house up for sale. Buyers want the extra storage space in a garage, especially in areas where houses don't have basements. In cold-weather regions, it's also very important to have at least one car in the garage during the winter. People also like the security of parking their car, closing the garage door, and walking directly into the house without going outside.

SUPER TIPS *for organizing sports and leisure items*

Create large cubbyhole bins. Organize your outdoor equipment into a series of cubbyhole-type bins made from plywood. Ask your lumber supplier to split a few sheets into 2-foot x 8-foot pieces to use for the sides, vertical dividers, top, and bottom. Screw rails to the sides to hold shelves and you have several large bins to store folding chairs, coolers, and camping equipment. Adjust shelf distances to fit the contents and you'll have a place for everything from golf clubs to tackle boxes.

Separate children's playthings. Make sure balls, toys, and other children's items are stored together and within easy reach. You don't want little ones to get into dangerous areas while looking for something to play with. It's always a good idea to keep an eye on young children whenever they're in the garage.

Hang your helmet on your bike. It saves searching for a good place to keep it and helps remind you to wear it. Strap it to the bicycle seat or the handlebars and you'll always know where it is.

SUPER TIPS for organizing auto care items

Make use of nooks and crannies between studs. If your garage doesn't have interior walls, then you have a bonanza of storage space between the bare studs. Any number of shelves and hangers can be attached to the studs themselves, or you can make simple shelves by nailing boards between the studs. Stand up pieces of lumber between the studs and attach a board, strap, or bungee cord across the front to hold them in.

Attach clothespins to studs. Use the spring-loaded kind and you've got a great clip for goggles, car wash rags and chamois, gloves, and other small items. Drill a hole to keep the clothespin from splitting and attach with a finish nail or small screw.

Wheel supplies where you need them. Keep all your automotive maintenance supplies together on a set of shelves equipped with wheels. Then when you want to wash your car in the driveway, just roll out the cart, and your buckets, sponges, and soap are right there. The same is true if you're checking the oil, antifreeze, or washer fluid inside the garage.

Guard against lost keys. Never again misplace your keys. Install a hook in the wall next to your garage door and hang your house and car keys on the hook. Leave them there when you come into the house, and they won't be lost when you're ready to leave. If you have too many keys for one hook, put several on a small, narrow board and attach that to the wall.

SUPER TIPS for organizing home care items

Hang your ladders to save space. When you lean them up against the wall, ladders take up valuable floor space and can tip and fall on people or vehicles. Shorter stepladders can hang vertically, but longer ladders need to be horizontal. Consider using the space above your garage door for hanging ladders.

Use scrap lumber to make a storage rack. If you've decided to keep that perfectly good scrap lumber but don't know where to put it, sort through it for some 2x4s you can use  to make a storage rack. A design that works nicely has one end hanging from the rafters and the other anchored to a wall stud. Fasten them with lag bolts for strength. Put up two or more sections and lay the lumber across them. Then you've got your valuable wood in an out-of-the-way place, and you can find it when you need it.

Stack trash and recyclables. Take advantage of vertical space with a shelf above your garbage can for lightweight recycling bins. Heavy bins, for things like newspapers, should stay on the floor.

Hang a rope shelf from the ceiling. When attaching a shelf to your wall just won't work, try making one out of rope so it can hang from the ceiling. Drill holes in the corners of an inch-thick board either 4 or 6 inches wide and as long as you want the shelf. Thread a piece of rope through each hole and attach one end to eye-hooks in the ceiling. Tie knots at the bottom to keep your shelf level. You can add shelves by using a longer rope, but only use them for lightweight items.

SUPER TIPS for organizing pet care items

Give an old dresser a new purpose. You might be solving two clutter problems at once. Does that old dresser, buffet, or cabinet no longer serve a purpose in your house, but you think it's too good to get rid of? Use it in the garage to keep your pet food and supplies high, dry, and where you can find them.

Clean up after your pooch with newspaper bags.
Those long, plastic bags your morning paper comes in
make perfect pooper-scoopers for picking up after your
pet. Use the same technique of slipping it over your
hand, picking up what you don't want to touch, peeling
it off inside out, and throwing away the bag to deal with
other undesirable items, such as poison ivy. Stuff several
of these bags into another bag, or use a tennis ball sleeve
or old baby wipes container and keep them where you
can find them in your garage.

Step 4 Keep it clean

Now your challenge is to keep your reorganized garage looking
neat and clean. You'll want to sweep it out occasionally — more
often during bad weather when your car brings in mud and
snow — and give it a thorough cleaning once a year. The best
thing you can do is clean up messes as they occur. Sweep up
the sawdust, put tools away, clean up oil spots, and don't use
your garage as a dumping place for unwanted items. Try these
tips to keep your garage as clean as a whistle.

SUPER TIPS for cleaning your garage

Spruce up your garage with a leaf blower. Dirt. leaves,
and grass clippings make a mess in your garage the same
as they do outside. So when you're using your leaf blower
to tidy up your driveway and sidewalks, start in your
garage. It's a lot quicker than sweeping and you can get to
hard-to-reach places without moving things around.

Catch dirty drips with a floor mat. If your car drips mud, slush, oil, or antifreeze onto your garage floor, consider buying a protective mat made just for garages. They can be found at auto supply and home improvement stores or on the Internet, usually for less than $2 a square foot. They're made of rubber or vinyl and go under your car to catch all the dirty drips. That way, you don't track the mess through the rest of your garage and into your house. When the mat gets dirty, just pull it outside and hose it off.

Triumph over bugs. Lots of little critters like to live in your garage, so getting rid of them should be part of an occasional thorough cleaning. Empty out the tub of your shop vac and put a little powdered bug-killer in it. Move everything away from the walls and vacuum everything in sight, including edges, crevices, and cracks in the concrete. When you're finished, spray liquid bug-killer around the entire perimeter of your garage.

Chapter 12
The Car

Today's busy, mobile lifestyle translates into more time in your car than ever before. The average American spends about an hour driving each day.

But you don't just drive, do you? You eat. You transport groceries, grandchildren, and your bridge club. You pick up dry cleaning, potting soil, and Fifi from the groomers. Every trip you take leaves its own special souvenir on your car's upholstery, carpet, dashboard, windows, and trunk.

You may think no one notices the clutter, but they do. Since you spent quite a bit of money buying that car and almost as much keeping it running, isn't it worth a little TLC?

Take your best guess on how long it will take you to complete each task

Remember...

✓ make a wish list

✓ be realistic

✓ set priorities

✓ identify your clutter
   problems

✓ label your zones

✓ set a timeline

for each zone. Keep in mind you may need time to shop for new storage containers. Remember, this is just an estimate to help you plan your car decluttering project.

Zones	Step 1: Cut the clutter	Step 2: Increase storage	Step 3: Get organized
Car interior			
Car trunk			

Step 1 Cut the clutter

Be honest. There's stuff in your car you can't even identify. But don't worry, this is going to be easy. Almost everything will belong somewhere else in your house or garage, or go in the Toss pile. You'll keep a few things and possibly add a few important items that might make your travel easier and safer. Grab a trash bag and let's get started.

Keep in mind

Make a decision:	Follow purging rules:
✓ keep	✓ decide quickly
✓ toss	✓ handle items once
✓ donate	✓ set limits
✓ sell	✓ pass the "keep" test
✓ pass on	✓ recognize garbage

SUPER TIPS for sorting your car interior

Dash off a note to yourself.
It's amazing how many good ideas you get while stuck in traffic — or how many errands you forget because you don't write them down. But you don't want to clutter up your car with scraps of paper. Instead, place some Velcro on the back of a notepad and stick it to your dashboard or glove compartment. Stick a pen nearby, too. That way, you'll always have a way to jot down a thought or a to-do list.

DON'T STORE...

- ✓ cans of gasoline
- ✓ open or perishable food
- ✓ receipts you accumulate while on the road
- ✓ mail
- ✓ books or magazines
- ✓ work papers
- ✓ bags of clothes or other items you've been meaning to donate
- ✓ sporting equipment

Vanquish clutter with visors. Wrap a few rubber bands around your sun visors, and you'll have a handy place to slip maps, pencils, directions, parking stubs, toll tickets, or to-do lists. A big clothespin will do the same trick.

SUPER TIPS for sorting your car's trunk

Start from square one. There's only one way to declutter your trunk — take out everything, except your spare tire and jack, and inspect every last thing. Make a decision and sort the items into piles. Save time and keep a trash can handy to toss things that are broken. When your trunk is empty, only put back the items you absolutely need to keep there. Donate and relocate everything else.

Leave your golf clubs at home. Storing sports equipment in your trunk wastes precious space and hurts your gas mileage. It also makes it more difficult to retrieve your spare tire if you get a flat.

Step 2 Increase storage

You are working with a small amount of space here. That's why it's important to use the space to its full potential. Here are lots of clever ideas for storing the things you need.

Remember...

✓ map your space
✓ shop for containers

But first, just like any room in your house, measure before you decide on containers. Don't forget the space between your front seats, the width of your seat backs, and the depth of your trunk.

SUPER TIPS *for storing inside your car*

Carry your clutter in a crate. Even if you were an octopus, you wouldn't have enough arms to carry all the stuff from your car to your house. Make things easier on yourself. Use a milk crate, cardboard box, or laundry basket to transport items to and from your car. Before you leave your house, fill up the crate with video rentals, library books, dry cleaning, your briefcase, or any other materials you need. Then, instead of performing an elaborate balancing act, simply carry the crate to your car. Any items you accumulate over the course of the day go right in the box. When you come home, just bring the box in with you and unload the items where they belong.

Toss without a thought

✓ broken or scratched sunglasses

✓ pens that don't work or broken pencils

✓ outdated maps or maps to places you don't visit

✓ food containers and other trash

✓ extra or broken umbrellas

Give car clutter the boot. Here's an easy way to "shoe" away clutter in your car. Drape a plastic shoe organizer over the back of the front seat, and use the pockets to hold items you need, like books, cassettes, toiletries, maps, tools, or medication. Your grandchildren can even use it to store their toys or portable listening devices during trips. However you use it, a shoe organizer can keep everything in its place and prevent clutter from filling your back seat and floor.

Change the way you store change. Stop fumbling for change every time you come to a tollbooth or parking meter. Keep quarters handy by storing them in an empty film canister in your car. You won't waste time digging through your pockets or purse.

SUPER TIPS for storing in your car's trunk

Swap trunk junk for kitty litter. Don't let icy winters catch you unprepared. Keep some sand, rock salt, or kitty litter in your trunk for emergency traction. Plastic containers with pour spouts or handles make things even more convenient.

Give your trunk a helping handbag. You might not want to carry that old handbag or briefcase anymore, but your trunk will be happy to. With all the pockets and zippers, a large handbag or tote makes a handy, portable storage system. Use it to hold things like jumper cables, flashlights, maps, and scrapers. You can also fill an old briefcase with tools and store it in your trunk in case of an emergency.

Step 3 Get organized

You should have a couple of goals here. One is to stow things in your car so you have what you need when you need it. Plus, you want to be able to find things while you're driving without endangering life and limb, or emptying the entire trunk to get at your spare tire.

Remember...
✓ pack properly
✓ label

SUPER TIPS *for organizing inside your car*

Keep car info in your car. Your home records include a neat, detailed folder labeled "Car," but that doesn't do you much good when you break down on the road. Keep your car's repair records, or at least copies of the repair records, and warranty information in your glove compartment. That way, you'll have access to them when you need them most.

Find your way with a folder. Tired of asking for directions all the time? Save yourself the trouble by keeping all your maps and driving directions in a folder. If you travel often, you can even create several folders and organize them by state. When you set out on a trip, just grab the appropriate folder along with your suitcase. A small photo album also works well to store and protect your driving directions.

Make room for menus. In today's fast-paced world, sometimes you need to grab dinner on the go. Give yourself a head start by keeping your favorite takeout menus in your glove compartment. Use your cell phone to call in your order from the road, and pick up your meal on your way home.

Arm yourself for accidents. Accidents happen. But a few simple items can make dealing with them much easier. Keep a notebook and pen in your car to jot down the details of the accident — the date, time, street, city, weather, road conditions, and a description of what happened. Include the speed you were going and the direction you were traveling. Make sure to get the names, license plate numbers, and insurance information of the other drivers involved. Also keep a disposable camera in your glove compartment to snap photos of the accident scene and the damage to your car. It will come in handy for your insurance company.

SUPER TIPS *for organizing your car's trunk*

Transport car fluids in clever carrier. Next time your family orders takeout, save the cardboard multiple-drink carrier the restaurant gives you. Reinforce the bottom with some tape. Then use the pockets of the carrier to hold your bottles of oil or transmission fluid. It will keep them from sliding around in your trunk when you make sharp turns.

Cleaning out your car? Don't get rid of everything. Here are 10 essentials that need to stay.

❑ blanket

❑ first-aid kit

❑ flashlight

❑ ice scraper

❑ emergency phone numbers

❑ jumper cables

❑ tire gauge

❑ spare tire with jack

❑ flares

❑ shovel

Step 4 Keep it clean

Once you've organized your car, you'll want to clean it. Be thorough. Vacuum the carpeting, wipe down the dashboard, and spray the windows. Make sure you wash the exterior, too.

You can wash your car in your driveway or take it to a car wash — the important thing is that it gets clean. After all, a clean car discourages clutter.

Here are a few tips to help you keep your car clean and clutter-free.

SUPER TIPS for cleaning your car

Keep your car neat as a pin for 2 bucks. Here are two things to add to your car to keep it neat as a pin — baby wipes and a bag for trash. Wipe up spills and dust the dashboard with baby wipes, which also come in handy for sticky hands and faces. Stash a recycled grocery bag or plastic newspaper bag in your car. Put any trash in the bag, and throw it away each day. Your car will stay clean at a total cost of less than two dollars.

Empty trash as you fill up. Cars have a way of accumulating trash, especially during long trips. Whenever you stop for gas, use that time to clean out your car. Most gas stations have large trash cans near the pumps, so you can kill two birds with one stone.

Banish grime from wheel covers. You want your car to look clean on the outside as well as the inside. But you don't want to spend too much time or energy washing it.

When those spoked wheel covers get dirty, there's no need to hand scrub them. Just put them in your dishwasher and set it on the pots and pans cycle.

Make a date with your car. Now that your car is clean, put it on a schedule so it stays that way. Every month, go through your car to get rid of any trash and make sure everything else is in its place. Then take it to the local car wash for a wash and an interior cleaning.

Going away for a while? Keep these tips in mind when putting your car in long-term storage.

❏ **Store your car indoors.** A climate-controlled facility is best. It doesn't have to be a garage. You can find ministorage places that fit cars. Just make sure the facility is dry and clean.

❏ **Clean your car thoroughly inside and out.** Don't forget to clean under the car, as well.

❏ **Take pest precautions.** Set mousetraps and place them around your vehicle. Rat poison and mothballs will also keep critters away.

❏ **Fill up the fluids.** Change the oil and fill up the gas tank. A full tank keeps out moisture.

❏ **Remove the battery.** You can even hook up a trickle charger to make sure it won't conk out on you.

❏ **Put a car cover over your vehicle,** and bid it farewell.

CHAPTER 13
The Attic or Basement

C all it the black hole of storage. It's usually where you dump everything that doesn't fit or belong anywhere else. And heaven help you if you need something from the basement or attic right this minute.

Clearing your way through this storage space is different from tackling a junk drawer in your kitchen. It's almost impossible to accomplish this project a little bit at a time.

For one thing, you're bound to make a mess, and you don't want that hanging around for too long. Get mentally prepared for a full weekend's worth of work.

As you look at this space, what do you want to achieve? When you've created your ranked list of objectives, you'll have goals that may be unique

Remember...

✓ make a wish list

✓ be realistic

✓ set priorities

✓ identify your clutter problems

✓ label your zones

✓ set a timeline

to your space and lifestyle, but some common ones are:

- store off-season clothes

- pack up and pass on family memorabilia

- easily locate holiday items

These goals naturally translate into three zones. Later in this chapter, you'll learn the best ways to purge, sort, and store clothing, memorabilia, and holiday items.

If you've come up with more or different zones for this space, write them into the following table. Then take your best guess on how long it will take you to complete each task for each zone. Keep in mind you may need time to shop for new storage containers. Remember, this is just an estimate to help you plan your attic or basement decluttering project.

Zones	Step 1: Cut the clutter	Step 2: Increase storage	Step 3: Get organized
Off-season clothes			
Family memorabilia			
Holiday items			
Additional zone			

Step 1 Cut the clutter

If you're lucky enough to have a finished or partially finished, well-sealed, and insulated attic or basement, you have fewer hurdles to overcome. You can start decluttering. Otherwise, you might have to deal with these problems first.

- environmental issues — heat, cold, moisture, and air circulation

- pests

- difficult or inconvenient access

Decide if you should spend the time and money fixing a water problem or temperature extremes. If you must live with the situation as it is, you'll have to think carefully about what you can store in this space and how you should store it. For instance, you simply can't keep Christmas candles in an attic that hits 100 degrees during the summer.

Do you have room to sort out the clutter right there in your attic or basement, or will you move everything to another area?

Keep in mind

Make a decision:

✓ keep
✓ toss
✓ donate
✓ sell
✓ pass on

Follow purging rules:

✓ decide quickly
✓ handle items once
✓ set limits
✓ pass the "keep" test
✓ recognize garbage

Wherever you end up, mark out some floor space or lay down a sheet for each zone. This will help you keep things separate. Don't forget bags or boxes for trash. Now, you're going to evaluate every item in your space and make a decision.

Move as fast as you can without getting caught up in trips down memory lane. After everything is sorted and tidy, you'll have plenty of time to enjoy family mementos at your leisure.

SUPER TIPS for sorting off-season clothes

Make purging easy on yourself. Having trouble letting go? Here's one way to get motivated. Before you begin purging, pick one or two charities or organizations you feel strongly about and donate your items to them. Having a worthy destination in mind for your things should make the decision to let go a little easier.

Outfit a little one's imagination. What to do with those sequined gloves from Aunt Mae. And then there's the hat collection no one else in the family wants. Rather than tossing out some of your more interesting clothing discards, start a dress-up box. Add to it as the year progresses and you purge another season's wardrobe.

Before you tackle this unique space, you may need to gather some special equipment, like:

❑ plastic gloves   ❑ broom

❑ flashlight   ❑ shop vac

❑ insect spray   ❑ dust mask

Then give it to a young grandchild or other family member for a special birthday or Christmas present.

Offer items to shelters.

Women's shelters are usually eager for donations, with certain clothing items topping their most wanted list. Call those in your area or check them out online. Also, offer luggage if you have pieces to donate.

Encourage local actors.

Your community theater or local high school's drama department might jump at the chance to inherit some of those unusual or formal garments you don't know what to do with. Make sure everything is still wearable and give them a call.

Give the hook to misfits.

An off-season wardrobe can too easily become an off-size wardrobe. The skirt that pinches at the waist or the pants that need suspenders settle into that extra closet space and watch the other clothes rotate in and out. Just apply the same purging rules to these misfits that you do to the rest of your wardrobe — if you haven't worn it in the last two years, let it go.

DON'T STORE...

Because of temperature and moisture problems, don't store items like these in a typical attic or unfinished basement:

✓ working electronics

✓ video or audio tapes

✓ vinyl albums

✓ important financial documents

✓ boxed food

✓ fur or leather

✓ paint or other flammables

✓ rare, valuable, or extremely fragile collectibles

✓ musical instruments

✓ any type of animal food, like birdseed or dog food, that could attract pests

If you get in a real storage jam — and have the money — consider storing out-of-season clothes at your local dry cleaners. Originally designed for furs, many offer this service for all types of clothing. The garments are stored in a vault that protects them from mildew, insects, fire, and other home disasters.

SUPER TIPS for sorting family memorabilia

Rank mementos to ease the parting. At first glance, all that family memorabilia is equally important to you. So how on earth are you going to declutter? Ask yourself this question. "If I could save five things from a fire, what would I choose?" Those five items are definite keepers. Now work your way through everything else, ranking as you go.

Share family treasures now. As soon as family members are old enough to take care of special memorabilia, start giving them as gifts. This can apply to furniture, clothing, linens, knickknacks, or whatever. It's a great way to start doling out all those photographs you have stacked up.

Outsmart clutter with a keepsake quilt. Special memories come in many forms — baby's first blanket, a sports jersey from the championship game, your prom dress, souvenir T-shirts by the truckload. And there can be no better gift than a quilt made from pieces of memorable clothing. Find a theme, whether it's for one person, from one trip, or representing one decade, and gather articles of clothing that fit the theme. If you can sew, tackle the project yourself. Otherwise, contact a local quilting guild and see if you can commission the piece. You'll not only clear out boxes of old clothing, you'll create a new and special piece of memorabilia.

Rescue family heirlooms from never-never land. You can save attic space and money at the same time — simply get those beautiful keepsakes out of storage and onto your dining room table, living room display shelf, or guest bed. Whether it's family china, heirloom crystal, or hand-embroidered linens, use them. Dinners will feel special and guests pampered if there's a memory or story behind every item. And you won't spend money on things you already have. Just think how happy that would make Grandma.

Turn memorabilia into art. While you're wavering between the "toss" and the "keep" piles, take another look at the thing in your hands. Is there a way to turn this half-trash, half-treasure whatever into something decorative or useful? Take those scarves you flaunted in the 80s. How would that geometric one look as a drapery tieback in the guest bedroom? There are bronzing companies that preserve such diverse pieces of memorabilia as pacifiers, hats, cleats, footballs, and boots. These could make interesting bookends or doorstops. Laminate small items. Frame sheet music. Put a delicate fan into a shadowbox. Get creative with the things that have special meaning to you, and you may find a way to enjoy them every day.

Display collectibles with style. What a surprise to discover you have enough snow globes from around the country to make an interesting collection. And surely those signed concert tickets deserve a special viewing. A tasteful grouping of almost any kind of memorabilia can turn clutter into art. Instead of hiding these special mementos, show them off — whether it's a shelf over a window, a shadowbox hung in the study, a pretty scrapbook, or a special display case. Just remember — your collectibles will be easier to clean if they are behind glass or inside an album.

Curtail keepsakes with a steamer trunk. It's easy for memorabilia to get out of hand. Set limits by purchasing a storage container, like a steamer trunk, for each family member. Here's the catch — you may only keep whatever will fit into your trunk.

Save space with a snapshot. If a sentimental item is taking up valuable space, and you don't really like it, take a picture of it for posterity, then give it away or donate it to a worthy cause.

Appraise antiques before you sell. Everyone's heard the story of the million-dollar garage sale find. And while you rejoice with the lucky buyer, what about the seller who unwittingly gave away a fortune? Don't let that be you. If there's even a chance you could have a hidden gem in your "sell" pile, get a professional opinion before you open your yard sale to the public. Call on a local antiques dealer and see if they'll offer a bid on any of your pieces.

Uncover valuable family gems. Inherited jewelry deserves better than a box in your basement. First, take everything you find to a reputable jeweler for a once-over. See what's worth repairing, cleaning, or resetting. Ask which pieces should be appraised and insured. Even if you don't discover the mother lode, consider wearing things you like and passing special pieces on to family members.

Give an old fur a new life. You've inherited Aunt Edna's fur coat, but you can't seem to work it into your wardrobe. So there it sits in storage — year after year. Fortunately, many enterprising companies are just waiting to turn that beautiful fur into something you'll love. The choices are endless, but if you want to simply restyle it into something more modern, consider some of these:

- the lining for a jean jacket
- trim on a leather coat
- a sporty vest
- detachable collar and cuffs
- a hat or earmuffs
- a purse
- a throw or pillows
- slippers

But perhaps the most charming makeover idea is turning your old fur into a soft, cuddly teddy bear. These heirloom bears are terrific for display or gift-giving. Look in your Yellow Pages or search the Internet for companies specializing in fur makeovers.

Divvy up treasures at family gatherings. The perfect time to pass on heirlooms is when family members gather together. Schedule time at your next reunion or holiday dinner for others to look through items you don't want. You may be surprised to learn that your sister has always wanted that old armoire gathering dust in your attic. Just make sure you've arranged transportation for the larger pieces so they can leave at the same time your family does.

Hold a ceremony to help you let go. It can be especially hard to let go of personal possessions of family members who have died, and experts say don't trivialize this. Instead, turn it into an opportunity to honor them. Decide what you are comfortable with — whether it's a formal ceremony with family and friends or simply a quiet moment by yourself — but choose a manner to say goodbye to special items, then give them to a worthy organization.

Preserve items for posterity. A piece of your family history might also be a piece of local history. Consider donating the family memorabilia that's cluttering up your attic to a local history museum. The museum curators will probably take better care of your stuff than you do — and you can always visit your exhibit. Museum-worthy items include those related to a war or local business.

SUPER TIPS for sorting holiday items

Hand down childhood ornaments. At some point, all your children's handmade holiday ornaments and decorations become family memorabilia. If you no longer display them and your children have homes of their own, pass these treasures on to them.

Trim gifts with unused ornaments. Don't throw out ornaments you no longer use. Instead of spending money on bows, use these extras to decorate gift packages. Simply tie them on securely with coordinating ribbon and you've cut clutter and saved money at the same time.

Slipcover your pillows to save space and money. If you buy fancy holiday pillows, you'll clean out your wallet in

Avoid duplicate decorations. Know what holiday items you have before you go shopping, and you won't impulsively buy that second turkey platter. If you shop the after-holiday sales, your current decorations will still be fresh in your mind.

a hurry and then have to find space to store them. Instead, buy holiday fabric just after the holiday — when it goes on sale — and use it to make slipcovers for pillows you already have. It's a lot easier to store slipcovers than whole pillows.

Now that you're left with just the items you're going to keep, and they are spread out all over the floor, use this as an opportunity to document your possessions for insurance purposes. This will help limit your losses in case they are destroyed, damaged, or stolen and will make sure you get the money you're owed if you have to file a claim.

❑ **Use a regular camera** or video camera to make a record of everything.

❑ **List serial numbers,** make, model, purchase date, and purchase price of special items.

❑ **Ask your insurer** for a home inventory form to make this easier.

❑ **Store all documentation** in a safe deposit box.

Simplify your gift wrap collection. Instead of buying a mountain of specialized holiday wrapping paper, cut down on the amount and variety you need to store by choosing just a few solid colors. White, gold, silver — and red or blue — will take you through almost every holiday or celebration. Keep this multipurpose collection easy to get to since you'll be tapping into it throughout the year. Buy ribbons and bows as needed to personalize the package.

Let baskets do double duty. Don't create more clutter by buying a special basket for little ones every year at Easter.

Take any basket you have around the house and decorate it to match the occasion. When Easter is over, it can go back to its original duties.

Donate and toss without delay. Your final purging step is to dispose of all boxes and bags right away. Contact family members and commit to a date and time for the handoff of any items you're passing on. Take trash to the bin or the curb. "Donate" boxes go straight into the trunk of your car. There can be no detour to your back porch, guest bedroom, or garage. You absolutely must move all these items out of your house and on to their next home before you forget what's going where and why.

Step 2 Increase storage

Unlike most other rooms, basements and attics are often uniquely configured. Yours may have strange little angles or odd bits of space tucked here and there around pipes. Measure and map it all. You want to take advantage of every bit of potential storage. When you're evaluating how to use wall space, consider building shelves under your stairs, between wall studs, or under the eaves.

Remember...

✓ map your space

✓ shop for containers

SUPER TIPS *for storing off-season clothing*

Nix the cardboard. Because you're working in a space that might be exposed to moisture and pests, use only sturdy, waterproof, airtight storage containers — not cardboard boxes. Choose ones with handles and snap-on lids.

No more wire hangers. Experts say to replace all your wire hangers with sturdy wooden or plastic ones. They won't rust onto your clothes, and because they are wider, they'll allow more air circulation between garments.

Box the bedlam. Clear plastic, shoe box-size containers are great for everything from winter accessories to handbags to — well — shoes. They stack neatly, and you can easily see what's inside.

Shield shoes from dust. Keep sturdy, gallon-size, self-sealing plastic bags on hand. They are great for keeping shoes dust-free until you're ready to wear them next season.

Shrink storage woes down to size. Vacuum-sealed storage bags may be the best storage investment you

Toss without a thought

✓ clothes you haven't worn in the last two years

✓ decorations you haven't put up in the last two years

✓ old high school or college textbooks

✓ original packing cartons unless you plan to move in the next two years or they contained electronics that must be returned for repair in their original carton

✓ things that go to things you no longer own

✓ clothing that's mildewed or moth-eaten

✓ appliances beyond repair

✓ duplicate items

can make. These sturdy, plastic bags come in a variety of sizes and are perfect for storing linens and clothing. You simply fill, zip shut, and remove the air inside with a vacuum hose. The contents compress to a fraction of their original size while remaining safe from insects, dust, moisture, and odors because of the airtight seal. You can find these vacuum-sealed bags at most home stores and on the Internet.

Recycle product bags as free storage. Whenever you bring something home from the store, stop and examine its container before you throw it away. For instance, the plastic zippered bags that sheets, blankets, duvet covers, and comforters come in are perfect for corralling swimwear, ski socks, or whatever. You might want to put these bags into something sturdier, like a plastic tub, but since they are clear, you can quickly see what's inside.

The National Cleaners Association wants you to take the plastic dry cleaner bags off your garments before storing them. These experts say the long-term use of plastic covers will suffocate the garment, possibly causing stains, mildew, or other problems. They recommend hanging garments for storage inside unbleached, ventilated, cotton covers. An unbleached white sheet works perfectly.

Repel critters with cedar. Cedar's essential oils smell good to people but not to pests. A well-made cedar trunk will keep away nearly every kind of animal or insect that might have designs on your stored duds.

Seal out unpleasant odors. A secondhand wooden trunk or other storage unit is an economical way to corral off-season clothes. But if it came with the lingering odor of mothballs, you may be rethinking your bargain. Get rid of the smell by sanding the inside, then coating with polyurethane.

Put your luggage to work. Suitcases make great storage containers. Put last season's clothes inside old pillowcases, then into your suitcases. This way, you can simply remove the filled pillowcase when you need the suitcase for a trip. Don't let this overlooked space go to waste.

Stored furniture offers extra storage. Why let that piece of furniture you're saving for posterity just sit empty? Fill it with off-season clothes, papers, or what have you, and you'll double your efficiency. First, make sure it is appropriate storage for your items. You may still have to protect the contents from moisture, dust, and pests.

Look up for inspiration. Exposed ceiling joists don't have to be an eyesore. Think of them as storage opportunities. If you have the headroom, hang any kind of sturdy bar or pole from hooks and, voila, instant clothing rods.

Calm clothing chaos with garment racks. Leave your off-season clothes on hangers, and you'll make switching wardrobes a snap. If you've got the space, set up a portable garment rack, preferably one on wheels. Then make sure everything is on good quality hangers — wooden or sturdy plastic instead of wire. Protect with cloth garment bags or drape sheets over the whole rack.

Dangle boots for smart storage. Boots will always be a winter wardrobe staple, and they will always pose a summer storage problem. But now you can keep them out of the way during the off-season, while still helping them maintain their shape. Simply stuff a bit of crumpled paper inside, then clip the top of each boot onto a sturdy skirt hanger — one clip for each boot. Cut a slit in an old pillowcase and slip over the boots, hanger and all. Tie the bottom shut with a twist tie or bit of string for even more dust protection. Now suspend the hanger from a ceiling rod or wall hook.

SUPER TIPS *for storing family memorabilia*

Recycle kitchen cabinets for added storage. Someone is always remodeling a kitchen. It may even be you. Don't let those old cabinets wind up in the landfill. They make excellent storage in a basement or attic. Who cares if they are Early American?

Consult experts when storing valuables. Historic documents and other important, but fragile, pieces of history should not be tossed willy-nilly into the family trunk in the basement. They shouldn't even be placed in there carefully. If you want to preserve something of value, talk with an expert. For instance, the Library of Congress Preservation Directorate does not recommend laminating newsprint since it damages the paper. They say to make a photocopy and store the original in a flat, custom box available from archival suppliers. Keep it away from moisture, heat, pollutants, dust, and pests. If you have a special item to preserve for future generations, call an antiques dealer for advice.

File school memories. An accordion file is useful for storing school papers — a partition for each school year. Remember, you don't need to save every piece of homework or every story. Pick ones that have special meaning to you. Then label the file with your child's name plus "School K-12."

Roll up cherished art. Save children's artwork by rolling it up inside empty paper towel or wrapping paper tubes. Stick a label on the outside with the child's name and date. These are easy to store and won't ruin little treasures.

Keep special flowers uncrushed. Store your wedding bouquet, anniversary corsage, or other sentimental arrangement inside an old, clean, plastic food container. Poke a hole in the lid and thread the flower stems through from the inside. Snap the lid onto the container, and your flowers should rest safe and secure inside.

SUPER TIPS for storing holiday items

Discover neglected wall space. The walls on either side of your basement or attic staircase are often overlooked areas for extra storage. Measure carefully and see if you have room for Pegboard, shelves, or cabinets. At the very least, you should be able to hang slim items, like wreaths.

Drape with cloth for simple storage. Sometimes you have an item to store that's simply too large to fit into any container. Painter's dropcloths are fairly inexpensive and perfect for this situation. In some cases, an old sheet will work if you just need to keep the dust off. If possible, tuck in or tie the bottom.

Store decorations with ease. Get a sturdy skirt hanger and clip hanging decorations to it. Cut a small slit in the bottom of a plastic trash bag and slip it over the hanger, working the hanger's hook through the slit. Tie the bottom of the bag shut to keep dust out. Label the bag so you'll know what you've got inside. Another option is to use a recycled dry cleaning bag. These are already set up to slip over a hanger, and they are clear, so you can see your decoration.

Wage war on wrinkled linens. Last year, you carefully folded and packed away your poinsettia tablecloth. Unfortunately, now it's a mess of wrinkles and creases. Avoid this hassle next year by using well-padded hangers or rods to store your linens. You can either buy sturdy hangers at your local home store or suspend a large wooden dowel from the ceiling. Drape your linens over the hanger or rod and cover with a clean sheet.

Give holiday tins a new life. Holiday tins filled with cookies, popcorn, candy, or nuts make great gifts. If you are the lucky recipient, why not find a new life for the tins after the treats are gone? They make attractive and handy storage bins for ornaments and holiday lights.

Cushion your treasures with air. Don't lose precious ornaments to packing mishaps. Keep them safe until next year by storing them in sealable plastic bags. Place one ornament in each bag and use a straw to blow air into the bag while sealing it. Pack these little "balloon" bags loosely in a sturdy storage box.

Battle breakage with egg cartons. If an egg carton can safely guard a dozen fragile eggs, it can do the same for other small breakables. Use egg cartons to store all your delicate holiday treasures.

Put an end to ornament bedlam. Go shopping after the holidays and pick up some specialty storage containers while they are on sale. The ones that have smaller, divided sections inside are particularly useful for keeping ornaments organized. That means you can throw away all the individual boxes cluttering up your attic. Store the ornaments by type, color, or use. Label each box and see how easy decorating is next year.

Wrap lights to avoid tangles. Don't throw away those empty gift wrap cardboard tubes. Wind your holiday lights around them, and you'll never have to wrestle with snarls and knots again. Cut small slits in each end of the tube and slip in the wire near the plug. A piece of tape over the slit will hold each end of your light strand securely in place.

Keep gift bows perky. Even if "Thrifty" isn't your middle name, you probably recycle gift bows. But it's hard to pass one off the second or third time around if it's smashed flat. Here's a great way to store them. First, decide on a type of bag to use — self-sealing plastic, small trash or grocery, paper — then fill loosely with bows. Now hang your bow-filled bags from the ceiling, and you'll be ready to wrap at a moment's notice. If you really want to be organized, group your bows by theme or color.

Think vertically when storing wrapping paper. Stand up rolls of wrapping paper in a tall trash can. Put the bin in a corner or against the wall, and you've barely used any space at all.

Step 3 Get organized

You might find broken treasures, mildewed boxes, or surprises of a creepier kind. If you want to turn this place of the unclaimed and forgotten into a bright and well-ordered space, you must learn about careful storage.

If water is an issue, make sure everything is up off the floor. Get wooden pallets from local stores or businesses and place your storage containers on top. Even a few pieces of lumber will save treasures from accidental flooding.

Remember...

✓ pack properly

✓ label

Check the floor structure of your attic, too, making sure it's sturdy enough to bear the weight of anything you plan to put up there. Placing sheets of plywood over the exposed floor beams is a good idea.

Don't stack large containers more than two or three high or two deep. You don't want to work too hard to get the container you need.

For even easier retrieval of your stored goods, consider some type of inventory system. Take the diagram of your attic or basement you sketched out earlier in this chapter and pencil in — either generally or specifically depending on your level of organization — where items are stored. Put this labeled diagram in a clear plastic bag or page protector and hang it by the door. Not only will it help you remember where you put things, it will also guide other family members in finding and replacing items. Update the map as needed.

Some organizing experts recommend numbering every container. Then on numbered index cards, list the contents of each corresponding box. You can see at a glance that Box #3 contains your Christmas stockings and tree skirt. A small file box keeps all the index cards neat and handy.

If you want to take this system to a higher level of technology, use a simple spreadsheet program on your computer. Keep a running alphabetized list of all your stored items in one column and the corresponding box number in a second column. You can easily sort, group, and find anything on your list.

SUPER TIPS for organizing off-season clothing

Let a photo do the talking. Need a particular sweater before winter arrives? Don't spend hours hunting through every sweater box. Take a snapshot of each container's contents and tape it onto the front. You'll know at a glance which one houses your favorite argyle without opening a single lid.

Clean before you store. The National Cleaners Association says to always dry-clean or launder your clothes before you store them. Stains, body oils, and perspiration attract moths and other pests. For even more protection, you can have your dry cleaner mothproof your clothes before you pack them away. This is a chemical treatment that guards against insects but doesn't leave an odor, like mothballs and other preparations.

Keep off-season ready to wear. Organizing experts recommend you keep off-season clothes always in "ready-to-wear" mode. That means you should be able to grab an item out of storage and put it on immediately. Who knows when an exciting trip to a different climate could pop up. So if you've packed things away dirty, torn, or otherwise unwearable, you might have to cancel that last-minute holiday to the Caribbean. What a shame.

Reward special clothes with tender, loving care. You may have a few pieces of special clothing you don't wear too often — like a tuxedo or formal gown, a costume from a special party, or a uniform from your younger days. They don't belong all jumbled together in one box.

Instead, separate them into your zones. The evening wear deserves special storage and labeling all its own. A formal occasion could spring up any time of the year, and you need to be able to put your hands on that elegant black dress quickly. Consider hanging this type of clothing near your off-season storage and inside a clean, moth-repellent garment bag to avoid wrinkles and pests. Costumes can logically go with your holiday storage, and your cheer-leading sweater is a piece of memorabilia you'll want to hold on to for posterity.

Chase away pests with cedar chips. Not everyone can afford a cedar chest to store woolens. But a simple trip to the pet store solves that dilemma. Buy cedar chips designed for small animal cages and fill bags of cheese-cloth. Tie them and place in your storage container.

Overpower moths with a fragrant spice. Moths hate mothballs, but so do people. Why not protect your clothes with something that works great and smells good, too? Put whole cloves in the pockets of wool coats before stor-ing them. You can also make a moth repellent using cloves and cheesecloth. Take a square of cheesecloth, drop some cloves in the center, gather the four corners together, tie shut, and hang it with your clothes. Your storage area will have a pleasant scent, but moths won't bother to stop by.

Do away with moths. Here's a moth repellent you'll find in your pantry — black pepper. Sprinkle some on clothes before storing them for the season, and you'll send moths away sneezing.

Neutralize unpleasant odors. Stick a dryer sheet inside containers, especially those containing shoes. The contents will smell fresh and clean next season.

Retain shape with newspaper. Stuff hats and handbags with newspaper so they'll keep their shape in storage. If you're putting sneakers away for the season, crumple up newspaper and put it inside each shoe. This will get rid of that locker room odor.

SUPER TIPS for organizing family memorabilia

Color-code your family. Many organizers say you can cut down on storage confusion by assigning each family member a color. This way, you'll know at a glance that all of John's mementos are in the blue boxes and Sandy's are in green. If you can't find containers to match your colors, use stickers, markers, ribbon, or yarn.

Store framed items upright. Don't lay pictures, paintings, or mirrors flat to store them. Stand them up and they're less likely to crack or sustain other damage. Sandwich them between sheets of cardboard or Styrofoam for even safer storage.

Put an end to mildew. Before boxing up books for storage, put a piece of activated charcoal inside to absorb moisture, which encourages mildew to take up residence. You can find activated charcoal at pet supply stores.

Freeze out odors. Older books stored in a basement or attic can develop a musty smell. Place them in a frost-free freezer overnight. In the morning, they'll smell fresh once more.

Halt mildew with cornstarch. Old or stored books are magnets for mildew, but you can use simple cornstarch to get rid of the problem. First, brush off dry or loose mold with a clean, soft cloth. Then sprinkle cornstarch on the pages to absorb any moisture. Let the book sit open, with the pages fanned out, for several hours. After that, gently brush off the cornstarch.

SUPER TIPS for organizing holiday items

Simplify holiday decorating. Take the guesswork out of holiday decorating next year by snapping photos of different areas of your home. Tuck the photo inside the box with all the supplies for that spot. For instance, if you've got your mantel decorated perfectly, photograph it and store the photo with the garland, beads, pine cones, and bows, right down to the twist ties you need to hook everything together. Then label the storage box "Mantel."

Locate holiday essentials fast. After a long afternoon picking out the perfect Christmas tree, the last thing you want to do is dig through storage boxes to find your tree stand. Avoid this yearly hassle by boldly labeling one box "Open me first." In this box, put your tree stand, extension cords, and anything else you'll need to kick start the holidays.

Use colors to categorize decorations. Color code your holiday storage containers and you'll never pull out shamrocks in December again. Use red for Christmas, orange for Halloween, and so on. If you can't find colors to match the holiday, at least be consistent — a single color for each celebration. Then label, label, label. If you don't have a label maker, large holiday-themed stickers help distinguish between gray rubber totes.

Deck the halls with ease. Who says you have to take everything apart to pack it away? Leave the lights on your wreaths or garland and simply place the whole setup in a storage container. Look at each item critically as you prepare to put it away. Are there parts or pieces that can stay where they are without becoming damaged in storage?

Pack parts with their partners. Pieces that go together should be stored together. Put your wreath hanger in the box with your wreath. Keep an extension cord with your lighted village set. If you need twist ties to attach your garland to the mantel, tuck those in your storage container.

Keep spares handy. Place a package of extra bulbs inside your holiday lights storage container. That way, if one burns out, you won't have to make a special trip to the store.

Hang wreaths to store. If you don't store your wreaths in special storage boxes made especially for them, consider placing them inside a trash bag or sheet to keep the dust out and then hanging them on the wall. It's a great use of underutilized space.

If you don't have any other system for storing your holiday decorations, at least keep like items together. You may be surprised at your collection of snowmen once you have them in a group.

Recycle solo socks. Don't discard those unpaired socks your dryer occasionally spits out. Save them to cushion delicate holiday ornaments. Slip a treasured decoration inside an old, heavy sock and then into your storage container.

Protect holiday china. Don't take up valuable kitchen space with special holiday dishes you only use once a year. Pack them in sturdy storage containers and label them clearly. Just be sure you take the time to protect them inside the storage containers. A coffee filter is an inexpensive way to separate plates and bowls. It keeps them from scratching each other during storage. And slip a toilet paper tube over the spout of your holiday china teapot, and it won't get chipped.

Re-roll wrapping paper to keep it safe. You saved all your leftover wrapping paper from last Christmas, but it managed to unravel and tear in the storage box. This time, unroll all of the leftover paper, then roll it tightly to fit inside the cardboard tube. Your paper will be in perfect condition for next season.

Dispense wrapping paper like the pros. Take an empty wrapping paper tube and cut it lengthwise. Slip it over a new roll and feed the end of the paper through the slit. Now you can neatly pull out and tear off just the amount you need, and the roll won't unravel and tear during storage.

Step 4 Keep it clean

Before you put even one shoe box back into your basement or attic, get the space as clean and safe as possible.

- Sweep, mop, vacuum, wash, and dust whatever surfaces you can.

- Paint the last step of your dark basement stairs with white enamel. Even if your basement is a dungeon, you'll see it coming and avoid a fall.

- Add or update lighting if possible. You want to be able to see, so put in maximum watt bulbs. If there's no light switch right at the entrance, install a wall-mounted flashlight within easy reach of the door. Check its batteries periodically.

- Install smoke detectors and carbon monoxide alarms.

- If you're always bumping your head on the basement stairwell, it's unlikely you can rip out the header beam. The best thing to do is paint the overhead a bright or even neon color.

SUPER TIPS *for cleaning the attic or basement*

Access attic storage with ease. A folding or disappearing stairway is a great way to access your attic storage. They are available in aluminum, wood, and steel, and you can buy them from most home improvement and hardware stores, as well as from specialty companies online. Installing one

When cleaning out your basement, don't get rid of everything. In fact, you may need to add some important supplies. In case of an emergency, such as a natural disaster or terrorist attack, here's what every home should have. These simple items could save your life.

❑ bottled water

❑ sleeping bags

❑ canned food

❑ first-aid kit

❑ portable radio with batteries

❑ flashlight with batteries

yourself takes a little construction know-how, usually two people, and a bit of muscle, so make sure you're prepared. Otherwise, hire someone to do the installation for you.

Tim Carter, who writes a nationally syndicated column called *Ask the Builder*, says many folding attic ladders are poorly constructed and dangerous. He offers this advice:

❑ **Look for thick steps and sides** — at least three-fourths of an inch — with a metal rod under each tread.

❑ **Do the math** to make sure the weight bearing capacity of the ladder is sufficient for you plus anything you'll be carrying up and down the stairs. The minimum should be 250 pounds.

❑ **Check all the hardware.** Heavier means more durable.

❑ **Choose a system that matches** the amount of use it will receive.

❑ **Read the warranty** so you know how long the staircase should last.

❑ **Follow the instructions very carefully** if you install it yourself.

Conduct an annual checkup. Inspect everything in your attic or basement at least once a year. This way, you can get a jump on problems that have cropped up and deal with any damage.

Regulate extreme attic temperatures. Here's how you can protect belongings stored in your attic from extremes in temperature:

- Make insulation a top priority. The recommended level for most attics is to insulate to R-38 or about 10 to 14 inches deep, depending on the insulation type. A quick way to tell if you've got enough is to see if the floor joists are visible. If they are, you probably need more insulation.

- Plug any gaps you find around plumbing, light and electrical fixtures, chimneys, and under the eaves.

- Install attic vents and open them during the summer to let hot air escape.

- Suck hot air out during the day and blow cool air in at night by installing a reversible fan.

Keep your basement dry. Check your basement regularly for leaks or damp areas. A water problem can play havoc with anything you store there. Hang a mirror on the wall overnight. In the morning, if the mirror is fogged, you have a problem with moisture in the air — or condensation. If the mirror is dry while the wall is damp, you probably have one or more cracks in the wall allowing moisture to seep through. Follow these suggestions for a dryer basement:

- Buy a dehumidifier to remove moisture in the air.

- Repair any damaged faucets and pipes under your house.

- Use mold-resistant paint on the floor and walls.

- Seal cracks or contact a professional.

Do away with musty basement smell. Want an easy way to get rid of that musty basement smell once and for all? Mix 10 pounds of cat litter with 5 pounds of baking soda. Every week, put 2 inches of this mixture in shallow pans and place them around your basement.

Watch out for safety hazards. In your organizing zeal, don't forget to leave a clear path to and from important mechanical systems, like the furnace. And don't stack anything too close to them. Besides avoiding a potential fire hazard, you must leave enough room for a mechanic or repairman to have access.

Try these home remedies for deterring attic- or basement-bound critters, big and small.

❏ **Scatter mothballs** around walls to discourage mice, spiders, and silverfish.

❏ **Tuck steel wool into cracks** and holes. Mice can't chew their way through.

❏ **Sprinkle baking soda** anywhere you suspect mice are visiting.

❏ **Leave out mint leaves** or cotton balls soaked in peppermint oil extract. Mice can't stand the smell of peppermint.

CHAPTER 14
Garage Sales

Your house is decluttered, and you're ready for a garage sale. You might call it a yard sale or a tag sale, but the principle is the same — you're getting rid of your clutter by offering others a bargain.

You can make big bucks on a garage sale if you have enough of the right kind of stuff. If not, you're still a two-way winner because you're reducing your clutter and putting cash in your pocket at the same time. Whatever the amount, it's money you wouldn't have had, and it might be enough so you can afford to redecorate some of the newly uncluttered areas of your home.

On the following pages are insider secrets from garage sale gurus for getting the most for your stuff.

Here are four great tips to get you started:

- *Organize early.* Make plans well ahead of time for when and where your sale will be. When you ask others for help with inventory or manpower, give them plenty of lead time.

- *Advertise wisely.* The more customers you attract, the better your selling chances. You have more potential buyers, and people in a crowd are more apt to grab an item before someone else gets it.

- *Price competitively.* Remember, your goal is to get rid of it all for the best possible price. Do some research to find the going rate for things and set your prices accordingly.

- *Sell sensibly.* Create an atmosphere that encourages buying. Be willing to negotiate and don't be greedy. You're better off selling something cheap than being stuck with it at the end of the day.

Pick the best day for your sale. Friday and Saturday are the traditional days for garage sales, but some people start on Thursday to get a head start on the competition. Pick a weekend when you can give your full attention to the sale and check local schedules for other activities that could either enhance or take away from your event. Stay away from major holidays, like Memorial Day and the Fourth of July, but don't be too concerned about Mother's Day and Father's Day.

Be aware of local restrictions. Checking for restrictions is one of the first things you should do when planning your garage sale. You may need to register your sale or

You need to have room for extra cars to park at your garage sale. If not, you could have problems with potential customers, neighbors, and even the police. Without adequate parking, you're better off having your sale at someone else's house or renting space at a community garage sale or flea market.

obtain a permit from your city, county, or homeowners association. Sales might even be banned completely in your neighborhood. Find out also about parking regulations and local policy on temporary signs.

Talk with your neighbors. Multiple-family garage sales attract more customers so check with your neighbors, friends, and family to see if anyone wants to join you. You can share advertising costs, get extra help, and have a wider variety of items to sell. Even if your neighbors don't want to participate, they'll appreciate knowing your plans so the extra traffic won't come as a surprise.

Be ready for unpleasant weather. Your garage sale doesn't have to be inside your garage, but you're better off if it is. Then you have everything in a sheltered area in case it's rainy, windy, or unbearably hot in the sun. If your sale is actually a yard sale or a driveway sale, consider rigging a tarp over some or all of it in case the weather report isn't on your side.

Accumulate garage sale items as you go. An excellent decluttering tool is a box in your basement or some other out-of-the-way place for potential garage sale inventory. Whenever you run across an item you don't think you need any more, retire it to the box. If it stays there for several months, it's safe to say you won't want it again. When you're ready for a garage sale, you already have a head start on merchandise to sell.

Advertise according to local custom. Get in tune with the garage sale culture in your area and advertise the way other people do. That's where your buyers will be looking for information. If there isn't an established custom, then look for the most effective way to reach people who will come and buy things at your sale. Your primary tools will be newspaper ads and signs. Other methods are flyers,

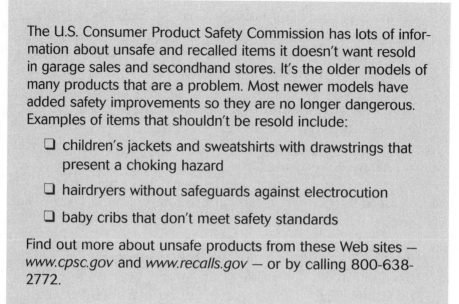

The U.S. Consumer Product Safety Commission has lots of information about unsafe and recalled items it doesn't want resold in garage sales and secondhand stores. It's the older models of many products that are a problem. Most newer models have added safety improvements so they are no longer dangerous. Examples of items that shouldn't be resold include:

❑ children's jackets and sweatshirts with drawstrings that present a choking hazard

❑ hairdryers without safeguards against electrocution

❑ baby cribs that don't meet safety standards

Find out more about unsafe products from these Web sites — *www.cpsc.gov* and *www.recalls.gov* — or by calling 800-638-2772.

word-of-mouth, and the Internet. There may even be a local radio station that has a buy and sell call-in program. If there aren't many other sales going on, you'll want to start advertising a week or two in advance. At the height of the season, wait until the previous week's sales are over before you start advertising yours.

Pump up your ad with important details. Time, date, and place are the most essential elements of all your pre-sale advertising. How big the sale is and the fantastic bargains you offer make no difference if people don't know when and where to come. Signs you only put up on the day of the sale still need directions, but sale hours aren't very important. Flyers and newspaper ads should mention something about the merchandise to attract buyers' attention. Tools, antiques, furniture, and children's clothing are some of the standard eye-catchers. Other categories vary from region to region. If you have room in the ad — and if it's important in your market area — you can include details, like sizes and name brands, but generally use as few words as possible.

Pick a paper that delivers customers. The newspaper advertisement for your garage sale will likely be your largest single expense, so you want to make sure it does some good. In large cities, an ad in the major daily paper may not be worth it because you're paying more to reach people who live miles away and will never come to your sale. Instead, find a community weekly or a free distribution newspaper that everyone in your neighborhood reads. Do a little research and find out where the serious shoppers look before setting out on their weekly trek to all the sales.

Plant signs to get the word out. Start putting out signs in your neighborhood several days before your garage sale, and make sure the dates are clear. You don't want people showing up before the actual day of the sale. Put them at high-traffic intersections and streets within a two-mile radius of your house.

Find out what the local rules and regulations are before you start putting up your signs. In some places, it's illegal to put signs on a public right-of-way. Sometimes it's allowed as long as you don't leave them up too long. If you put a sign in someone else's yard, get their permission first. Utility poles are not a good idea because leftover nails and staples become a safety hazard — and it might also be illegal. Your best bet is to see where other signs are posted and follow suit.

Create easy-to-read signs. Make sure your signs are big enough that drivers can read them as they go by. Use large letters, few words, and eye-catching colors — yellow and lime-green work well for backgrounds and bright red and basic black are best for lettering. If you print well, then hand-letter your signs. Otherwise, consider stencils or your home computer printer. Attach your signs to heavy cardboard or light plywood for stability. Test the readability of your sign by putting it up in your front yard and driving by yourself.

When you let a political candidate put his sign in your yard, hang on to it after the election. You can use it later to advertise your garage sale. It's a perfect framework and backing for a temporary sign. Just staple your own sign on top of the original and stick it back in the ground.

Spread the word to attract a crowd. Word-of-mouth is both an effective and a cost-effective form of advertising. Tell friends, family, and coworkers about your sale and ask them to spread the word. You can also hand out flyers and put notices on community bulletin boards in grocery stores, self-service laundries, and other places. Use your computer to design and print an attractive flyer or hand letter one and use a copy machine for a larger supply.

Consider advertising on the Internet. You might be able to advertise your garage sale on the Internet. Look for a local Web site that is frequented regularly by people in your community.

Learn what the market will bear. Every area has its own customs and pricing structures. If you're not familiar with this culture, attend a few sales while getting ready for your own. Read the ads, check out the signs, and see what's selling and what's not selling. Then you'll have a better idea of how to market and price your merchandise. Just remember, your goal is to clear your clutter, not add to it, so don't be tempted to buy things at the sales you visit.

Get a handle on fair pricing. Pricing is your biggest task, but you should have a price on every item before you start your sale. Then you have a price you've thought about instead of making it up on the spur of the moment. Customers are more trusting when they don't have to ask about prices. Mark the price on pieces of masking tape or special stickers, and use bigger stickers on bigger items so they can be seen easily. A general rule is to price at 20 to 25 percent of retail cost, but take into consideration the demand for particular items. You may be able to get more for some things and considerably less for others.

Sometimes certain collectibles, furniture, or antiques can be quite valuable. If you think an item you're selling has extra value, have it appraised. You can also check printed guides or online to get a feel for the going price.

Leave some wiggle room in your prices. Garage sale shoppers are notorious bargain hunters, so it's a good idea to set your prices just a little higher than what you want to get. Then when a buyer wants to haggle, you can jump right in. Don't price so high you scare the customer away. Getting a good price is secondary to getting rid of your junk.

Size up the situation. The best-selling clothing is usually kids' clothing, but even adult clothing will sell if you price it cheap enough. If you have a lot of adult clothing that's still in style and good shape, you might get more money for it at a consignment or secondhand shop. Make it easier for buyers by labeling and sorting clothing according to size and call attention to popular brand names. Don't price clothes with stains or excess wear higher than a quarter.

Sell faster with group pricing. Bundling is an old but effective retailer's trick. Dishes, cups, and things that come in sets will sell faster if you price them six for a dollar instead of 15 cents apiece. Books, albums, and things with titles seem to do better individually, but you can still give bulk discounts such as 25 cents each or five for a dollar. You can also give bundled prices for unrelated items. Set up a table with just items priced at $5 each and put up a sign offering any three for $12.

Code price tags for multifamily sale. Use different colored labels for price tags when you go in with someone else for a garage sale. Stick each person's price tag on a different page of a notebook as items are sold. At the end of the day, add up each page to see how much money each seller has coming. Be sure and change the amount when you sell something for less than the tag amount.

Attract customers with organized display. A disorganized garage sale will quickly turn customers away, but do it right and your merchandise display can be your best advertising. Put smaller things together and arrange them attractively on tables where they can be easily seen. Don't make shoppers sort through piles of clothes or boxes of junk. Get as many tables as you can find — card tables, Ping-Pong tables, plywood-on-sawhorse tables — and leave room to walk between them. Set larger items in your yard or along your driveway, with high-interest items the most visible.

Entice drive-by shoppers to stop. Set your more-interesting items nearest the street to attract people driving by. Be sure to emphasize things many men are interested in, too. Although many women put "I Brake for Yard Sales" bumper stickers on their cars, their husbands might be just as happy to drive by. A garden tiller or a table saw is almost guaranteed to draw a crowd.

Keep items you don't want to sell out of sight. Otherwise, those might be the things your customers want the most. If you can't put them away somewhere, put up a tarp or curtain in front of where they are stored.

Clean up your inventory to boost sales. Bright, shiny merchandise sells a lot better than dull, dusty garage sale stuff. Just a little cleaning effort can really boost your sales. Run dishes through your dishwasher to get rid of dust and grime, and throw some clothes in your washing machine. You'll get a better price for clean, fresh-smelling clothing on hangers than for stained and rumpled items tossed into boxes.

Lure customers with freebies. Appliances that need repair, games that don't have all the pieces, and old T-shirts that are only good for rags don't have to be put in the trash right away. See if you can't give them away first. Most garage sale shoppers think they can turn junk into something valuable, and they're all looking for a bargain, so give them the chance for a free treasure. The "Free" sign will attract attention, and you can always throw the leftovers away later.

Provide playthings to keep kids busy. Children can be a distraction at a garage sale. Help shoppers at your sale focus on buying things with a table of toys for kids to go through. You could even have a "Free" box and let each child keep one toy. Another distraction is sidewalk chalk. Let them draw on your driveway, then hose it down when they're gone.

Spruce up your yard. Mow the lawn, sweep the driveway, and tidy up the patio before your sale. An attractive home is more inviting than a junky one, and people are more likely to stop when your place looks neat and well-kept.

Announce your sale with balloons and flags. Put your best sign up in your yard the morning of your sale to show that this is the place to come. Attach balloons or strings of colored flags as eye-catchers. Put additional signs at streets and intersections leading to your house to show people the way. Staple arrows pointing in the right direction and labeled "Today" over the dates on signs you put up earlier in the week to get double duty from your pre-sale advertising.

Use large, paper grocery bags for signs pointing the way to your garage sale. Write "Garage Sale" and an arrow on a bag and put a couple of pounds of rocks or sand in it. Make sure your lettering is big and bold, and you have a perfect directional sign. Another way is to slip the bag over a couple of stakes and staple the bottom.

Refresh your customers with a cold drink. If it's going to be hot the day of your sale, ice down some cans of soda and offer them for sale. You could also offer water, coffee, or lemonade. Then add doughnuts, brownies, or something else to eat. It will mean more work and you'll need extra trash cans, but there's a method to this madness. Eating and drinking detains people a little longer, and the longer they stay, the more likely they are to buy something. Even if they just stand around, it may lure others to stop. Nothing attracts a crowd like a crowd.

Set the mood with nice music. A pleasant atmosphere encourages shoppers to linger longer and, hopefully, buy more merchandise. Set up a CD player or radio and play easy-listening, middle-of-the-road music to create this atmosphere. Stay away from loud extreme sounds that might offend some people. Not only is the music soothing, it provides background noise so customers can discuss potential purchases without worrying about being overheard.

Send your dog away for the day. No matter how much you love your dog, many people are uncomfortable around them, so make sure your dog is not around for your garage sale. If your dog bites someone, jumps on them, or just scares them with a low growl, you're the loser no matter whose fault it is. The dog could get hurt, too, with all the excitement and extra traffic. It's better all around if Fido stays in your house or visits a neighbor while the garage sale is going on.

Enlist extra help. You need at least two people all the time for your garage sale — one for the check-out table and one to greet customers, answer questions, and watch out for shoplifters. You might need more when it's busy early in the morning. Pick the most enthusiastic salesperson to work the crowd. But make sure they don't overdo it — getting in people's faces will drive away more business than it generates.

Start saving grocery bags now. Save plastic or paper grocery bags before your garage sale so you'll have something to put sold items in. Also have old newspapers on hand to wrap fragile items. A pad of paper, extra price labels and markers, a calculator, and some pens or pencils will be helpful, too. For your customers' convenience, have a tape measure handy. Make sure you have batteries to test items that need them. If you have things that need to be taken apart to transport, have the necessary tools available.

Be prepared for people to want to go in your house — and be prepared to tell them no. It's not worth the trouble that can arise when strangers use your telephone or bathroom. Have an extension cord handy for customers to test appliances. Keep unattended doors locked so no one will be tempted to go inside without asking.

Start out with plenty of change. It never fails — your first customer pays for $1 worth of stuff with a $20 bill. So go to the bank before your sale and get at least $100 in change. Start out with plenty of $1 bills — 20 or 25 at least — but have enough 5s and 10s to make change for those 20s. If you're running out of small bills, be willing to haggle on the price if the buyer has the correct change. Don't be tempted to solve your change problems by taking personal checks unless you fully understand the risks involved.

Stash cash in a fanny pack. The best way to protect your money is to keep it with you in a fanny pack or carpenter's apron instead of an open cash box. As the sale goes on, move the large denomination bills into a separate pocket so you're not flashing a big wad of cash every time you make change.

Save yourself a headache by pricing your items in 25-cent increments. All you'll need is quarters. You won't have to figure change involving nickels, dimes, and pennies. Leave the tempting $1.99 and $9.95 pricing to slick retailers with cash registers that calculate the change.

Decide how to handle early birds ahead of time. Have all your preparations done the night before your sale, because someone will surely show up early, maybe even the night before, to get first shot at your bargains. Decide how you want to handle these eager beavers. You might want to let them go ahead, especially if they're only 10 or 15 minutes early. If you think it'll be a problem, include "No early birds" in your newspaper ad, or only advertise your general location and let them find your house by the sign you put up at opening time.

Be ready to bargain. Some buyers will expect you to haggle with them, so stay flexible and let them know you're willing to negotiate. Listen to every offer. If you don't want to cut prices early in the day, tell them you think the item is worth the money but ask them to come back later and see if it's still there. They may worry that someone else will buy it and offer more. Just remember, you're selling something you don't want which means anything you get is gravy.

Move merchandise around during the sale. Regroup and reprice your merchandise as things get sold and empty spots appear on the tables. Keep your displays neat and attractive and lower the prices on slow-moving items. Your goal is not to have anything left at the end of the day, so shift to "Everything must go" tactics an hour or so before quitting time.

Take down your signs before your sale ends. Just before you close up shop, ask a friend or family member to take down the signs you put up. This helps to keep stragglers from coming by looking for bargains after you're finished. It also prevents neighborhood clutter that has your name or address on it. In some communities, you can be fined for leaving your signs up.

CHAPTER 15
Shopping

We've all had them — painful shopping expeditions that steal away too many hours and dollars. Or shopping memories forever spoiled by the product you had to return or overpaid for.

And perhaps the worst is the guilt and embarrassment after you've been tempted into making an impulse purchase. But this chapter can show you tricks that help you avoid getting lured into impulse buys by sneaky stores and supermarkets.

You'll also find secrets to help you make more satisfying buying choices and purchase only what you really need. So discover how to organize your shopping, and start saving more time, effort, and money right away.

Curb impulse buying. Ask yourself these three questions before you buy anything — from a kitchen gadget to new outfit.

- Do I really need it?

- Will I use it in the next week or the next month?

- Do I have a place to put it right now?

If you answer "no" to any of these questions, then walk away from the purchase. Only buy items that meet these criteria, and your home will stay clean and uncluttered.

Re-channel your shopping urges. You don't have to stop shopping completely to rout clutter. Honestly assess what you have and what you need. Have too many clothes but need new light fixtures? Then the next time the urge to shop strikes, head to the home improvement store instead of the department store. Shopping for what you actually need will feel great. You'll get your fix, avoid adding useless clutter, and get what you really need in the bargain.

Take advantage of libraries. Libraries carry books, movies, and even music these days. So why buy when you can "rent" it all for free? Trim your bookstore budget by shopping at the library instead. If you want a book they don't carry, chances are the librarian can order it for you.

Inventory your items for smart shopping. Before you walk out the door to the store, stop and take an inventory. How many pairs of shoes do you own, and how many of those do you actually wear? Are your shelves loaded with books you haven't read yet? Then you don't need any more. Take honest stock of your belongings before you splurge on more of the same.

Limit multiple items. More is not better. Who really needs two grills, 10 vases, or three pairs of boots? If you want the new item that badly, then you should give away one you already have.

Create space before buying. Establish a rule about bringing things home. You can't buy an item until you have space for it. You may have to get rid of a few items you don't use to create room for the new one. Carve out space first, then buy the new object, and you'll continue to live clutter-free.

Plan out your shopping day. Write down all the stops you need to make and what items you are picking up. Figure out the most efficient route to run your errands. Then stick to the plan. Resist making unplanned stops for garage sales or department store sales, and only pick up those items on your list.

Don't fall for "spectacular savings." Sales events promise big savings — 50, 60, even 70 percent off. But is a "deal" really a deal for an item you don't need or will rarely wear? No. You may reason you'll save lots of money buying something on sale, but in truth you'll save even more by not buying unnecessary stuff.

Shop sales without losing your shirt. By now you should know to be wary of sales — they can quickly put an end to your junk-free lifestyle. But when you absolutely must brave a great sale, remember this advice.

- Make a list of exactly what you need — black shoes, new pants, a white turtleneck. Only shop a sale with specific items in mind.

- Ask a sales associate where things are instead of wandering the store looking for what you need. Wandering can lead to unplanned purchases.

- Find what you came for, buy it, and leave as quickly as possible. No lingering.

Sleep on it for a firm decision. Unplanned purchases, whether large or small, can get you into trouble fast. Before you walk out of the store with something you don't need, try this. Tell yourself you may come back and buy it, but you need to think about it first. Then go home and sleep on it. Wait at least three days. If you can't stop thinking about the item, then you can seriously consider buying it. Make sure you can afford to pay cash and that you have a place to put it once you get it home.

Resist the lure of easy credit. Save up for large purchases instead of buying them on credit. This gives you time to consider whether you really want the item. Plus, the cost will seem more real to you — since you'll be paying with cold, hard cash — than if you bought it on credit. Place a picture of the item inside your checkbook or wallet, so every time you start spending money, you'll be reminded of what you're saving for.

Pay cash to avoid overspending. Pay cash when you go shopping, whether at the grocery or department store. You are more likely to overspend if you pay by check, credit, or debit card. Limit your purchases to the cash on hand, and you'll never blow your budget again. Remember to figure in sales tax when deciding how much you can afford to buy.

Let go of unwanted gifts. Everyone gets a gift they don't need or can't wear, and everyone gives these gifts occasionally. Don't keep items you can't use or don't like. They just create more clutter. Return them to the store immediately for a refund. If you miss the return deadline, then donate them to charity. Someone else could surely use that too-small coat or spare pair of slippers.

Maybe you can't pass up a "good deal." Or you go to the store for one pair of shoes and leave with eight. Are you struggling with debt because of your shopping habits? Do you hide purchases from family and friends for fear of criticism? Then you might be a "shopoholic," otherwise known as a compulsive shopper.

Shopping can be addictive, especially in a society that urges you to buy, buy, buy! Shopoholics get a temporary rush, or high, from buying — but then guilt, embarrassment, shame, and money worries sink in. In order to feel better, they go shopping again.

They tend to buy things they don't need and often justify their spending by buying for loved ones. They usually shop:

- ❏ to make themselves feel good.

- ❏ when they are anxious, depressed, worried, angry, or lonely.

- ❏ on credit, rather than paying with cash.

- ❏ even when they can't afford to, sometimes maxing out credit cards and going deeply into debt.

Experts stress that compulsive shopping is treatable. First, seek out help managing debt and finances through an organization like Debtors Anonymous (DA). They offer a 12-step program to help people curb spending and get out of debt. Look for a DA group near you by visiting the Web site *www.debtorsanonymous.org*, or call 781-453-2743.

And talk to your doctor about your shopping impulses. She may recommend a counselor to help you control your habits and, in some cases, medication to treat the underlying anxiety, depression, or mood disorder that sends you to the stores.

Empty your pockets to control spending. Remove your credit cards and checkbook from your purse before you go to the store. Leave them at home, and you are less likely to overspend or buy things you don't really need.

Avoid shopping therapy. Never go to the store when you feel anxious, depressed, or lonely. Take a walk, greet your neighbors, or work in the yard — anything else to lift your spirits. Buying stuff may make you feel good temporarily, but the bill is guaranteed to make you feel worse.

Hunt for other hobbies. Shopping is an expensive pastime. If you browse because you're bored and need entertainment, find another source of fun. Visit the park and people-watch, read a good book at your local coffee shop, or take up a hobby like gardening. You and your home will feel and look better when you stop buying junk out of boredom.

Cut back on gift-giving. Almost every holiday involves a gift nowadays, and that can take a financial toll. Buck the trend. Sit down with your loved ones and agree to give each other one nice gift every year to celebrate all the combined holidays. Then plan to spend each holiday together as family instead of focusing on the gifts. You'll minimize shopping stress and take the financial sting out of year-round gift-giving.

Control mail-order madness. Catalogs can be so tempting — all those slick, glossy pages filled with beautiful things. Go ahead and enjoy flipping through them. Savor every page, choose the items you want, and fill out the order form. Place the order in an envelope, write the total cost in large numbers on the outside, then leave it someplace where you will see it every day. Wait at least one week. Can you remember what you ordered? If not, toss the envelope.

Share catalogs — and the cost. Gather a group of friends and create a catalog club. Pass around the booklets you each get, and combine your orders on one form. Designate one person's name to use so you don't all end up on the mailing list. Combining orders may save you money, too. Some companies offer discounts or free shipping on orders over a certain amount. Read the fine print before placing your order to see if you qualify.

Place one order from a catalog, and you could find your mailbox stuffed with glossy junk for years to come. Evade this clutter chaos. If you place your order by phone, tell the salesperson not to include your name on any mailing lists. If you order by mail, check the box on the order form excluding you from future mailings.

Check return policies to avoid surprises. Before ordering from a catalog, ask the company if they guarantee your satisfaction with a product, and get details on their return policy. They may offer store credit instead of cash refunds, which may not make you happy if you have to return a product.

Choose classic clothes for long-term savings. Allow yourself one or two trendy pieces of clothing each season, but make a classic style the core of your wardrobe. Classic cuts and basic colors never go out of fashion, and separate pieces mix and match well together. Find a look that works for you, and focus on it. You'll save loads of dough over time.

Get a real feel for shoe fit. To get a feel for how shoes will fit, you need to test them in real-world conditions.

Carpeting makes the soles seem deceptively soft and comfortable. Walk around the store on the hard floor for a more realistic feel.

Repair, don't replace. Have clothes, shoes, and handbags repaired instead of replacing them. Fixing zippers, heels, and torn hems is downright cheap compared to buying new items.

Make men's shirts last longer. Cuffs and collars are often the first things to go. Stretch a shirt's life by taking it to a tailor or dry cleaner and having the cuffs or collar turned. You'll spend a few dollars, but less than you would buying a new one.

Shop sensibly for other people. You can be clutter-free and still buy clothes for other people. Simply ask your family what size clothes and shoes they wear and if they need any particular items. Make a list, and keep it in your purse or wallet. When you stop to shop a sale, you'll have accurate measurements for everyone and less chance of returns later on.

Find fitting furnishings. Avoid buying furniture, fixtures, or knickknacks that don't fit your space or decor. Create a house bag. Buy a notebook with folder pockets. Write down important measurements for each room, including room dimensions, window sizes, and door width. In the pockets, place samples of the paint chips and wallpaper you used in each room. Stash the notebook in the glove compartment or trunk of your car. You'll always have a handy guide to help you choose furnishings and accessories.

Look for double-duty furniture. When you get ready to buy new furniture, look for pieces that double as storage containers. Coffee tables with drawers and ottomans that open to hold blankets keep your house clean and clutter-free.

Split subscriptions with friends. Make your magazine subscriptions work harder for you, and for less, by sharing them with friends. Go in on a subscription with another person, and each of you pay half. Or each of you order a magazine, split the cost evenly, and swap when you finish reading your copy. You'll save money and paper, and reduce clutter.

Win with this insider secret. Even the world's most organized pantry and fridge can run out of storage space, but you can help prevent that with an insider secret. Do what some restaurants do before they post each week's daily specials. Plan a week's worth of meals and snacks around the supplies you already have, and then make your grocery list. You'll win in three ways. You won't come home with more food than your pantry and fridge can handle, you won't waste money on duplicates or "splurge" items, and you'll only bring home items you're sure to use.

Get the best deal every time. Never miss an opportunity to check a unit price. Although the economy size is often a bargain, you will find cases where the smaller size saves you money. Always take a calculator to the supermarket when you shop. Figure up the price per ounce, per liter, per pound, per serving size, or per unit. Then you'll know for sure where the best deals are. And you might free up some fridge and pantry space, too.

Discover the #1 way to slash grocery spending. No, it's not coupons. According to USDA research, a shopping list works as a key money saver for people on limited income. What's more, consumer experts recommend this strategy for anyone because it helps prevent impulse buys. These little purchases may seem harmless, but they can fatten up a grocery bill fast. After all, if you scour the shelves of every aisle to help you remember what to get, you're more likely to find extra things to buy. Avoid that expensive, pantry-cramming trap. Make a shopping list and stick to it.

Breeze through your shopping. Get a store map or directory list the next time you're at the grocery store. You can use it to organize your coupons and your shopping list by aisle and product. This will help you zip through your coupons, and you'll spend less time slogging through the supermarket.

Start a system for easy restocking. The key is to keep a "resupply list" near your refrigerator, pantry, or trash can. Every time you run out of something or throw out an empty container, add that item to your list. Keep the list on an erasable whiteboard, chalkboard, or a tablet with tear-off sheets so you can make changes as needed. When you make your grocery list, simply add these items to whatever else you need.

Prevent the forgetful syndrome. You've just come back from the grocery store when you realize you forgot to add dog food to your list. You have no choice but to return to the store. Here's how you can prevent this frustration from happening again. Save your grocery lists from five or six trips. Then use them to compile a list of items you buy regularly as well as other staples. Either type this list into your computer and print multiple copies, or hand write the list and make a small batch of photocopies. Before going to the supermarket, grab one of your list copies and strike through what you don't need to buy on this trip. If you need to add any items, write them in at the bottom of the list. You can relax knowing you'll never forget your poor dog's food again!

Make your list do double-duty. Write your grocery list on the back of an old envelope, and then drop the coupons you'll be using inside. You'll have everything at your fingertips and save time in the store.

Choose a clever coupon keeper. If your coupons always end up buried in your junk drawer, take heart. All you need is the right container, and your coupon-searching days are over. Try filing your coupons in a small index-card file box, a bank-check-sized accordion file, a binder with top-loading sheet protectors, a recipe box, or even a shoe box with dividers. A few minutes of organizing is as good as money in the bank.

Decide which of these three popular ways to organize coupons will work best for you.

❏ File them by expiration date. If you put the nearest expiration dates first, you'll be more likely to use those coupons before they expire.

❏ Group them by category to match your grocery aisles or departments or the way you think of them in your own mind.

❏ Arrange coupons alphabetically by product or brand name.

Get the most out of your clipping. Don't waste precious time and effort clipping coupons for items you wouldn't normally buy. You'll just end up spending more money and struggling to find extra pantry space. And be sure to compare prices even when you have a coupon. Buying a store brand will sometimes save you more money than using a coupon on a name brand.

Streamline your coupon cutting. Grab a pair of scissors and your coupon file or organizer whenever you sit down to read the newspaper or other publications. You can file your coupons as you clip them so you're less likely to lose coupons or forget to clip them out later. Just put your coupon file back in your purse or car when you're done, so you'll be sure to have it when you go to the store.

Prune your coupon crop. When you sit down to clip coupons out of the Sunday paper, finish up by clearing expired ones out of your organizer. That will make your coupons much easier to manage efficiently.

Resist pressure to buy. Don't risk bringing home an item you don't want. Save yourself with this advice from Susan Samtur, co-editor of the *Refundle Bundle* rebate magazine. Read the fine print on coupons ahead of time. Make sure the coupon applies to an item you truly need, is in the size or style you want, and won't require you to spend extra money on additional products or multiple purchases. If you discover the coupon doesn't cover the item you have, don't feel obligated to purchase the product even if you're standing at the checkout.

"C" your coupons at a glance. How many times have you returned home lugging coupons you were supposed to use? Here's an easy way to make sure you never forget again. Put a mark — such as a C, a check, or a cent sign — next to the items on your grocery list you have coupons for. You'll know at a glance how many you have to use.

Reap some extra savings. Get extra mileage from your coupons with these tips.

- Visit the customer service desk to find out when the store offers double-coupon days.

- Check the packages of items you regularly buy for instant coupons.

- Use coupons together with rebates, online coupons, or sales to get the most savings.

Practice precision shopping. The serving size you prefer may differ drastically from the one listed on the box, bottle, basket, or package. So tailor your storage and your spending to the precise amounts you need. Pull out your measuring cups, measuring spoons, and a kitchen scale, and keep them handy. Then start measuring all your food before you serve it so you can determine your serving size — or your family's. First, use your serving size to figure out how fast you use things up. Then use it to figure your cost per use — which may be far more accurate than cost per ounce. Armed with these valuable numbers, you'll know how often to buy, whether to buy in bulk, and when a "bargain" is truly a bargain for your household. You may also find that your groceries fit into your storage space more easily.

Solve the just-need-a-little problem. Your recipe calls for a small amount of a particularly expensive or perishable item. Obviously, you don't want to buy the whole package, but what can you do? Check to see if your supermarket or health food store has the product in bulk bins. If so, you can scoop out exactly the amount you need.

Get bulk bargains in smaller packages. You'd like to buy in bulk — or buy the economy size — to take advantage of the cheaper per-unit price, but you can't possibly finish it before it goes bad, or you just don't have the storage space for the large package. Solve this in three steps. Find someone else with the same problem, agree to split the cost, and then repackage the item into smaller containers. Now you can get the bargain without running out of storage or wasting food.

Reap rewards far from the maddening crowds. Extra minutes in the supermarket may mean more money spent,

---

Despite what you may have heard, the truth is, buying in bulk is not always cheaper. Consider these points before you take the plunge.

❑ **Figure out the cost per ounce,** per liter, or per serving. Some products in larger containers are more expensive than the same product in smaller containers. They're tougher to store, too.

❑ **Determine whether you have room** to store large packages and boxes before you reach the checkout line — or work out how you can repackage them into smaller containers and where you'll store them. Non-perishables may last for ages, but that's no help if you have no place to put them.

❑ **Find out the product's shelf life** before buying any perishable item in bulk life, and estimate how long you'll take to use it up. You only save on what you use. A big package of perishables may spoil, harden, or become stale long before you finish it.

❑ **Ask yourself whether your family** will feel obligated to overeat in order to finish a product before it goes bad.

❑ **Don't break the bank** if you don't have the money to pay for bulk products right now. Even if you buy products to use over the next few pay periods, the credit card interest paid on your bulk purchase bill will probably erase your "in bulk" savings.

research suggests. Those minutes give the store more time to break down your resistance to impulse buys — including the ones you don't have space or money for. But you can fight back and make shopping faster, easier, and less stressful at the same time. Just shop during the days and times when the stores are less crowded. According to the Food Marketing Institute, Tuesday is your best bet, followed closely by Monday or Thursday. If you must shop on the busy weekends, go early in the morning or at other off-peak times.

Beware the supermarket's double-edged sword. "Loss leaders" can save your food budget or sink it. These are the items advertised at an amazingly low price in order to lure you into the store. Grocers hope you'll also buy less favorably priced products and spend more than you meant to. Loss leaders are only budget helpers if you can stock up on them without overspending or making unplanned purchases. If you can be tempted into impulse buys, you're better off staying home.

Boost your shopping efficiency. Shop with a hungry child, and you'll probably buy more. Food marketers know that wise shoppers might resist impulse buys, but the children with them probably won't. You'll do your most efficient shopping and bargain-hunting alone. If possible, offer to do someone else's grocery shopping for them if they'll keep the kids while you're at the supermarket. But if you must shop with children, make sure they're well-fed before you enter the grocery store.

Practice no-guilt grocery shopping. You'll almost surely buy more if you grocery shop when you're hungry. So eat before you shop. Also, try not to shop when you are rushed, tired, lonely, or angry.

You aim to buy less so you'll have less clutter and expense, but grocers strive to make you buy more. Guard against supermarket gimmicks like these.

❑ **Recognize a bargain.** Displays at the end of the aisle aren't always a bargain. Compare prices to find out whether you're getting a discount or paying extra. Do the same for displays near the checkout line.

❑ **Watch out for hitchhikers.** If you've always eaten apples without caramel dipping sauce, why buy the sauce because it's next to the apples today?

❑ **"Get a free container of item X** with a minimum purchase of item Y." Don't consider this unless you were planning to buy both X and Y anyway.

❑ **Don't be tempted.** Free samples of food are meant to tempt you to buy an item, especially if you hadn't planned to.

❑ **Look high and low.** Grocers place expensive items at eye-level hoping you won't notice the bargains near your feet or above your head.

❑ **Keep on moving** You'll find the products people buy most often at the back of the grocery store — or near it. Grocers hope you'll spot some extra items to buy as you wheel your cart through the store.

Fight the pantry clutter monster. Try this if you can't totally eliminate impulse purchases. Limit yourself to three — or even better, just one. Pick the one that has the lowest price or will create the least clutter. Or just pick a favorite — but be sure to stick to your limit.

Watch for checkout mistakes. Supermarkets ring up the wrong price on more than 10 percent of their products, according to research. So make a point to know what you should pay for an item — especially if it's on sale. When you finish at the checkout, step out of the flow of shopping cart traffic, and check your receipt. If you were charged full price for any items on sale, or if you were charged twice for an item, see customer service for a refund.

Get the right groceries at the right price more often, and you'll probably recover storage space, too. Use these tips to help.

❑ **Consider buying** an item in a bag instead of a box. Bagged foods often cost less and may fit more easily into odd spaces in your pantry or fridge.

❑ **Learn which fruits and vegetables are in season** so you can take advantage of those bargains. If you can't possibly finish the bunch of produce before it goes bad, ask the store if you can buy a smaller amount. You'll save money and gain space.

❑ **Start checking shelf price tags** for the price per pound or ounce. You may discover opportunities to save. For example, unit prices will tell you when generic brands are cheaper than name brands.

❑ **Spot sales more quickly** by memorizing the prices of foods you buy regularly.

❑ **Shop on senior discount days** if you qualify.

CHAPTER 16
Time Management

T ime is money. Time is of the essence. Time waits for no man. You've heard these sayings about time, but did you ever really stop to think how important time is? Probably not — you're probably too busy scrambling to get to work.

Just as your possessions can turn into clutter, so can your schedule. With deadlines, household chores, family events, and day-to-day errands ganging up on you, it seems like you never have enough time. Unless you know how to manage it.

Read on to discover how to make the most of your time. Get organized at home and the office. Discover time-saving tips for cleaning, working, and running errands. Learn how to stop procrastinating and form new habits. After all, your time should be spent on more important things — like you.

Tidy up with minutes you'll never miss. Here's how to keep your entire house "white glove clean" in just a few minutes a day during time that's usually wasted. Do your cleaning during television commercials. Instead of just sitting there watching ads, use the time to dust, vacuum, or pick up stray items. You're just five minutes to the perfect home. Sound impossible? Just try it — the results are astounding. Not only will your house look great — you'll have lots of extra time to enjoy it.

Ban shoes and clean less often. For centuries, the Japanese have removed their shoes before entering a home. Keep your floors clean by adopting this ancient custom. If your family and guests follow the "no shoes in the house" rule, you'll have less dirt to deal with. You'll give your vacuum a break — and cool your feet at the same time.

Aim high when dusting. Are you dusting twice as much as you need to? Just follow this simple strategy and save yourself some sweat. The best way to dust for cleanliness and efficiency is to clean from top to bottom. Dust and dirt fall as you clean. If you start at the bottom, you'll end up cleaning some areas twice.

Make knickknacks bite the dust. Want to slash your dusting time in half? Just follow this one sneaky tip. Get rid of half your knickknacks. Whether you sell them, donate them, or just box them up in a closet, you won't have to dust them anymore. With half as much to dust, dusting should take only half as long.

Wipe out clutter while you dust. Just dusting? You're missing a great opportunity to pull double duty. Take a plastic grocery bag with you if you want your house neat as a pin. As you go from room to room dusting, toss garbage in the bag. Or use the bag to collect items that

A good leader knows when to delegate responsibilities. Rather than waste precious time hand washing certain items, just stick them in your dishwasher and let it do the work for you. You'd be surprised how much your dishwasher can handle. According to Maytag, here are just some of the things you can wash in your dishwasher:

❑ baby toys

❑ plastic cutting boards

❑ baseball caps

❑ golf balls

❑ vases

❑ dish scrubbers, scrub brushes

❑ sink or bath mats

❑ combs

❑ toothbrushes

❑ sponges

❑ light fixtures

❑ cans or bottles you plan to recycle

don't belong in one room and transport them to their proper spot in another. With just one trip around the house, you can get everything dusted and put away.

Put the heat on wrinkles. No time to iron? No problem. Just dampen your clothes and toss them in the dryer on low. Then hang your garments right away. This five-minute solution should get the wrinkles out.

Give yourself a head start on tomorrow. Here are five small things to do each night before bed to make the next day a breeze.

- recycle newspapers
- go through your mail
- load the dishwasher.
- put dirty clothes in the hamper
- lay out your clothes for the next day

Controlling your clutter can help you save even more time than you think. According to a recent study, the average American wastes 55 minutes a day — about 12 weeks a year — looking for things they know they own but can't find.

Save trips with stair basket. Going up and down the stairs all day might be good exercise, but it's lousy time management. Instead, place a basket at the foot of your stairs. During the day, fill it up with things that need to go upstairs. When you finally go upstairs, bring the basket with you and put the items where they belong. Then leave the empty basket at the top of the stairs, ready to be filled for the trip back down. You won't waste time and energy running up and down the stairs several times a day.

Arm yourself with an errand basket. Running errands can be hectic enough without scrambling to collect everything you need before you leave the house. So keep an errand basket by your door. Fill it with things that need to leave the house with you — video rentals, library books, dry cleaning, your shopping list and coupons, or anything you've borrowed and need to return. When it's time to run errands, just grab the basket and go.

Put job requests in writing. Tired of constantly reminding your spouse to do something? Sick of being nagged by

You sure would like to get organized ... tomorrow. Putting things off may feel good now, but you'll be in big trouble one of these tomorrows. Check out these 10 ways to break the habit of procrastinating.

❑ **Break a big project** into several smaller tasks. It will be much more manageable that way.

❑ **Set deadlines** for yourself.

❑ **Visualize yourself** completing the task, step by step.

❑ **Think positive.** Ignore those doubts, excuses, and rationalizations that creep into your mind.

❑ **Do the most difficult** or most distasteful task first. It's all downhill from there.

❑ **Reward yourself** for completing tasks along the way.

❑ **Prioritize.** Don't get sidetracked from an important project by a less-important one.

❑ **Eliminate distractions.** Don't let a messy desk, the Internet, radio, or TV get in the way of the task at hand.

❑ **Take care of yourself.** When you don't feel well, whether physically or emotionally, it's harder to get things done. Get enough sleep, eat a healthy diet, and exercise every day.

❑ **Get started now.** Just do something, no matter how small. Taking the first step will lead to more.

your spouse? Instead, each of you can post a "Honey Do" list for the other on the refrigerator. It's much quieter — and more effective. When you think of a task you would like your spouse to do, add it to the list. When you complete a task on your own list, cross it off. You can treat it as a competition, to see who can cross the most items off the list. Better yet, work on tasks at the same time and reward yourselves with something fun — like a night out — when you're both done.

Save over $1,000 in three minutes a night. Packing a lunch packs quite a punch when it comes to savings. If you make your lunch the night before, you save time the next morning. You can also save calories with healthier choices and smaller portions than you'd find in a restaurant. Packing your lunch is also an unbelievable cost cutter. Do this three-minute tip each night, and you'll save over $1,000 a year for a great vacation. How? Instead of spending $5 a day on take-out food, you'll spend only about $1 on food from home. That's a savings of $4 a day, $20 a week — and more than $1,000 a year.

Time yourself when doing chores. How can you accurately plan your day if you don't know how much time you need to spend on each task? Consider timing yourself as you pay bills, run errands, or clean your house. Next time, you'll have a better idea of how long these things take. Always remember to leave yourself a little extra time in case you get stuck in traffic or something unexpected pops up.

Consolidate appointments on one calendar. You try not to mix business and pleasure, but there's one place you should — on your calendar. Instead of keeping separate calendars for work and personal obligations, consolidate all your appointments and important events on one calendar.

With one glance, you'll know your entire schedule. It's a simple way to avoid conflicts and confusion.

Use color to organize your calendar. With your busy schedule, your calendar can get pretty cluttered. Help make sense of it with a color-coding system. Highlight special dates, like birthdays and anniversaries, in red.

They say you can't teach an old dog new tricks. Good thing you're not a dog. It's never too late to change your bad habits and become more organized. Just ask management consultant and author Marilyn Paul, who earned a Ph.D. in organization and management from Yale. In her book *It's Hard to Make a Difference When You Can't Find Your Keys*, Paul provides these 10 steps to forming new habits.

❑ **Pick one small habit** you'd really like to change.

❑ **Estimate what it costs** you to keep this habit.

❑ **Become aware of your thoughts** that accompany it.

❑ **Check your deeply held beliefs** for validity.

❑ **Create a picture of a new, better habit.** Actually act it out.

❑ **Remind yourself** how your new habit will nurture your vision and purpose.

❑ **Interrupt your old habit** with a shout, music, or a "No!"

❑ **Reinforce your new behavior** with new thoughts.

❑ **Reward yourself** for the new behavior.

❑ **Get lots of support.** Ask for help from all your support sources.

Use green for work obligations and blue for doctor's appointments. You'll transform your bland, confusing calendar into a rainbow of organization.

Write it down to get it right. You may have a great memory, but why risk forgetting something important? Write things down. As soon as you make an appointment, put it on your calendar. Make lists or leave yourself notes. No more running back to the store for a forgotten item or letting an important deadline pass. Written reminders come in handy, and writing something down will reinforce it in your mind.

Group tasks for greater productivity. Variety may be the spice of life, but jumping randomly from task to task wastes time and leaves a bad taste in your mouth. Group your activities to take better advantage of your time. For instance, make all your phone calls or send all your e-mails in one sitting. Run all your errands at once, so you don't waste time and gas making several small trips during the day.

Take time to smell the roses. You're motivated by a challenge, so you want to aim high. But if you have unrealistic expectations, you're setting yourself up for defeat. Remember, you don't have to cram everything into one day. You can plan an ambitious schedule, but keep it flexible. You'll function better without so much pressure, and you'll enjoy life so much more.

CHAPTER 17
Relocating

G etting your home ready to sell, and then moving all your belongings, can be over-whelming. The key to any big job is to take it one step at a time.

First, declutter each room, including the closets. Crowded rooms seem small, and buyers like large, airy spaces. You may need to donate, sell, or pack up some of your belongings.

Next, stage your home. Clean it thoroughly, and arrange furnishings and decor to show the house to its best advantage. You may fall in love with it all over again! Once it sells, start packing and inter-viewing moving companies.

Sounds easy, but where do you begin? Right here. This chapter is jam-packed with advice on how to declutter your rooms, decorate to entice buyers, dress up the exterior, pack for a smooth move, and even hire movers. You can also check other chapters for more tips on clearing clutter room-by-room to help sell your house.

Sell your house with the right colors. Certain colors can make a room look serene and tidy as well as make a space seem much larger than it really is. Use this to your advantage when trying to sell your home.

- Choose neutral colors like beige or taupe, or light, soft shades of green, blue, or yellow for the walls and furniture.

- Keep colors within the same color family.

- Use flooring that blends into the wall color.

Enlarge a room instantly. Make a small room seem big — with just a few easy changes. Stuffing too much in any one room can make it seem super small. Pare down your furniture, and your rooms will look bigger and cleaner, without spending a dime! Try to look at each room the way an outsider would. What does your eye focus on first? If too many things catch your eye, you need to pare down furniture, plants, pictures, and other items. Can you see the tops of tables, bookcases, and furniture? If not, clean off the knickknacks covering them. Remember, clean lines, open spaces, and fewer items make a room seem larger. And rather than move the clutter from one part of the house to another (like the basement), hold a garage sale, give it to charity, or rent a storage unit until the house sells.

Lighten up to entice buyers. Light streaming through the windows makes a room seem open and cheerful. Make sure your home has plenty. Wash curtains and blinds, leave them open during the day, and turn on all the lights when showing your home at night. If you still notice dark corners, including in the basement, then add more light. Set lamps atop bookcases or end tables, put different bulbs in light fixtures, and cut back plants blocking windows on the outside.

Clear counters of clutter. Buyers these days often look for large bathrooms and lots of kitchen counter space. That may not describe your home, but simply clearing off surfaces in the kitchen and bathroom can make these spaces seem larger. You don't have to throw out all your kitchen appliances. Simply keep them hidden in cabinets when not in use. Wipe down anything you leave sitting out, like the coffee maker. Use attractive baskets or other containers to hold bathroom items if they must sit on the counter.

Pack up family photographs. Buyers need to picture themselves in your home, but that's hard to do when every inch of space is covered with your family photos, personal mementos, or unusual decor. While trying to sell your house, go ahead and pack up these objects and store them until you move. Soon, you'll have a new place to hang your hat — and your photographs.

Get help staging your home. Cable television shows such as "Designed to Sell" and "Curb Appeal" can give you simple ideas for staging the inside and enhancing the outside of your home. If you have trouble doing it yourself, get advice from a pro. Ask your real estate agent to recommend an Accredited Staging Professional (ASP), a professional home stager. You can find one yourself by visiting the Web site *www.stagedhomes.com*, or calling StagedHomes.com at 800-392-7161.

Make small spaces seem large. Proper staging can make a room seem larger and more open. Pull furniture away from the walls, and try arranging pieces at interesting angles. Placing a sofa diagonally across a long, narrow room can make it seem wider. Group pieces into cozy seating areas to create a warm, welcoming feel.

16 tips to make your home irresistible to buyers.

- ❑ Clean, clean, clean! Focus on the kitchen and bathrooms.
- ❑ Clear off kitchen and bathroom countertops.
- ❑ Put out fresh towels in good condition.
- ❑ Repair running toilets and leaky faucets.
- ❑ Do dishes as soon as you dirty them.
- ❑ Replace burned-out light bulbs.
- ❑ Wash curtains and blinds.
- ❑ Clean windows inside and out.
- ❑ Replace torn screens.
- ❑ Paint walls in neutral colors.
- ❑ Remove rugs to expose hardwood floors if in good condition.
- ❑ Shampoo dirty carpets.
- ❑ Replace worn carpet or cover with neutral rugs.
- ❑ Oil squeaky hinges.
- ❑ Fix, polish, or replace old door handles and cabinet hardware.
- ❑ Set thermostat so your home stays at a comfortable temperature.

Clean house thoroughly for a better showing. The house doesn't have to be spotless, but the cleaner it is the better it will show. Focus on kitchens and bathrooms. Scrub toilets, wipe down counters and sinks regularly, and wash dishes as soon as you dirty them. Attack mildew in the bathroom mercilessly — mold and mildew can seriously turn off buyers. Bleach tile grout, too, if necessary. While you're at it, dust furniture and decor throughout the house. Vacuum rugs and carpets, and shampoo them if needed. Gently wipe dirt off walls if you don't plan to repaint, and wipe down baseboards, chair rails, and blinds.

Bring the outdoors in. Bright blooms and green foliage can dress up a drab room and make a house feel fresh and airy. A few attractive, well-placed plants, either live or silk, may even help hide minor flaws. Keep only healthy, vibrant plants indoors — no hosta hospitals — and remember to water and dust them regularly.

Create a handy fix-it list. Walk through your home with a friend or your real estate agent. Ask them to help you make a list of everything that needs fixing — doors that stick, leaky faucets, gouges in walls, loose doorknobs, and other problems. Then fix as many as you can before putting your home on the market. Remember, you are competing with brand new construction, so your property needs to be as like-new as possible. Plus, the fewer problems a buyer has to fix, the fewer chips they have to bargain with when asking for a lower price. Some sellers even get a professional home inspection before putting their house on the market to catch potential problems before it goes under contract. Talk to your Realtor if this option appeals to you.

Make a great first impression. The entrance to your home is the first thing buyers see when they arrive. And they have plenty of time to examine the porch, paint, doorknob, siding, windows, and shrubs while they wait for the real estate agent to unlock the door. Keep this area especially nice. Wash mildew and dirt off the siding, porch, and rails. Sweep leaves and debris off the steps and walkway. Trim shrubs to below window-level, and prune

The first thing any prospective buyer sees is the outside of your house — the yard, driveway, porch, and front door. Tidy it all up to attract buyers.

❑ Mow the lawn regularly.

❑ Sweep, clean, and repair driveway, walkway, and steps.

❑ Pick up toys and tools in the yard.

❑ Remove dead trees and plants.

❑ Rake leaves and yard trimmings.

❑ Prune shrubs away from windows.

❑ Water, prune, and fertilize outdoor plants to keep them healthy.

❑ Clean and repair gutters.

❑ Make sure doorbell works properly.

❑ Lay out cheerful, clean welcome mats.

❑ Pressure wash siding and windows, and repaint if necessary.

❑ Clean cobwebs from around doors, windows, and porches.

❑ Repaint exterior doors and trim if needed.

❑ Sand down and repaint flaking porch paint.

❑ Repaint or replace old mailboxes and house numbers.

❑ Polish or replace exterior door handles.

nearby plants. Wash windows inside and out, and repaint the porch if you must. Last, consider jazzing up the entrance with colorful, cheerful, blooming potted plants. All of this helps create a good first impression.

Roll out the welcome mat. Lay a cheerful welcome mat at each exterior door to welcome buyers and remind them to wipe their feet before entering. This should cut down on tracked-in dirt, help your home stay clean, and make the buyers feel welcome.

Rent storage for faster sell. To present your house in its best light, you will likely have to declutter both furniture and decor. Don't clog up the basement or attic with extra stuff. New owners need to see those spaces, too. Instead, pack up those items, and move them into a temporary storage unit, along with anything you currently have stored in the attic and basement. Consider getting a climate-controlled unit, and ask about access hours and security.

Protect valuables while showing home. After you put your house up for sale, consider packing up or otherwise hiding your valuables — jewelry, collectibles, or any other treasures someone could easily pocket. Lots of strangers will be trooping through your house. Real estate agents try to keep an eye on people when showing your home, but they can't watch everyone at every moment. Tuck these items deep in a drawer, or go ahead and pack them up.

Keep your home ready to show. The person who will buy your home could walk through the door at any moment. Is your house ready to show right now? Sellers need to keep their home clean and tidy all the time. These four strategies can help.

- Make your bed every morning.
- Take out old newspapers and trash every evening.

- Make a daily "clutter sweep" through the house, and return objects to their proper place.

- Keep a lidded basket in each room so you can quickly toss in items when a buyer arrives on short notice.

Document valuables in case of loss. Some organizers recommend you make a list of every item in every box you pack. That's not realistic for most people, but you should at least inventory your valuables. Get all the information you would need if you had to file an insurance claim for lost or broken belongings.

- Write down the serial numbers on televisions, computers, and other expensive electronics.

- Photograph or videotape valuables, including electronics, furniture, jewelry, and antiques.

- Note the make, model, purchase date, and purchase price for each of these items, if possible.

- Call your insurance agent for more advice on how to document your belongings before a move.

Use up excess to avoid overpacking. Don't buy groceries or personal care items before a move. Instead, try to use up all the food you have, both fresh and canned. And if you run out of toilet paper, get just enough to make it through the move. The less you buy, the less you have to pack and take with you.

Be an early bird to lessen stress. Think about it — most things you own, you don't use every day. Box up these items early to lessen the stress of moving later. Leave out the things you do use every day, like toothbrushes and a couple of towels, and pack these last.

Keep the IRS in the loop. Notify the IRS when you move so any tax notices follow you to your new home. Call the IRS at 800-829-1040 and request Form 8822, or download it from the Web site *www.irs.gov*. To deduct moving expenses, request Form 3903 as well.

Simplify the packing process. Pack one room at a time, and put items from the same room in boxes together. When you arrive in your new home, you can simply place boxes in the right rooms and unpack an entire room at once.

Keep parts together to avoid losses. Whenever possible, pack smaller pieces with the items they go with. For instance, pack light bulbs with lamps, TV cables with televisions, and bookends with books. Should you need to take apart any furniture, place the matching hardware in a zip-lock plastic storage bag, and tape it to the bottom of the furniture. Do the same with the cables, screws, nuts, brackets, and other small, loose parts that match other items.

Make good use of suitcases. Stash clothes you wear regularly inside suitcases. These often have wheels for easy moving and are much easier to spot than boxes.

Cushion breakables with blankets. Use towels, sheets, and blankets to wrap breakable items and cushion them from the sides of the box. Lay folded linens between glass picture frames to cushion the glass. You'll save space by not having to pack towels and sheets separately, plus avoid having to wrap with newsprint.

Store electronics in original boxes. Pack delicate electronic items such as video players, printers, and stereos in their original boxes whenever possible. Often, these items come packed in molded Styrofoam or other materials, which offer better protection than newspaper and other packing materials.

Wrap up messy electrical cords. Keep unruly electrical cords under control. Neatly loop dangling cords. Tie them with twist ties or rubber bands, and secure them to the back of their appliance with tape. For electronics with more than one cord, like computers, color code the cords with different-colored twist ties or rubber bands.

Remember the 50-pound rule. Don't load more than 50 pounds into one box, and follow this rule of thumb — if you can't lift the box, it's too heavy. It's all right to pack heavy and lightweight objects together. Just put heavy items on the bottom and lighter ones on top.

Create an "emergency" box. Designate one box as the "emergency" box you will open first when you move to your new place. In it, stow things you will need in the first few days, like a telephone, alarm clock, instant coffee, snacks, cups, utensils, paper plates, trash bags, paper towels, and a can opener. You may also want to include a pen, paper, and address or telephone book; tools such as a flashlight, screwdriver, hammer, tape measure, scissors, and extension cords; and linens and bath items like fresh sheets, towels, toilet paper, moist towelettes, aspirin, and soap. Write the words "Open me first!" on the top and sides of the box so you can quickly find it after moving.

Color-code moving boxes for instant ID. Color-code boxes according to which room they belong in your new home. Buy brightly colored stickers, and designate a different color for each room — kitchen, master bedroom, bathroom, and so on. Slap the corresponding stickers on boxes as you pack. On moving day, go to your new home and place a sticker on the doorway to each room based on the colors you assigned. You and your moving helpers will have no trouble identifying where boxes go.

Label boxes for easy unpacking. On each box, write the contents and the room it goes in. Be as specific as possible when labeling the contents to help you find items when you unpack. For instance, "good sweaters" is better than

Take this advice to hire an honest mover and protect yourself from scam artists.

❑ **Get written estimates** from at least two movers before signing a contract.

❑ **Don't settle for over-the-phone estimates.** Have a representative from the moving company come to your house to give you an estimate.

❑ **Try to get a "binding not-to-exceed" estimate.** If the movers refuse, ask for the regular "binding" variety. Avoid signing a "non-binding" estimate. It offers you little protection from fraudulent movers.

❑ **Ask for references,** and check them yourself.

❑ **Call the Better Business Bureau** or your state's consumer protection agency to learn about complaints filed against the movers as well as their on-time record.

❑ **Be suspicious of low-ball bids.** Beware movers who issue an estimate far below the others you get. They could be planning a scam.

❑ **Check out Web sites** such as *www.movingscam.com* and *www.moving.org* for more advice on hiring professional movers and avoiding con artists.

"clothes," and "coffee mugs" tells you more than "miscellaneous kitchen."

Carry important items with you. Keep valuables like jewelry, silver, and heirlooms with you when you move rather than load them on a moving truck. The same goes for important papers. Gather together wills, birth certificates, social security cards, passports, car titles, marriage or divorce papers, medical records, financial information, pet documents, closing papers, and any current bills you need to pay. Place these in a briefcase, and carry it with you during the move. Remember, any item you put on a moving truck or in someone else's vehicle could get lost, and some things are too important to risk.

Cats love empty boxes — a little too much. Keep pets away from packing boxes and moving trucks on the day of the big move. You don't want to discover them missing after the moving van drives off.

Unpack in a snap. Ask the movers to place boxes in the room they belong in your new home. This should be easy if you have clearly labeled where each box goes.

Hire a professional organizer. A professional organizer can make your move virtually stress-free. Senior moving managers (SMMs), a particular kind of organizer, cater to the needs of older adults. These professionals specialize in helping seniors downsize a lifetime worth of belongings and move into a smaller home. They help decide what will fit in the new home and where to donate or sell the rest. They can also act as a buffer between the senior homeowners and well-meaning family and friends. SMMs can hire professional movers and supervise the packing. They'll even travel to the new home, unpack, and prepare it for your first night there. Some senior moving managers specialize in moving people with dementia and can help ease this confusing transition. To find one near you, visit the National Association of Senior Move Managers on the Internet at *www.nasmm.com*, or ask your real estate agent for help in locating one.

CHAPTER 18
Holidays and entertaining

Birthdays and holidays should be joyous occasions. Unfortunately, struggling to organize gifts, decorations, and parties can suck the joy out of otherwise happy events. Stop the madness and start enjoying the holidays again!

You'll find in the following pages the simplest ways to shop for gifts, how to snag the biggest bargains, and what to do with these gifts until the big day.

Once your gifts are organized, it's time to start entertaining. Hosting parties can be a breeze with a little planning. This chapter will show you how to organize and host stress-free parties, including quick cleanup tips and decorating secrets, along with special advice for holiday gatherings.

Take the hassle out of buying gifts. The best time to buy Christmas presents is often right after Christmas when stores advertise big clearance sales. But you don't have to wait until then. You can shop for gifts year-round. Think about the upcoming year. Are you expecting any weddings, baby showers, or children's birthdays? Make a list of occasions you need to shop for and carry it with you at all times. You can pick up gift items on sale as you spot them. You may find particularly unique items while traveling. Check off your list, and make a note of what you bought for each occasion. A spare cedar chest makes a perfect place to store gifts until the holidays or special occasion. Inexpensive plastic bins work well, too.

Shop till you drop — from home. Catalogs, and now the Internet, have revolutionized holiday shopping. If you hate fighting crowds, you'll love these options. Catalogs from your favorite retailers allow you to browse and order from the comfort of your home at your leisure, plus curb impulse buying. Simply tear out the pages that interest you along with the order form, then toss the rest. Shopping online can be just as easy. And when you shop from catalogs or Web sites, you can have the gift mailed directly to the recipient. Many large online retailers also offer gift-wrapping for an extra charge.

Create a gift list and keep it handy. Carry a list of gift ideas in your purse year-round. Friends and family often mention in passing things they need, want, or simply like, such as a favorite author. Jot down your notes and you'll never be without the perfect gift.

Wrap gifts as you buy them. Don't wait to wrap your gifts. Wrap them as soon as you get home from the store. Cover holiday gifts in festive paper, and birthday gifts in birthday paper. Remember to apply the name tag. You'll save yourself the stress of last-minute wrapping and prevent prying eyes from spoiling the surprise. If you shop for gifts throughout the year, simply store the wrapped gifts in a closet, plastic bin, or any place that's dry and protected from temperature extremes.

Stow wrapping tools for easy access. Keep all your gift-wrapping tools together in a long, clear, plastic bin. Look for under-the-bed bins that can hold several rolls of wrapping paper. Store your paper, scissors, ribbon, name tags, bows, and tape you need to wrap in the bin. Tuck it under your guest bed or sofa for quick access.

Ask for gifts that won't clutter your home. Try giving your family these gift suggestions when you don't want more stuff but love their thoughtfulness.

- gift certificates to your favorite restaurant, grocery store, or department store
- donations to a charity of your choice
- a plane or train ticket to visit far-away loved ones
- tickets to a theater, museum, concert, or sporting event
- gift card to a nearby bookstore
- a personal service, such as a massage, manicure, or facial
- homemade holiday goodies
- a gift basket of fruit or other healthy foods

Recycle old greeting cards. Reuse the fronts of Christmas and other greeting cards as unique gift or luggage tags. Simply write the recipient's name or your luggage's home address and phone number on the back. Alternatively, a local kindergarten, preschool, or elementary school might be able to use them for children's crafts. St. Jude's Ranch for Children no longer accepts charitable

donations of greeting cards, but your church or an
Internet search may help you locate organizations that do.

Get organized with a greeting card organizer. You'll
never miss another birthday. These notebooks contain a
page for each month where you can write down birthdays, special occasions, and holidays, plus a pocket for
each month to hold all the cards you'll want to send.

Make updating your address book a breeze. Save the
envelopes from greeting cards you receive during the year,
and file away the return addresses. Either copy the address
into your address book or clip it off the envelope and paste
it into a notebook. You will have updated addresses handy
when it comes time to send cards of your own.

Bid farewell to unloved decorations. You don't have to
keep all the decorations you own. Make room for the new.
Keep a black trash bag by your side as you unpack holiday decorations and when you put them away. Trash
those ornaments that are broken or in poor condition.
With a black trash bag, you are less likely to see what you
tossed and have second thoughts. Consider donating the
decorations you've simply grown tired of looking at.

Photograph decor for next year's decorating. Do you
go all-out decorating for the holidays? Take pictures of
your hard work. Snap photographs of the outside of your
house and each adorned room. Tuck the prints in with
your holiday decorations. Next year, you'll have photo-
graphic blueprints to tell you exactly where it all goes.

Label lights and garlands for decorating ease. If you use
garlands and lights to trim more than just your tree, consider labeling each strand so you know where it goes next
year. For instance, if you cut a stretch of garland just the
right length for your banister, tie a colored ribbon around

it when you pack it away and write "stairs" on the ribbon. The same goes for the strands of lights you swag over each window and the garland you hang from the mantle.

Start a party journal for easy entertaining. Like making lists, keeping an "entertaining" journal can make hosting events easy. Use it to keep track of specific guests' food allergies, likes and dislikes, and medical conditions that affect what they can eat. You can also note what you served at your last gathering, as well as what worked and what didn't. Jot down how many people attended, how much of each dish you made, and whether it was enough or too much.

Plan ahead to throw the perfect dinner party. Food and get-togethers go hand-in-hand, but complicated dishes don't always take the cake. Consider this expert advice when deciding what to make.

- *Keep it simple.* Choose a dish you know you do well, and build the rest of the meal around it. Don't try new recipes on unsuspecting guests.

- *Pick a dish you can make in advance* and either reheat or cook just before the gathering. This way, you won't spend the whole party sweating away in the kitchen.

- *Select side dishes and desserts* you can prepare ahead of time and serve cold or reheat.

- *Let your local bakery help.* You don't have to make it all yourself. Sometimes a store-bought dessert really hits the spot! Simply remove it from the package and serve on a nice dish.

- *Avoid serving foods with delicate sauces* or complex garnishes.

Make greasy pan cleanup a snap. Choose disposable cookware when possible if cooking for a large group of people. For instance, invest in a disposable aluminum roasting pan for your holiday turkey. Once baked, transfer the turkey to a serving platter and toss the pan. You'll save yourself lots of grimy cleanup afterward.

Serve foods that won't spoil. Keep your guests safe from food poisoning by serving foods that won't spoil if you plan on having an all-day gathering. To make things easy on yourself, use dishes you can easily refill.

Inform your guests with clever invitations. Whether your gathering is formal or casual, be sure to include this information in your invitation.

- the occasion for the party
- the kind of event
- who is hosting
- the date and time
- the address
- directions, when necessary
- how to dress
- whether children, spouses, and other guests are welcome
- an RSVP deadline
- a phone number and, if you use the Internet, an e-mail address to respond to

Give foolproof directions. Your guests need to find the party for it to be a success. If you are holding the event at a church, restaurant, or hotel, ask the staff for printed directions. Otherwise, write your own, and include a map. Give directions from major roadways. Drive the route with a friend and note specific mileage measurements, as well as major landmarks. Include these in the directions, along with a phone number where you can be reached the night of the party in case anyone gets lost. Enclose the directions and map with the invitation. Internet Web sites such as MapQuest at *www.mapquest.com* offer relatively reliable driving directions to and from almost any location, plus maps to go with them. Just double-check the MapQuest directions before handing them out to friends.

Save the day with simple, elegant decor. Don't lose your head over last-minute decorations for the event you're hosting. Flowers and candles never go out of style, and they're available year-round. Seasonal blooms and greenery, plus a few scented candles, go a long way in dressing up any space. Sometimes simple arrangements are the most elegant and effective.

Turn unusual bottles into beautiful vases. You don't need fancy vases to grace your table at a dinner party. The most eye-catching containers are sometimes the least expensive. Visit a local flea market or thrift store and look for old glass bottles or jars. Hand-blown glass often comes in unique shapes, and unusual colors truly brighten up a table.

Hide dust while adding atmosphere. So you didn't have time to dust before your guests arrived. Don't panic! Dim the lights and break out the candles. The soft lighting hides dust, while the gentle glow creates the perfect setting for laughter and intimate conversation.

Turn an old basket into a serving piece. Put old baskets to work serving at holiday parties. Line them with cloth napkins, plastic wrap, or foil and use them to hold silverware, candies, or fresh-baked rolls. Place another in your bathroom for rolled hand towels or extra toilet paper. You can even surprise holiday house guests with a small gift basket holding toothpaste, soap, and other necessities. Be sure to save one to fill with hostess gifts the next time you are someone's guest.

Get excellent free advice from design specialists. Why pay a fortune to get good ideas from designers when you can view their work for free? New home and condominium developments are perfect playgrounds for gathering ideas. Developers often hire a designer to stage a model home or condo. Visit the sales office and make an appointment to view the model, and take a notebook with you to jot down ideas as you walk through the home. Established neighborhoods may hold an annual "tour of homes" during the warm months, giving you a chance to visit 10 or more homes, all exquisitely decorated. Real estate open houses and television channels, such as HGTV and DIY Network, are also rich in ideas. Watch for shows like "Designed to sell," or visit the Web sites to look for specific advice at *www.hgtv.com* and *www.diynet.com*.

Set the stage for enjoyable conversations. Create intimate conversation areas for your guests by arranging several cozy seating areas. Include at least one end table or coffee table for holding beverages in each cluster of chairs. Dim the lights or use lamps to softly illuminate each seating area.

Arrange guests to encourage table talk. Dinner parties sometimes need a little help to get the conversation going. You can do that by assigning seats with place cards. How you arrange people depends on the size and shape of your table. To encourage particular people to chat at round or wide tables, seat them next to one another. At long, narrow tables, place them across from each other.

Lay out tableware in advance. Set the table at least one night before your dinner party. You'll have time to shine up the silver, wipe spots from dishes and glasses, iron table linens, and notice any missing touches.

Dress up place settings with simple favors. Place a small gift for each guest atop their place setting for special dinner parties. Try to choose a gift to match the holiday or season — baked treats at Christmas, miniature gourds in autumn, or a single flower during spring. Even a very simple gift will make the evening more memorable.

Speed clean before your party. You needn't spend days slaving away to clean for your party. A quick sweep can have it nice and tidy in plenty of time. Chances are, your guests won't see every room of your home. Focus on the areas they will spend the most time in — the downstairs bathroom, living room, dining room, and kitchen, for instance. Then follow this to-do list for a speedy cleanup.

- *Grab a laundry basket.* Go to each room and toss in items that don't belong there. Stash the basket some-place guests won't go, like your laundry room, and close the door.

- *Wipe down the dining table,* bathroom, and kitchen counters with a disinfectant wipe.

- *Lay out fresh towels* and check toilet paper levels.

- *Vacuum visible dirt* on rugs and hard floors.

- *Dust coffee tables and shelves* with special dust-grab-bing cloths.

- *Empty kitchen and bathroom* wastebaskets.

Plan for the unexpected. Give yourself twice as much time as you think you'll need to finish final preparations for any party. Inevitably, problems will crop up at the last minute. Follow this golden rule and you won't be a mess of stress when your guests finally arrive.

Make room for guests' coats. Clear out your coat closet before hosting a party, and leave plenty of empty hangers for guests' coats. They won't have to store their outerwear in a spare bedroom, and that's one less room you will have to clean.

Set out serving tools in advance. Dig out every utensil, serving tool, plate, and bowl you will need for the party beforehand. That includes corkscrews, cutting knives, pie plates, and spatulas. You don't want to keep your guests waiting as you hunt for a lost serving spoon.

Make changing trash bags a snap. Before the party begins, put a few unopened trash bags in the bottom of your trash can, then line the whole thing with a fresh bag. When one bag fills up, the kind soul who empties it during the party will find a fresh bag waiting underneath and won't have to search your cabinets looking for a refill.

Stock up on clear containers for leftovers. Buy clear, cheap, disposable plastic containers to send leftovers home with your dinner guests. You won't have to worry about getting your good dishes back, and if the container is clear, your guests will know exactly what it holds.

Accept praise graciously. When a guest compliments your party, don't point out all the things that went wrong. Accept the praise and pat yourself on the back for a job well done.

Chapter 19
Traveling

C lutter inside your house is bad enough, but if you carry clutter when you travel, it can ruin your vacation. You need to know how to pick just the essential items and how to pack them in the least amount of space.

Clothes, jewelry, shoes, cosmetics, toiletries, and more all have to fit into your suitcase. If you take too much, it's in the way and you'll struggle with baggage the whole trip. If you don't take enough, there could be a problem when you need something you left behind.

Read the following tips and learn how to organize your suitcase the way travel pros do. Pack everything you need and nothing else — and have a wonderful trip.

Conquer overpacking with a clothing diary. Start your packing process long before you leave on your trip. Come up with a clothing diary and make a list of things to take. Sit down with your itinerary and plan what you'll wear every day you're away. Mix and match and try to use each piece of clothing several times. If you find you're wearing something only once or twice, choose something that's more versatile. Keep your list with you and check it off when you repack to come home. Don't forget to add new things you acquire on your trip.

Mix and match to stretch your wardrobe. Plan your wardrobe thoughtfully when you get ready for a trip. If you just throw in an outfit a day and a couple of extras, you'll be saddled with way too much baggage. Stick to one style and color scheme and try to make sure everything goes with everything else. Pick pants, skirts, and tops that are interchangeable. Two outfits can become four just by switching combinations. Add a jacket, sweater, or colorful scarf, and it will look like you brought your entire closet.

Pack only what you can carry. Your trip will be a lot more fun if you don't have to constantly worry about getting your bags from place to place. Solve that problem by taking only as much luggage as you can handle by yourself. It cuts down on stress, tips to baggage handlers, and — most importantly — the amount of clutter in your suitcases.

Most hotel rooms come equipped with hair dryers, so check ahead before you use valuable space in your luggage to pack one. If you're staying at someone's house, it's better to take your own.

Divvy up clothes to prevent problems. Consider packing two smaller bags instead of one large, heavy suitcase. They'll be easier to handle and won't necessarily have to be checked baggage if you're flying. On family vacations, pack a change of clothes for everyone in each suitcase. If one bag gets lost, everybody will still have something to wear.

Leave your jewelry box at home. Losing your jewelry or having it stolen can turn an exciting vacation into a disaster. Don't be tempted to take your most expensive gems with you. Wear only small items that are not flashy advertisements for thieves. Store them in a container that doesn't look like a jewelry box — an empty 35 mm film canister is good for rings, earrings, and small pins. Then you know where they are and you can keep them with you when you're not wearing them. If you must take larger pieces, make use of the hotel safe.

Steer clear of aerosol cans. Large aerosol spray cans of hairspray, deodorant, and insect repellant are a huge waste of space in your luggage and may be banned on airplanes. The Transportation Security Administration says only limited quantities of personal care aerosol cans are permitted in either checked or carry-on baggage. Replace those big, bulky spray cans with travel size, nonaerosol containers.

Streamline your cosmetics bag. Stick to the basics when getting your makeup together for a trip. Mascara, lipstick, and blush are about all you really need. And don't get hung up on taking several shades of makeup. If you seldom wear pink lipstick at home, why would you wear it on vacation? You still have to take care of your skin, so buy travel size moisturizer and other skin care products or stop by a department store cosmetic counter and ask for samples. Look for products that have several uses, like a moisturizer with SPF 15 sunscreen. Once you get all these items together, put them in a special cosmetics bag just for traveling. Replenish it after every trip, and you'll always be ready to go.

Squeeze bottles when packing to prevent leaks. When you have to pack liquids, like lotion or shampoo, pour just enough into a small plastic bottle to get you through your trip. Leave some air space and then squeeze the bottle as you put on the top to create suction, which will cut down on leaks and spills. Put all your bottles into a plastic zip-lock bag for extra protection.

Use a new contact lens case for cosmetic items that just require a dab or two. Put eye cream in one side, for instance, and petroleum jelly to ward off chapped lips on the other side.

Pack a carry-on to avoid luggage disasters. The Aviation Consumer Protection Division of the U.S. Department of Transportation says that although relatively few bags are damaged or lost, you should never put the following items in checked baggage:

- small valuables — cash, credit cards, jewelry, cameras

- critical items — medicine, keys, passport, tour vouchers, business papers

- irreplaceable items — manuscripts or heirlooms

- fragile items — eyeglasses, glass containers, liquids

Keep these things and anything else you can't afford to lose with you at all times. It's also a good idea to put things you'll need the first 24 hours at your destination, like toiletries, a bathing suit, or change of underwear, in your carry-on bag.

Pack carry-on items in a cooler. Here's a cool idea for a carry-on bag. Put your valuables, breakables, and have-to-have-with-you items in a small but sturdy cooler — one with straps or a handle so you can carry it easily. When you reach your destination, take out your toiletries and valuables and pack the cooler for a picnic or day trip. That way, you don't have to buy one of those cheap foam coolers you throw away after a day's use.

A diaper bag makes a great carry-on bag — even if you don't have a baby. It's easy to handle and has plenty of room for valuables and a change of clothes. It also has extra pockets to keep things separate. Besides, it's much less likely to be stolen than a traditional carry-on bag.

Leave the sand at the beach. About the only downside to a trip to the beach is the sand you take away when you leave. Avoid some of the mess with a mesh bag. Buy one or just use the kind oranges and onions come in. Put your beach toys, suntan lotion, seashells, and other washable items in it and when you're ready to leave, dunk bag and all in the water or run a hose over it to rinse away the sand.

Safeguard valuables in a zip-lock bag. When you're boating, camping, or hiking, put maps and other important papers in a zip-lock plastic storage bag, and you can read them and keep them dry at the same time. In a boat, put valuables in a zip-lock bag and blow into it before you seal it so the bag will float if it goes overboard. These bags also work well for keeping important papers and items separate, clean, and where you can find them in your luggage. Put clothing, either clean or dirty, in a large zip-lock bag and press the air out of it before you seal it so it takes up less space in your suitcase.

Save precious space in your cosmetic bag. Use cotton balls and a plastic zip-lock bag instead of bottles that might break or spill in your luggage. Just soak some balls with nail polish remover, insect repellant, or other liquid and seal them in the bag. This idea is great for items you'd like to have along but can't really justify the space they take up.

Roll clothes to save space and reduce wrinkles. Save suitcase space and cut back on creases and wrinkles when you roll your clothes instead of folding them. It makes your suitcase neater and helps use all the available space. Increase efficiency by rolling like items together — three pairs of trousers in a roll are only a little larger than a solo roll. You can also save cardboard wrapping paper tubes and roll clothes around them. Roll bulky things, like sweaters, and stuff them inside a section of pantyhose to keep them from unrolling.

Preserve the shape of your shoes. Stuff your shoes with socks and underwear when you pack. It keeps the shape of your shoes while it saves space in your suitcase. If you're not worried about damaging your shoes, you can also use them to pack small items you don't want to leave loose in your luggage.

Put your shoes in those plastic bags the newspaper comes in and you can pack them right alongside your nicest clothes. Use the bags to keep other things, like brushes and combs or all your medicine bottles, all together, too.

Divide your suitcase for easy packing. Make a divider for your suitcase from a piece of heavy cardboard. Pack your shoes, toiletries, and other heavy items in the bottom of your bag and then add the cardboard. Continue packing soft items on top of the cardboard divider. You can lift up the cardboard and get to things in the bottom without messing up the top layer.

Smooth out wrinkles with plastic bags. Keep the plastic bags that cover your clothes when they come back from the dry cleaners and use them between layers when you pack. The plastic reduces friction and helps clothes slide around instead of bunching up in your suitcase. One way is to hang several pants on a hanger, then add a shirt and a jacket. Slip the plastic bag over the whole thing and fold it to fit the top of your suitcase. You'll be amazed at how wrinkle-free your clothes are when you arrive.

Arrive with unwrinkled garments. Don't pack your clothes in a suitcase for a car trip. That's how they get wrinkled, so you either have to find an iron or look frumpy when you get where you're going. Leave clothing on hangers, put them in a garment bag, and lay the bag in the back seat or the trunk. A leftover dry cleaner bag or large, plastic trash bag works, too. It takes up a lot less room than a bulky suitcase. You can also hang clothes from a rod inside your car.

Sneak an extra suitcase onboard. An extra suitcase comes in handy when you do a lot of shopping on vacation and have more to bring back than you took with you. Gain some extra space by packing a collapsible suitcase or duffel bag. For the trip home, put your dirty laundry in the duffel and your new stuff in the regular suitcase. Another solution is to pack a medium suitcase for the trip, and put it inside a larger one.

Ship your suitcases home. One seasoned traveler says the most liberating thing she's ever done is to ship her luggage home. Before you leave for home, spend a few extra dollars and have the hotel send your bags on ahead. Or go to FedEx or UPS and do it yourself. You'll have nothing but your carry-on for the rest of the trip and miss the stress of lugging, checking, and retrieving baggage all the way home.

Index